WRAP THE SHROUD

Chronicle of a Passion

A former monk's life-changing odyssey into the enigma
of Christianity's most revered relic

Joseph G. Marino

Foreword by Barrie Schwortz
Shroud of Turin Project Documenting Photographer

Cradle Press
St. Louis, MO

WRAPPED UP IN THE SHROUD:

Chronicle of a Passion

Copyright © 2011 Joseph G. Marino
Cover Art copyright © Laura L. Seeger
Cover design by Joseph G. Marino
Front cover photo, Giovanni Battista della Rovere painting—circa 1625—copyright unknown—courtesy STERA, Inc.
Back cover photo, shrouded body—courtesy of *shroudtv.com*
Back cover photo, M. Sue Benford—courtesy of *Columbus Dispatch*

ISBN: 978-0-9789499-6-9
Library of Congress Control Number: 2011939698

ALL RIGHTS RESERVED

No part of this publication may be reproduced in whole or in part, or stored in a retrieval system, or transmitted in any form or by any means, electronic, mechanical, photocopying, recording, or otherwise, without written permission from Joseph G. Marino

Published by:
Cradle Press
P.O. Box 8401
St. Louis, MO 63132

Printed in the U.S.A.

Every effort has been made to seek permission for use of and to properly credit all copyrighted sources included in this book. However, in some cases the author was unable to locate the copyright owners or received no response when he did contact them. Should you find your copyrighted materials in this book without proper attribution, please contact the author immediately and the proper corrections will be made in the next printing.

The whole outward, visible world with all its being is a signature, or figure of the inward spiritual world; whatever is internally, and however its operation is, so likewise it has its character externally; like as the spirit of each creature sets forth and manifests the internal form of its birth by its body, so does the Eternal Being also.

Jacob Boehme in <u>The Signature of All Things</u>

ACKNOWLEDGEMENTS

I would like to thank my parents, who provided me with the physical and spiritual means to grow and mature. To my brothers and sisters, who have always been loving and supportive of whatever path I chose. To Father Tom Santen, for his sage spiritual advice over many years. To Margot Martin, whose friendship has been a sustaining factor in my life over the years. To all previous and current Shroud researchers, who have spent much time and money trying to educate others about the mysteries of this object, especially John Jackson and Barrie Schwortz, without whose focus and tenacity the Shroud would not be as well known as it is. Barrie also graciously agreed to write the Foreword for my book. Even though he's Jewish, he's one of the best "Christians" I know, and our friendship has been a real treasure over the years. Barrie is on good terms with most Shroud researchers, due to the fact that he, unlike most, is able to not let intellectual disagreements (of which there are many) ruin friendships. Even one Shroud skeptic was moved to say about Barrie during a radio debate with him: "He's the best of a bad lot." (!) To the monks at St. Louis Abbey, who graciously let me pontificate about the Shroud for more than 18 years and allowed me to spread the news to the wider community. To Dick and Sandy Nieman, whose encouragement and financial assistance enabled me to further my own research and that of others, as well. To fellow Shroud researchers, Mark Antonacci, John Schulte and Chuck Hampton, whose enthusiasm for the Shroud was contagious. To artist and physicist Isabel Piczek, who prodded me in her most gentle style to write this book. To Laura Clark, for her tremendous help and guidance as my publisher and for her warm friendship. To Joanna Emery, who despite having a young family with all of its demands, donated her time to read over the manuscript and make many wonderful suggestions. To Carol Gregorek, for her loving support and constant encouragement. To my fellow author Annette Cloutier, who also reviewed the manuscript, for her suggestions. To friend and student of history and languages Diana Fulbright, for eleventh-hour editorial suggestions. To another friend, scholar Mary Hines, who also supplied her expertise. To Laura Seeger, for her artful cover design work. To my stepdaughters Erika and Alexis, who had to endure the many years of frenzied Shroud activities of their mom and stepdad. To all those who have given me permission to use material for this book. To many others whose goodness to me is known mainly to God alone. I wish I could name each one. Lastly, I would like to specifically thank my remarkable late wife, Sue Benford, whose amazing love, support and very presence brought an indescribable richness to my life that words could never describe. She also helped me fulfill my destiny with the Shroud, and I know she is still looking over my shoulder.

This book is dedicated to my late wife, M. Sue Benford, one of most amazing women I have ever met or ever will meet.

TABLE OF CONTENTS

Chapter One – "Is This the Face of Jesus Christ?" 19

Chapter Two – Life in a Monastery Begins 27

Chapter Three – "Are You Going to the Shroud Conference?" 35

Chapter Four – C-14 Test: "1260-1390!" 47

Chapter Five – Sindonologists Strike Back 59

Chapter Six – A Fire and Two Phone Calls 71

Chapter Seven – Where Are We Headed? 85

Chapter Eight – It was a Repair! 95

Chapter Nine – Controversies in Dallas 105

Chapter Ten – Controversies in Turin 119

Chapter Eleven – Invisible Reweaving Hypothesis Gathers Steam 131

Chapter Twelve – Retesting the 1988 C-14 Sample 149

Chapter Thirteen – Déjà vu in Dallas 163

Chapter Fourteen – Moving Forward—Without a Key Player 171

Chapter Fifteen – "She's Gone" 181

Chapter Sixteen – New Horizons 191

Epilogue 201

References 205

Appendix A – Dr. Robert Dinegar's notes during 1985 Trondheim C-14 Conference 213

Appendix B – Shroud Symposia held since 1939 219

Appendix C – Correspondence (1990-1999) between Dr. Walter McCrone and Author 221

Appendix D – Documents from 1986 Turin Workshop on Dating the Shroud 243

Appendix E – Letter (1987) from Archaeologist Paul Maloney to Father Peter Rinaldi 251

Appendix F – Article (1988) on Shroud C-14 Dating in *St. Louis Post-Dispatch* 257

Appendix G – Column (1988) on Shroud controversy in *St. Louis Post-Dispatch* 269

Appendix H – Shroud article (1988) by Author published in *Shroud News* 271

Appendix I – Shroud Bibliography (1984-2009) by Author and Sue Benford 275

Appendix J – Correspondence (1997-1998) between Sue Benford and Author 277

Appendix K – Ian Wilson comments regarding 2001 Dallas Shroud Conference 293

Appendix L – Documents from Turin Authorities regarding 2002 Shroud Restoration 297

Appendix M – Correspondence (2001) between Ray Rogers and Author and Sue Benford 315

Appendix N – Letter (2003) from Ray Rogers and Bill Meacham to Turin's Cardinal Poletto 335

Appendix O – List of Major Shroud Researchers since 1898 339

FOREWORD
By Barrie M. Schwortz

It is always a great honor when someone asks you to write a foreword to their book, especially knowing how much work and time went into the project, and even more so since the Author is also a good friend and colleague. Such is truly the case with Joe Marino.

I have known Joe since he was a monk in the 1980s and remember looking forward to receiving the excellent Shroud newsletter he produced and distributed for many years. In those early days, I called him Brother Joe. Time passed and some years later, he was ordained and I started calling him Father Joe. And in 1998, when he decided to leave the monastery, he became just Joe. Through all those years, we stayed in close touch and he often advised me on both Shroud and personal matters. And he was always there for me, whenever I needed an honest, outside voice to guide me. In many ways, he served as my unofficial "priest" (yes, I am Jewish) and I have even called him that on many occasions.

Two years ago, in April, 2009, Sue Benford, Joe's loving wife, died unexpectedly after a brief illness. I spent many hours on the phone with Joe after Sue's passing and shared his grief with him, in some ways becoming Joe's unofficial "rabbi," thus reciprocating the kindness and friendship he had shown me over the years. So that is why writing this foreword is such an honor for me. He is not just my friend, but also my brother.

No matter what your personal opinions are of the conclusions Joe and Sue reached regarding the anomalous nature of the C-14 dating sample, there is no denying that their work had a major impact on Shroud studies. In fact, their contribution provided the impetus for Ray Rogers to dig back into Shroud research in the last few years of his life, even though he was already seriously ill (and probably prolonged his life for a few years, until his work was completed). There is also no denying that their combined efforts led to the first scientific paper to appear in the peer-reviewed scientific literature that challenged the 1988 radiocarbon dating results. In the end, they opened the door to what I personally believe to be the most plausible explanation for the medieval dating result that has been proposed to date.

As such, and with decades of other Shroud research and scholarship behind him, Joe has become a truly important figure in the history of the Shroud and its study. And that is why this book is also important. It is the honest, unconventional and often very personal story of one man's search for the truth, and more importantly, where that search has led him. I know I could easily say a lot more about Joe and his work, but frankly, nothing is better than hearing it straight from the man who lived it himself. I believe you will find this story as compelling and revealing as I did.

Barrie Schwortz
Shroud of Turin Project Documenting Photographer
Florissant, Colorado
June 28, 2011

PREFACE

Most people know that a "trekkie" is a person who is a fan of the Star Trek TV series/movies. Fewer people probably know that a "shroudie," inspired by the term "trekkie," is a person who is passionately involved in the study of the Shroud of Turin, the reputed burial cloth of Jesus that contains the mysterious front and back images of a crucified man. The study of the Shroud actually has a technical name, "sindonology," from the Greek word *sindon*, the fine cloth that wrapped the body of Jesus.

The Shroud is one of the most intensely studied artifacts in human history. Hundreds of thousands of hours have been spent studying the cloth, and although some people, mostly skeptics, have claimed to have solved the mystery, nothing could be further from the truth. It is still a mystery with a capital "M," and it's vastly more important than the face of Jesus on the doggy-door and tea towel and similar stories that surface from time to time in the news.

I have been a "shroudie," or to use the more technical and more reverent-sounding term, a "sindonologist" for more than half of my life (almost 34 years of my 56 years at the time of this writing). To say that the Shroud of Turin has been a big part of my life would be a gross understatement. It played a part in my joining a monastery, in my leaving that monastery, and in my marriage to someone whose life was also greatly affected by the Shroud.

The title and subtitle of this book are a double pun, being both about Jesus having literally been wrapped in a shroud after his passion and death, and about me having a passion about the Shroud and being wrapped up in it metaphorically. I have collected several hundred books on the Shroud, not to mention thousands of articles, letters, emails, videos and newsletters. I probably have one of the ten best English-language personal Shroud collections in the world. None of the previously published Shroud books focus on how the cloth affected the major events and the day-to-day life of the author, like the book you hold in your hand does.

Most Shroud books concentrate on the scientific, historical and theological aspects of the cloth. Those aspects will be touched upon here but will not be the main focus *per se*. I never really had a strong desire to write a book about the Shroud—I found writing papers for periodicals and conferences tough enough—but when I called a friend of mine to encourage her to take part in a questionnaire for shroudies, she in turn encouraged me to write a book about my incredible experiences over the years with the Shroud. With dozens of Shroud websites, blogs and already hundreds of books on the subject already out there, I wondered if another Shroud book was really needed. But as I had enjoyed in the questionnaire reflecting about my experiences, and as other people also encouraged me to write a book, I decided to take a stab at it. If you are reading this, I managed to complete it. The clincher was when one person said that it would be a good way to honor my late wife, M. Sue Benford, with whom I collaborated on some very significant Shroud work. Sue, the name she went by, did not get involved in Shroud work until 1997, but from that time until her untimely death in 2009, she made enormous contributions. In 2002 her autobiography, <u>Strong Woman: Unshrouding the Secrets of the Soul,</u> was published. It was republished in 2011.

The back cover of her book reads:

When Susie Benford was a child she almost died from cancer. However, she survived but with multiple handicaps. Thwarted by both physical and emotional challenges, an inner strength propels her to a miraculous physical achievement when she becomes the "strongest woman in the world" (three-time World Powerlifting Champion, holder of all the World Records in the 97 Ib. weight class).

Currently Benford is a registered nurse, health care researcher, and Executive Director of a non-profit biomedical organization in Ohio. Her education is diverse, from the in-depth study of religion to pursuing scientific testing of unexplained paranormal phenomena: i.e. the Shroud of Turin and Spontaneous Human Combustion.

Benford's experiences with psychic phenomena are responsible for the redirection of her life into the pursuit of spiritual enlightenment. In 1997, she contacted Father Joseph Marino, a Benedictine Monk and Catholic Priest at a St. Louis Abbey. Their divinely inspired meeting, and subsequent joining as life partners, served a research liaison that is credited with uncovering vital information leading to the authentication of the Shroud.

STRONG WOMAN is a real-life transformation story full of

hope, strength, encouragement, and inspiration that culminates in the understanding that there is much more to our existence than meets the eye. Susie's story is also your story. One of parallel courses of "strength" development: physical, emotional, and spiritual. It is the story of who we truly are—our spiritual heritage and our divine destiny.

Her back cover blurb includes the word "paranormal." I know that many Christians have a negative reaction when they see this word. Take for example the term "Spontaneous Human Combustion." Sue believed it to be just a rare medical condition. When she was interviewed about it for a television documentary, the footage of her explaining that it was no more than a rare medical condition, was left on the cutting room floor—after all, if it's just a medical condition and not an enduring mystery, there will be no opportunities in the future for lucrative documentaries. Due to such agendas, beware of most Shroud documentaries! The word "paranormal" did spark, as the English would say, a "row" between some Shroud conference organizers and me (along with Sue), which is described in some detail in one of the chapters. (Note: where there are documents or emails from Europeans, I have kept their spelling of words that are often are spelled differently in the United States.)

Although this is not a "scholarly" work as such, I believe there is much here to satisfy serious Shroud researchers. Letters and emails that I have reproduced, both in the main body when they are pertinent to the main focus of the chapter, and also in the appendices, will provide the serious Shroud scholar with some fascinating new information. Very few people have ever seen these communications. I have also included some previously unpublished material that is extremely significant from an historical point of view. These include the handwritten notes of a scientist at an important C-14 meeting, as well as personal correspondence with the most well-known Shroud skeptic. I have not cluttered the text with footnotes but there are extensive references, which give ample scholarly citations to books, articles, websites, and conference presentations. The citations list in parentheses the author's last name, and the year of publication (plus page numbers where appropriate). If the article does not have an author, the citation is listed by the title.

In cases where I reproduce important correspondence from people who are still living or discuss their involvement in various situations, I do not name them so as to protect their privacy, unless they have given me permission. Also, when mentioning certain persons or groups in the context of a negative situation, I am intentionally excessively vague in order not to be overly critical. In some cases, however, certain individuals and groups are named because the details and/or significance demand it. I don't relish relating these less-than-pleasant matters. I only bring up such situations because they are integral to the whole story. In addition, I have included some of the correspondence I had with Sue while I was still in the monastery. These emails can be found in one of the appendices. Hopefully, the scholarly material included throughout the book will not distract the non-scholar from the "human interest" aspects that make this such an intriguing story, and the non-scholarly portions will not deter the Shroud scholar from reading the whole book. I have not cluttered the text with footnotes, but there are numerous citations of books, articles and presentations in the "References" section.

Many readers might ask, "Is the Shroud really that important?" Considering the amount of time has been spent studying it, one must acknowledge that at least on one level, the answer is an unqualified "yes." Undoubtedly, the Shroud speaks deeply to people, many of whom, including myself, have spent decades researching this cloth. A *Harper's Magazine* article from 1981 relates the fact that one Italian researcher obtained Shroud samples from another researcher—at gunpoint!! From a theological point of view, however, the strict answer would be "no." Christianity neither stands nor falls on the authenticity of the Shroud. Yet, it can be for many people, as it was for me, a trigger of faith. The empty tomb of Jesus was not proof of his resurrection and neither is the Shroud. However, the empty tomb, in conjunction with the words and deeds of Jesus and the witness of men and women who claimed they saw him after he died, has convinced billions of people that Jesus was the Son of God. Similarly, the imaged Shroud, in conjunction with much scientific evidence and people's personal experiences, has convinced many that this cloth was actually in the tomb of the historical Jesus, and for some, is even an indication of his resurrection.

When I gave Shroud lectures, many people would come up to me afterward and tell me they wanted to learn more about it. I always gave them a friendly warning: "Be careful, if you get into studying the Shroud, you may never be able to get out of it." The Shroud has a way of penetrating and staying with a person once one is exposed to it. I have known only a few people who had been deeply into it and didn't end up making it a life-long commitment. In my own life, it has been an enormous catalyst that has taken me to Israel, France and Italy and has educated me in many disciplines of study, into which I would have otherwise never been bothered to delve.

Some of my own experiences described here will read like fiction, but I assure you, they are all true. I'm just not creative enough to be able to make up all of what I'll relate. Science will have a hard time coming up with a rational explanation for some of the events I will describe. There was an inner voice which gave me a strange command, which led me to participate in an on-air radio debate about the Shroud. There was a lost Shroud booklet that I definitely heard, but did not actually see, apparently reappear out of thin air. If you want real fiction, just read on the Internet or in books some of the explanations that skeptics offer for the resolution of the many mysteries of the Shroud. Many skeptics who have done little or no study of the Shroud make confident assertions about it being a forgery. Rarely, if ever, have I seen such skeptics state that they would have to spend more time on it before they would feel qualified to offer an opinion.

As mentioned in the Acknowledgements and as just noted, there are, as in any scholarly pursuit, intellectual disagreements. Although I shouldn't let it happen, skeptics sometimes get "under my skin." (I'm sure I get under theirs as well.) Frankly, I get irritated with would-be researchers who have perhaps duplicated a few of the cloth's characteristics, and then claim they have solved the whole enigma. It rarely seems to occur to these people to read scientific, peer-reviewed literature about the Shroud instead of a tabloid newspaper or a skeptic's book or website. The logic (make that, "lack of logic") of one argument that skeptics often use to say that the Shroud is a forgery leaves me shaking my head the most. The argument is: the Gospels say there was more than one cloth involved in the burial. The Shroud is only one cloth; ergo, it can't be authentic. What I say in rebuttal is: if someone lost a pair of earrings and then only a single is found, one doesn't conclude that it can't be part of the pair because two were originally lost. Two items that were originally together can easily end up in different places. Actually, another cloth called the "Sudarium of Oviedo," in Spain since the seventh century, is believed by many to be another one of the cloths used in the burial of Jesus. But that's another story. Suffice it to say, scientists from the United States' nuclear and space programs have studied the Shroud for decades and still have more questions than answers.

I have always felt that one of my missions in life was to spread information about the Shroud. A book is a good way to do that (but why does it have to be so much labor?). Fortunately, a labor of love feels more like love than labor. It is my hope that this book will be both entertaining and educational. Around the time I was writing this, I happened to come across the following noteworthy entry in an Internet blog: "After working 16 hours a day for 45 years, Rabbi Adin Steinsaltz has finished translating the Babylonian Talmud from archaic Aramaic into contemporary Hebrew." Whenever I think of the effort I put into writing this book, I'm going to think of that Rabbi! Even if only one person is affected by reading this, perhaps by inspiring that person to seriously research the Shroud, I feel that my effort will have been worthwhile. (For a list of all major Shroud researchers since 1898, see Appendix O.)

CHAPTER ONE

"IS THIS THE FACE OF JESUS CHRIST?"

The 1970s had some memorable and not-so-memorable events: the Beatles officially broke up, mood rings, gas shortages, pet rocks, Watergate, the Iran hostage situation, the death of Elvis Presley, and disco, to name a few. Looking back, the most significant event in that decade for me was learning in 1977 about a strange cloth known as the "Shroud of Turin." It was believed by many people not only to be the actual burial cloth of Jesus, but also possible evidence that he had arisen from the dead. The Shroud did show the distinct front and back images of a man who appeared to have been crucified, and what is seen there corresponds well with the Gospels. At the time, the Shroud was not well known in the United States, but that would change the following year, when a group of scientists called the "Shroud of Turin Research Project" (STURP), were given an unprecedented five days' access to the cloth and began to reveal incredible data. The STURP team, which consisted mostly of American scientists, many of whom worked in the United States' nuclear and space programs, essentially tried to determine if the image had been painted on the cloth, the most plausible explanation of how the image got there. (For a list of researchers and their institution affiliations at the time of the 1978 testing, see http://www.shroud.com/78team.htm. Although accused by some skeptics of being nothing but religious zealots, (despite the fact that team members included Christians, Jews and agnostics) many in STURP believed that the forgery would be quickly uncovered. STURP documenting photographer Barrie Schwortz once told me he expected to see the paint in less than five minutes. The late chemist Ray Rogers of STURP said " . . . I'll have this thing shot full of holes." The writer from whose article the Rogers quote came commented: "The minutes have become years" (Murphy 1981:44). The years have even stretched in the twenty-first century.

I was born and raised a Catholic in St. Louis, Missouri, the last child of five born to Mary and Joseph Marino, but like many young people in the 1970s, had become an agnostic. After graduating from high school in 1972, I attended the University of Missouri at St. Louis for two years, while working part-time for the Federal Government. Sports were a big part of my life from my earliest years—I played, officiated, and watched them often. In 1973, the men's collegiate basketball championship was held in St. Louis. I didn't have a ticket and had to be content with viewing it on television. Basketball was my favorite sport and I can vividly remember lying on the couch, watching the game, thinking, "Isn't this just the greatest?" Right after that thought, however, another one came into my head: "Isn't there more to life than basketball?" I proceeded to ignore that thought, deep as it was, and continued to go about my life. I wasn't sure what I wanted to major in during college and for a time considered some sort of career in sports, perhaps broadcasting. In 1974, I decided to quit school and took a job with a federal agency, the Veterans Administration. I had attended school for 15 straight years, which seemed like an eternity, and now decided to give my brain a vacation. Over the next two years, practically the only reading I did was the sports and comic sections of the newspaper.

Music was a big part of my life. I really liked to listen to my rock and pop music. Having grown up in the 1960s, I especially enjoyed the Beatles. They were easily my favorite artists. After their break-up, I followed their solo careers closely and kept the hope alive that they would reunite. I had also come to appreciate another British group called "The Moody Blues." Their music was characterized by a lush orchestration, which was unusual for a pop group. This group, or to be more specific, one of its members, would later play a role in one of the pivotal events in my life, which will be described later in the book.

At some point during 1976, I realized I needed to read something more significant than sports and comics. Apparently, the thought I had in 1973 about there being more to life than basketball was not completely buried. I began to read everything I could in the areas of religion and philosophy,

Christian or otherwise. Whenever I went to a bookstore, I would immediately head for the shelves containing those subjects.

In March, 1977, I went to the "Walden's" bookstore at Jamestown Mall near my home and as was my custom, headed to the religion section. My eyes were immediately drawn to a paperback that had on the cover the intriguing face of a man. It was like no picture I had ever seen. The face exhibited signs of various wounds, but the visage was surprisingly serene. The book was titled <u>The Fifth Gospel</u> and posed the question "Is this the face of Jesus Christ?" Leafing through it, I learned that the image was on a cloth known as the "Shroud of Turin," an object I had never heard of previously. Having attended Catholic grade school, I was familiar with the story of "Veronica's Veil," which although not biblical, is part of Catholic piety and even is included in what are called "The Stations of the Cross," which call to mind the various events surrounding Jesus' crucifixion. As the story goes, a pious woman named Veronica witnessed Jesus' death march to Calvary and pressed a cloth to his bloody face, thereby leaving a facial image on it. There have been many books and articles on this putative cloth, known generally as "Veronica's Veil." Much of that material is not in English, but recently a very good book in English by a German journalist was recently published. It explores the possible relationship between Veronica's Veil and the Shroud (Badde, 2010).

I decided to buy the Shroud book and headed home. I didn't know if I was going to "buy" the premise that the full-length cloth had wrapped Jesus and that it contained his image. After all, what were the chances that the linen could have survived intact down to our day? As it turned out, I read the book in one sitting and was totally fascinated by what was presented. The first pictures of the Shroud had been taken in 1898 by an amateur Italian photographer, Secondo Pia. Although the distinct images of the man can be seen on the cloth, they don't appear lifelike to the naked eye. However, when Pia developed his photographic plate, he was startled to see what *was* a lifelike image on his negative plate. In effect, the Shroud image appeared like a photographic negative. He recounted later that he was so amazed that he almost dropped the plate. Nearly 80 more years of study and analysis on the Shroud continued to produce amazing scientific results. Based on what I had read in 1977, the evidence seemed pretty compelling that the cloth was indeed authentic. Although I didn't realize it at the time, I was hooked. My life would never be the same from that point.

I studied the bibliography intently and went to my local library to find as many of the books and articles listed there as I could find. An extremely amusing incident happened one time when I found an article with a picture of that face—the serene face of the man in the Shroud—which had graced the front cover of the book I had seen that had so captivated me. I was at the photocopier getting ready to copy the article when a little boy about six years old happened to see the picture in the article and blurted out, "That guy is ugly." I said to him, "That's Jesus." The boy's older sister, perhaps about ten years old, who overheard this, looked at him and said, "Oh, you're in trouuubble!" as the expression on the little boy's face turned to horror. When I left the library a little while later, I happened to pass the little boy and girl on the way out and heard the girl say to her brother, "You're in trouuubble!" I hope that little boy wasn't scarred for life by that incident!

My new interest in the Shroud coincided with an event prominent in the news: the death of Elvis Presley. Elvis, who is mainly thought of as only a rock star, also made Gospel albums and was said to have been very religious. I heard from one of my Shroud contacts, an author, Frank Tribbe, that when Elvis died, he was reading a book that Tribbe had written called <u>A Scientific Search for the Face of Jesus</u>. It wasn't strictly on the Shroud, but did contain a great deal of material about it. I wrote Tribbe for more details about it. He wrote me back:

> Elvis had ordered another copy of <u>A Scientific Search</u> as he had lost his first copy. He apparently knew he was going to die. He was interested in the comments on the Resurrection. The day the copy arrived he told his girlfriend he was going into the bathroom for a few minutes. He took the S.S. with him. She fell asleep. When she awoke he hadn't come back. She went into the bathroom. Elvis was on the floor in the foetal position clutching the S.S. to his body (Personal communication, undated letter from the late Frank Tribbe).

I have a feeling that if Elvis had lived, he would have donated some money to the Shroud of Turin Research Project, which at the time was in the planning stage of what would eventually be its five days around the clock with the Shroud in October 1978.

One organization that did help STURP was the Holy Shroud Guild in upstate New York, run by several Catholic priests, including the late Father Peter Rinaldi and the late Father Adam Otterbein in upstate New York. I contacted the Guild, requested an order form and started to buy and collect materials, including slides. I kept a folder of all the articles I gathered, and when I had accumulated about seven or eight, I naively thought to myself, "I'm getting quite a collection here."

When one studies the Shroud, the Gospels come into play prominently, because if the Shroud is authentic, one will naturally closely compare the two. So I started rereading the Gospels and began to feel myself being drawn back to my Christian roots. My parish had a young priest named Father Tom Santen, who was a dynamic preacher. I wasn't quite ready to start going back to church completely, but I would find out when he was going to preach, plan my arrival to hear just his sermon and then leave, not staying for any of the rest of the Mass. One day I happened to see Father Santen out in front of church and stopped to talk to him. He mentioned that he led a Bible study at a parishioner's home every Wednesday and invited me to come. The next Bible study fell on the same night as a TV special hosted by ex-Beatle Ringo Starr. Video cassette recorders were just coming out around that time, but I didn't have one yet. I had to make a decision—would I stay home and watch the special with the Beatles' drummer—or would I attend a Bible study? Knowing deep down that there was more to life to basketball and even to the Beatles, I decided to attend the Bible study.

I eventually went back to church full-time around late 1977. I also felt like I wanted to do some type of Christian service. One suggestion I was given was to join the "Big Brothers" program, where one would be matched up to a boy from a fatherless home, and mentor him. I wasn't sure I wanted to do that, as I was the youngest in my family and had no experience being a "big brother." But I prayed and asked God to give me a sign if I should do that. A few days later, on a Saturday morning, I flipped on the TV and saw some idiotic show where famous athletes were huddled in a small room with a host. They were doing inane (or insane—both apply!) activities, and I asked myself why I was even watching it. The show broke to a commercial that showed a little boy walking along the beach. Eventually an announcer was heard and said, "This boy is lonely—what he needs is a Big Brother—call "Big Brothers . . . " Considering that a direct answer to my prayer, I immediately got up, called the number that had flashed on the screen, and applied to be a Big Brother. I was soon matched to a ten-year-old boy named Greg, who lived with his mother, sister and half-sister not too far from where I lived. I would see him an average of one time per week for the next eight years. I'm embarrassed to say that over the years, I used the fact that he was born when the Beatles' "Sgt. Pepper's Lonely Hearts Club Band" was released, to help me remember the year he was born!

The answer to my prayer (which can also be considered a "synchronicity," defined by the famous psychiatrist Carl Jung as a "meaningful coincidence") was the beginning of a series of spiritual synchronicities that I would continue to experience in the upcoming years. I didn't know it at the time, but more of them were right around the corner.

By now, early 1978, not only had I returned to church, but I had started to read the Bible on the bus to and from work. I even carried a small Bible with me to sporting events. One wintry night, I was coming back from a hockey game with an uncle. The roads were very slick and while on a major highway, the car began to spin out of control. At one point, we nearly went off the road where there was about a 15-foot drop. We continued to spin and ended up on the opposite side of the highway, facing in the direction of the oncoming traffic. Miraculously, even though it was one of St. Louis' main highways, not a single car was around for us to have to face head-on—literally. The car suffered some damage, but we managed to make it home safely. I felt that I had been under a special protection of some kind.

After that huge scare, life went on. I was still on the lookout for any information about the Shroud and continued to mentor Greg. It was during the fall of 1979 when I crossed paths with a grade-school acquaintance of mine named Gerard. Gerard also worked for the Federal Government and whenever we saw each other on the bus I took home from work, we would chat. He saw that I was sometimes reading my Bible, so religion became one of the topics that we discussed.

One day he mentioned to me that he was thinking about joining the religious life and was going to visit "Pius X Abbey," a Benedictine monastery located in a small community about 45 minutes south of St. Louis. He asked if I wanted to go along with him for the ride, and I told him I would. The next time I saw him he told me that he had left a message at the Abbey but no one had called back. He mentioned there was another Benedictine monastery right in St. Louis, named "St. Louis Priory." (A Priory is dependent on a founding monastery, whereas an Abbey is independent.) He was able to contact them and had arranged for a visit one Sunday in October, 1979. Once again he asked if I wanted to accompany him for the ride, and I said I would. We spent a good part of that Sunday with the monks, and I was happy to learn that one of them had an interest in the Shroud. He photocopied for me several Shroud articles that I didn't have. Although I had only come along for the ride, I actually found myself having thoughts about possibly joining the monastery.

I didn't mention to anyone at my job that I was thinking of joining. A few days after I had visited the monastery, while talking to someone at work about an expensive religious video that I had heard about, the person said something along the lines that "You would need to have a *monastery* buy it and show it." My ears perked up—how often does the word "monastery" come up, even when talking about religious topics? Also, I was playing in a basketball league at the time and was waiting to hear from a player on another team who had been trying to arrange a practice game. I hadn't heard from him so I called him. He said the gym he had first arranged for the game was no longer available, but he was able to line up a gym at another place. He asked, "Do you know where St. Louis Priory is?" "I do, as a matter of fact," I replied. It was amazing. I had just visited St. Louis Priory for the first time, immediately thought about joining, and within a few days found myself back there for a recreational activity. After the game, I dropped by the monastery to say hello to the monks, and I arranged another visit. Shortly thereafter, while on a lunch break at work, I was reading a national religious periodical when my eyes were drawn to the left part of the page. An advertisement there read "Do you like praying? Being part of a community? Working reasonably hard? Call Father Timothy at St. Louis Priory." All of these synchronicities happened within two weeks of my first visit to the monastery, which seemed to have become omnipresent in my life. The signs seemed pretty clear to me, and after some further prayer, I decided to join. On January 27, 1980 I moved to the monastery to become a "postulant," which is the first stage on the path to becoming a monk. There was no commitment at that juncture—one still had all the freedoms of a layman, and one was not even clothed with a monastic habit at that point. But this was definitely a new chapter in my life.

CHAPTER TWO

LIFE IN A MONASTERY BEGINS

I continued to work at my government job while living at the monastery. Postulants were called "Brother, so I became known as "Brother Joe." The monks had a weekday 6 p.m. Mass and as I attended regularly, I became familiar with many of the people that came. Most of them, usually numbering around 30, attended on a fairly regular basis, and it was rare to see a new face. Both monks and lay people were given the opportunity to do a reading at Mass, and one night, I was asked to do so. Despite the fact that I would simply be reciting a text, and it was before a relatively small group, I was very self-conscious. I had never done any public speaking before and found it rather nerve-wracking. I did the reading—but didn't dare look up—and nervously walked back to my place. At this 6 p.m. Mass, everyone was invited to stand around the altar during the "Eucharistic Prayer" part of the Mass. When I got up to join everyone there, I was still feeling nervous from having done the reading. I said a little prayer to God that he would have to help me overcome my fear of speaking in front of people. As I said that prayer, I happen to notice a woman, who I had never seen before, staring at me. Her look was piercing, and I had the odd sensation that she actually was reading my thoughts. At the "Sign of Peace" (where one gives a word of greeting to fellow worshippers), she came up to me, leaned closed to my ear and said, "You know, you read that very well." It was like a direct answer to my prayer. I immediately felt more confident about my ability to perform the readings. Interestingly, I never saw the woman again after that night. It was the first and only time I ever saw her.

With my newly found confidence to speak in front of people and my recently purchased slides on the Shroud from the Holy Shroud Guild, I resolved to put together a slide lecture. As I was still working my government job, taking part in most of the monks' daily activities when I was at the monastery, and mentoring Greg, the only time I had to work on it was late at night. I soon found myself toiling away each night until about 2:30 a.m. and then getting up at 5:30 a.m. for the first monastic prayers of the day. I marvel now that I was able to get by with little as three hours sleep (I am not a "morning" person), but I was much younger then and very enthusiastic about my idea of lecturing on the Shroud to others.

My very first lecture was at the monastery's parish hall (the monastery ran both a parish and a school). I discovered that because of my confidence from reading at Mass and my excitement about being able to talk about the Shroud, I wasn't even self-conscious. I eventually started giving more and more lectures to churches and other groups in the area. I always tried to add several bits of humor in the slide lecture, mixed in with hard facts about the Shroud. For example, in one part I stated:

> STURP applied organic and inorganic chemistry, radiography, bacteriology, immunology, vulconology, nuclear and molecular physics, entomology, mycology, endocrinology, geochemistry, pathology, hematology, physiology, ethnology, forensic medicine, criminology, photomicrography, aero-dynamics, computer technology, anthropology, palynology, and botany.
> They performed over one thousand chemical experiments employing visible, ultraviolet and infrared photography; visible, ultraviolet and infrared spectroscopy; x-radiography; thermography; macroscopy; polarization, fluorescence, phase contact and electron microscopy; microdensitometry; biostereometry; laser micro-probe spectroscopy; electron-energy-dispersive spectroscopy; and microspectrophotometric transmission spectra.

I would sum up with: "And those are the ones I can pronounce!"—which would usually generate a fairly good collective laugh. Another fact I mentioned was that the man in the Shroud was about five feet, ten inches tall and weighed about 175 pounds, which was very similar to my height and weight. I would then add that my parents' names were Mary and Joseph, and that people could make up their own minds regarding the relevance of all that! That would also always generate a few guffaws. In August, 1980, I quit my job and became a full-time monk.

Chapter Two: Life In The Monastery Begins

Other Shroud activities followed. I helped arrange to bring to the parish hall a traveling exhibit on the Shroud. The exhibit was quite large but fortunately, the hall was big enough to accommodate it. In the course of one week, several thousand people attended the exhibit. Sister Margaret, a nun stationed at the parish, told me one day that my name had come in conversation with a parishioner who asked her, "Isn't that the monk who's wrapped up in the Shroud?" Little did I know that the parishioner's remark would be the inspiration 30 years later for a book title! I also started corresponding with other Shroud researchers, and arranged to bring an historian and Shroud expert named Dorothy Crispino to give a lecture at the parish hall

In 1981, a worldwide exhibition of photos on the Shroud was to be held in Northbrook Illinois, not too far from St. Louis. As one of my activities with Greg, we drove there to see it. It was all very impressive. They handed out a pamphlet that contained startling preliminary results of the combined body of work STURP had performed on the Shroud since 1978. It read, in part:

> No pigments paints, dyes, or stains have been found on the fibrils. X-ray fluorescence and microchemistry on the fibrils preclude the possibility of paint being used as a method for creating the image. Ultraviolet and infrared evaluation confirm these studies. Computer image enhancement and analysis by a device called a VP-8 image analyzer show that the image has unique, three-dimensional information encoded in it.
>
> Microchemical evaluation has indicated no evidence of any spices, oils, or any biochemicals known to be produced by the body in life or in death. It is clear that there has been a direct contact of the Shroud with the body, which explains certain features such as the scourge marks, as well as the blood. However, while this type of contact might explain some of the features of the torso, it is totally incapable of explaining the image of the face with the high resolution which has been amply demonstrated by photography. The basic problem from a scientific point of view is that some explanations which might be tenable from a chemical point of view are precluded by physics. Contrariwise, certain physical explanations which may be attractive are completely precluded by the chemistry. For an adequate explanation for the image of the Shroud, one must have an

explanation which is scientifically sound, from a physical, chemical, biological and medical viewpoint. At the present, this type of solution does not appear to be obtainable by the best efforts of the members of the Shroud Team. Furthermore, experiments in physics and chemistry with old linen have failed to reproduce adequately the phenomenon presented by the Shroud of Turin. The scientific consensus is that the image was produced by something which resulted in oxidation, dehydration, and conjugation of the polysaccharide structure of the microfibrils of the linen itself. Such changes can be duplicated in the laboratory by certain chemical and physical processes. A similar type of change in linen can be obtained by sulfuric acid or heat. However, there are no chemical or physical methods known which can account for the totality of the image, nor can any combination of physical, chemical, biological, or medical circumstances explain the image adequately....

Thus, the answer to the question of how the image was produced or what produced the image remains, now, as it has been in the past, a mystery.

SUMMARY

We can conclude for now that the Shroud image is that of a real human form of a scourged, crucified man. It is not the product of an artist. The blood stains are composed of hemoglobin and also give a positive test for serum albumin. The image is an ongoing mystery and until further chemical studies are made, perhaps by this group of scientists, or perhaps by some scientists in the future, the problem remains unsolved.

[accessible at http://www.shroud.com/78conclu.htm.
Excerpt reprinted with permission of STERA, Inc.]

When one looks at the myriad of disciplines and the various tests applied to the Shroud and reads STURP's summary, one begins to understand why the Shroud has become one of the most intensely studied artifacts in human history. Besides the official investigations in 1969, 1973 and 1978, hundreds of Shroud centers and individual researchers around the world devote countless hours to study the mysterious cloth.

One of those individuals, Mark Antonacci, a lawyer from St. Louis who had been become very interested in the Shroud, called me after he heard that I had been giving lectures. Mark was another former agnostic whose whole life had changed once he had gained knowledge about the Shroud. We soon became friends, and in 1983, Mark decided to write a Shroud book (Antonacci 2000). I had begun to amass a pretty good collection of Shroud materials, so Mark would often call and ask me to check a fact or two. We soon were talking almost daily. Mark's book would eventually play a key role in events related to the Shroud that started to unfold in the year 2000.

Dorothy Crispino, whom I had recently invited to give a Shroud lecture for the parish at the monastery and who was publisher of *Shroud Spectrum International* (the only Shroud journal in the English-speaking world), lived in Indiana, a five-and-a-half hour drive from St. Louis. Dorothy invited me to come out and visit her for a weekend one summer to informally share about the Shroud. When I told her about Mark, she said to bring him along. We told other Shroud contacts about it, and several people expressed an interest to attend. Dorothy graciously hosted anyone who wanted to come and each summer for the next few years we had fairly large groups of people descend upon Dorothy's quaint, Civil War-era home.

There was no official agenda. It was simply a gathering of people interested in the Shroud, discussing theories and the latest news. I'll never forget one year when Dan, a member of the group, brought his girlfriend. As Dan introduced her to us, I could tell that this gathering was the last place on earth she wanted to be. When I extended my hand in greeting, she limply shook it and didn't even make eye contact with me. Her body language shouted, "Why did I agree to come to this?" I actually felt sorry for her. I truly wondered how she was going to make it through the weekend. Soon we were all discussing various Shroud matters. There were several discussions going on, and I decided that rather sitting in on just one conversation, I would just move around and try to hear bits of all of them. At one point, I blurted out—to no one in particular, "Isn't this great?" Dan's girlfriend looked at me in a way that I knew she was thinking I needed a mental-health evaluation. However, over the course of the weekend, I could see her demeanor slowly changing, and she even started showing interest in the conversations. While she and Dan prepared to depart on Sunday afternoon, she said that she hated to leave—and I could tell that she was being sincere. The Shroud bug had bitten again!

Studying the Shroud helped me to feel a strong connection to God. But I also soon experienced a very strong God-connection that had nothing to do with the Shroud. Every summer the monks had an annual retreat. We owned a small house in a rural part of Missouri and often used it for that purpose. One summer, I and several other monks came down to the house a few days before the official retreat began. During one of those nights, on what was a fairly cool evening for a Missouri summer, I left a window open when I went to sleep. At one point in the night, I woke up for no reason at all. As I felt a slight breeze flow through the window, I unexpectedly experienced a palatable presence of God in the room, and I felt unconditionally loved. Although I had experienced synchronicities before, they were nothing like this. It was powerful beyond words, and it has always stayed with me. I was later to have similar experiences, and most of those did involve the Shroud. (I will recount these later in the book.)

In June, 1985, a conference on carbon dating (C-14), used in archaeology in conjunction with other tests, to gauge the age of objects, was held in Trondheim, Norway. In 1983, six labs from around the world had participated in some tests, basically to see how they all of the labs compared in accuracy. Some of the labs that would later be chosen for the C-14 test on the Shroud took part. Zurich, which was one of the three later chosen to test the Shroud, was off by one thousand years on one sample because of improper cleansing. All six of the labs dated another sample and each one was 200 to 468 years out of range of the actual date (Petrosillo and Marinelli 1996:24). A chemist, the late Dr. Robert Dinegar, who eventually headed STURP's C-14 committee that made a proposal to the Turin authorities to date the Shroud, attended this meeting. He took handwritten notes of some of the events of the conference. I later met Dinegar and corresponded with him. Several times I encouraged him to write a book, as he had a key role in the events leading up to the C-14 dating. Unfortunately, I was not successful, and he died in 2005. He did, however, send me a copy of his notes for this particular conference. Although I have shared these previously with the Internet "Shroud Science Group" I belong to (consisting of about 100 scientists and researchers from around the world), they have never been made known to the general public. These are *very* significant from an historical point of view. (I have reproduced them in Appendix A.)

Also in 1985, I learned that the late Dr. Alan Adler, a chemist who was a blood specialist and a member of STURP, would be giving a lecture on the Shroud at an American Chemical Society meeting in St. Louis. I made plans to attend and was very excited to know I would be hearing for the first time one of the STURP scientists. (Adler didn't actually go to Turin with the group, but afterward studied samples brought back.) After the talk, many in the audience went to speak with him, and he continued to discuss his findings informally. I hung on his every word. Little did I know that I would be seeing Dr. Adler again very soon after that.

CHAPTER THREE

"ARE YOU GOING TO THE SHROUD CONFERENCE?"

A few months after I heard Adler give his talk in St. Louis, I learned through my Shroud network that a conference titled "The Mystery of the Shroud" would be held on February 15-16, 1986, in a small college town in Pennsylvania, Elizabethtown. (For a list of all Shroud symposia ever held, see Appendix B.) Naturally, my first thought was whether I would be able to make arrangements to attend. I looked at the calendar and based on the conference dates, was disappointed to see that it was apparently on a Wednesday and Thursday. I immediately thought to myself, "Why in the world would they have it in the middle of the week instead of a weekend?" I was involved in the monastery school as a teacher and coach and also taking theology classes at "The Aquinas Institute," which would make it impossible to get away at mid-week, so I put the idea of attending the conference out of my mind. I did, however, keep checking the media to see if there was any publicity about the conference, but I was disappointed that I couldn't find a single notice. I learned that the speakers included blood expert Dr. Alan Adler, physicist Dr. John Jackson, physicist Dr. Eric Jumper, archaeologist Paul Maloney, physician Dr. Gilbert Lavoie, as well as two skeptics, microscopist Dr. Walter McCrone and investigator Joe Nickell, a former stage magician, who wrote articles in such magazines as *Free Inquiry* and *The Humanist* and would later write for *The Skeptical Inquirer*.

On Sunday, February 9, it occurred to me that February 16 (the second day of the conference) would also be a Sunday. That meant that the conference was actually to be held on a Saturday and Sunday. I thought to myself, "Why did I think it was going to be on a Wednesday and Thursday?" I looked at a calendar and realized I had originally and quite mistakenly looked at January instead of

February. I immediately considered going again, but then quickly realized that it was less than one week before the conference. I figured I probably wouldn't be able to get permission from Father Prior ("Prior" is the equivalent in a Priory to an "Abbot" in an Abbey), the plane fare would be about $500 on such short notice, and I was scheduled to coach a seventh-grade basketball game on that Saturday. Also, one class at Aquinas Institute always had a paper due the Monday morning of each week and if I attended the conference, there was no way I would be able to get the paper handed in on time. My heart immediately sank as I realized I undoubtedly wouldn't be able to go.

After Mass that morning, a parishioner, Lucy McNamara, who knew I was interested in the Shroud, came up to me and said, "I heard there's going to be a Shroud conference in Pennsylvania. Are you going?" I was astonished that she knew about it since I had been on the lookout for publicity about the conference, but had not seen or heard anything. Here was a non-shroudie who had heard something I hadn't! "How did you hear about it?" I inquired. "I don't know—I saw it in some paper or something," she off-handedly replied.

I told her about the barriers that stood in the way of my attending and said that I would have to settle for watching videotapes of the conference. "Besides," I said, "I'm not sure Father Prior would even let me go." "Oh, but that's not like being at the conference," she said firmly. "You ought to go. Where is Father Prior? I'll ask him." I looked up, and to my amazement, he just happened to be walking straight toward us! Lucy stopped him on the spot and said, "Father Prior, there's a Shroud conference in Pennsylvania next weekend and Brother Joe would like to go, but he's reluctant to ask you. But if you let him go, I'll pay for his plane ticket." He looked at me and asked what sort of school obligations I had. I told him and he said, "If it's okay with Father Finbarr (the principal of the school), it's alright with me." I thanked Lucy profusely and eagerly waited to ask Father Finbarr for his permission.

At lunch, I related to Father Finbarr the situation, and he also asked me about my school obligations. I mentioned the basketball game and he said that if I get could get Rick Suarez, the other seventh-grade basketball coach, to substitute for me, it was alright with him. That day happened to be the school's annual fund-raising auction, so after lunch, I decided to go over to the auction to roam around. When I arrived, the first person I ran into was—Rick Suarez! I exclaimed, "Rick, just the person I need to see!" I explained the circumstances and asked if he would be able to substitute for me. He answered with three beautiful words, "Sure, no problem."

I now had permission to go, I had my plane fare paid for, and I had someone to substitute for me at the basketball game. There was still one obstacle left: I had a paper due for that theology class the day after the conference ended, and with travel and the busy conference schedule, there was no way I would have time to write it. I didn't know what I was going to do about the paper when I headed off to class on Monday morning, February 10. When I got to class, the first thing the professor said was, "We've fallen behind in our schedule so the paper that was due next Monday won't now be due until the following Friday." I internally screamed with delight. Amazingly, the last barrier had fallen. At that point, I felt like I knew how the Israelites felt when the Red Sea parted.

I was extremely excited, knowing that on Friday night I would be headed for my first real Shroud conference. I had made arrangements to stay at the hotel where most of the speakers were booked so that I could get extra time to talk with them and also to be able to get a ride to the conference site. After so many things had happened to enable me to go, I assumed nothing would go wrong now. On Friday morning, February 14, the day I was scheduled to leave, a huge snowstorm blanketed much of the Midwest and East Coast. I wasn't too worried though, as I wasn't scheduled to fly out until later in the evening, when I presumed the travel conditions would have improved. In the late afternoon, I called the airline to confirm my departure time and expected no problems. To my horror, I discovered that my flight would not be leaving as scheduled. "There's no equipment," said the representative. "What do you mean, there's no equipment?" I nervously asked. "The plane scheduled to fly out tonight was also the plane that was supposed to fly in this morning," he explained. "But because of the storm, the morning flight was cancelled, so there's no plane available to fly out." I suddenly needed a Plan B. I hurriedly tried to make other arrangements. I was told that I could take a flight out on Saturday morning to Harrisburg, but that would get me to the conference late. Or, I could fly into Philadelphia late on Friday night, take a Greyhound bus to Harrisburg, and take a cab get to Elizabethtown before the start of the conference. I took the latter option.

After a long plane flight (also delayed because of the weather), a Greyhound bus trip and a cab to the hotel, I arrived bleary-eyed at 6:30 a.m., less than three hours before the start of the conference. I hoped to find a ride to the conference venue from one of the speakers, so I approached the front desk and nervously waited for the clerk to get off the phone. "Are John Jackson and Eric Jumper here yet?" I asked anxiously. He informed me that they had been delayed by the weather. "But," said the clerk, "Al Adler is here." "Great," I said, "Could you please let me know when you give him his wake-up call?" "Oh, that's who I was speaking with," he replied. The clerk put me through to Adler's room, and I asked him if I could ride with him. Adler offered me the ride and told me to come to his room at 8:15 a.m. I breathed a sigh of relief. When I got there, he opened the door and immediately said, "I remember you." He was referring to when I attended his talk in St. Louis about six months prior. A friend of his actually drove and we arrived safely at the conference just before 9 a.m. I virtually had not slept since early Friday morning, but I was running on adrenaline at that point. It was going to be a fascinating weekend.

Shortly before the conference began, Jackson and Jumper arrived. Both had been young Air Force captains in the late 1970s when they co-founded STURP. Jackson and Jumper were to STURP what Lennon and McCartney were to the Beatles. I had been sending them my Shroud newsletter but had neither corresponded nor talked on the phone with them. It was a real thrill to meet both of them. During the course of the conference, I also met Paul Maloney and Dr. Lavoie for the first time. I had corresponded and/or talked previously on the phone with both of them. Father Otterbein of the Holy Shroud Guild also was in attendance at the conference, but Father Rinaldi was not able to make it.

Dr. Walter McCrone was a microscopist who had made a name for himself by supposedly debunking "The Vinland Map," which was owned by Yale University and was purported to be a fifteenth-century map that included information about the Norse exploration of America. I say "supposedly" because years later his conclusion would be contested by various other scientists. McCrone had been claiming since 1980 that the Shroud was a painting and that the blood on the cloth was just an artist's pigment. When STURP studied the cloth in 1978, their main objective was to discover how the image was formed. As a group, they concluded the image was *not* made by paint. (STURP didn't deny there were traces of tiny particles of paint that were left by artists who had been allowed to touch their copies to the Shroud.) STURP's documenting photographer Barrie Schwortz, when doing interviews, likes to ask how long would one expect a group of two dozen top-notch scientists to take to find out that paint was the source of the image. Nickell, on the other hand, claimed that the Shroud was the result of a dust-rubbing over a bas-relief statue.

When Adler gave his talk on Saturday, he incorporated arguments to counter what he knew McCrone would say when he gave his talk on Sunday. Adler, whose specialty was blood chemistry, asserted that without doubt, there was real blood on the Shroud. To this day I still chuckle when I recall him saying with a twinkle in his eye: "It's blood, "B-L-U-D, blood." McCrone wasn't present for Adler's talk, leaving Nickell as the only skeptic there on Saturday. Adler could talk about the Shroud for an hour and a half without taking a breath—and did. Adler also had the habit of constantly using the phrase "in fact" when he spoke. Adler's friend, who had driven us to the conference, informed Adler after his talk that he, "in fact," had used the phrase 27 times!

There was a supper break in the late afternoon, and, as is so often the case at Shroud conferences, people milled around during the break to continue to talk about the Shroud. When it began, I joined Adler, who was speaking with Jackson, Jumper and Lavoie. After talking away most of the supper break, Adler suggested to the group that everyone get together to eat after the last presentation of the evening. Since I was with Adler's party, I was excited to realize that I was implicitly invited to go to dinner with them. As planned, after the last presentation, we met later at a nearby restaurant with no need to worry about getting back to the conference. I had to pinch myself to make sure I wasn't dreaming. During the meal, many STURP matters were openly discussed. I suppose they figured a monk and a physician (Dr. Lavoie) could be trusted to keep confidences. When I retired for the night, it had been about 40 hours since I had any decent sleep. Despite that, I realized I didn't feel all that tired. It had turned out to be an exciting day as I had expected, and I was still somewhat wound up. But I eventually descended into a restful slumber.

On Sunday morning, I was invited to have breakfast with Father Otterbein and Adler. As the three of us headed to the restaurant, we ran into Jackson and Jumper. Father Otterbein invited them to join us, and they did. I, meanwhile, was hoping I wasn't still really just in my room and dreaming all of this. At one point, I said, "I wonder if Nickell told McCrone what Adler said in his talk yesterday." A few minutes later, I looked up and saw none other than McCrone and Nickell leaving. They apparently had eaten breakfast together, but I hadn't noticed them when I first arrived. As they had to pass our table to leave the restaurant, Nickell's eyes caught mine, and he bobbed his head up and down in a definite affirmative nod. He had obviously heard me express my question. Either I was talking louder than I thought, or he had excellent hearing—maybe it was both.

When McCrone began his conference talk, he apologized to Nickell because McCrone disagreed with the explanation that Nickell had presented in his talk on Saturday. After McCrone completed his talk, there was a question-and-answer session. I asked McCrone how his supposed forger was able to incorporate details that would not be known for several hundred years until certain instruments, such as the microscope, were invented. I still marvel when I remember his answer: "I'm not going to answer that."(!!) Needless to say, I didn't find that to be a satisfactory answer. I later corresponded with McCrone and brought this non-answer to his attention. (His reply and other exchanges between us can be found in Appendix C.)

After the conference ended on late Sunday morning, I bid goodbye to all the people I had been with and prepared to fly back to St. Louis in the early afternoon. The weather, however, that had caused problems before the conference, was still an issue. I was able to fly from Harrisburg to Pittsburgh with Dr. Jumper. I was glad to be able to get extra time to spend with him. However, my flight from Pittsburgh to St. Louis was cancelled due to the weather. The winter storm was still making its presence felt. I was unable

Chapter Three: "Are You Going to the Shroud Conference?" 41

able to fly out until Monday morning. Normally, travel problems are quite aggravating, but I was so thrilled to have been able to attend the conference, the travel woes didn't perturb me.

When I got back home, there was an *Associated Press* story, written by a Pennsylvania writer, in the *St. Louis Post-Dispatch* about the conference. The conference had featured seven speakers, five of whom basically said that the Shroud was a mystery. Two of those five had studied the cloth directly. The remaining two of the seven declared it a forgery (but disagreed on how it was done). Dr. McCrone had been saying since 1980 that the Shroud was a painting. And whose findings were featured in the article? Dr. McCrone's six-year-old assertion got top billing. I was absolutely furious at the slant and the fact that the article made it look like McCrone's findings were recent. If that wasn't bad enough, the story was carried on the back of the food section! I wonder how many of the stories that were deemed worthy to be on the front page that day are being discussed now more than the Shroud of Turin.

I immediately decided I would write a letter to the editor. I had a full day of duties at the monastery school, but I was distracted all day by the thought of writing the letter. When my school duties were over, I literally rushed to my room to write it when I experienced something out of the ordinary—something I can only describe as an inner voice—told me to go pick up trash. (I discovered later that, in theology, such communications are called "locutions.") Picking up trash on the grounds was not a job actually assigned to me, but something I actually did on my own because I couldn't stand to see the mess, and no one else was doing it. The last thing on earth I wanted to do at that point was to pick up trash, but as I knew the voice came from outside myself, I knew also I would have to heed it. It was so compelling, I unhesitatingly went out and picked up trash, unaware that something incredible was about to happen. After about an hour, I had picked up all the trash on the grounds and again started to rush back to my room to write the letter. As I headed for my room, I heard a car door close in the parking lot where I had just finished. When I turned around, I saw a man I recognized, someone who often came to the monastery church to pray. He was Robert Hyland, Regional Vice-President of the big CBS affiliate radio station in St. Louis, KMOX, a 100,000-watt station with a signal so strong it could be picked up in Canada. I asked him if he had seen the article about the conference. He said that he heard about it but hadn't actually read it. I then told him how biased and misleading it was. He proposed that I talk on the radio about it. KMOX had a Sunday program called "The World of Religion," which was recorded at the station's studios and sent out all over the country to other affiliates. When he told me to call John Angelides at the station to arrange an interview, I knew it would be a done deal. At KMOX, Robert Hyland's reputation and power were "second only to God." I called the next day and was told that they had already been planning to interview none other than Dr. McCrone, so they invited me to debate with him. Now, I had not given any radio or television interviews at that point and was very nervous about being baptized in a debate with a world-famous microscopist. Even though I felt it was a David-versus-Goliath matchup, I agreed to do it.

I paused to consider what had happened. I had just returned from my first Shroud conference and had met some of the key researchers. I had heard an inner voice instruct me to pick up trash and because I did, I was going to be on a radio program that would be broadcast across the nation. It strengthened the ever-growing conviction I felt that I was given a special calling with respect to the Shroud. However, I was unceremoniously brought back to my normal reality that night—I was on the monastic dishwashing crew after supper.

I went to the station later in the week to tape the segment and presented the case of the probable authenticity of the Shroud as best I could. After the show, the moderator told me he was not very impressed with Dr. McCrone's arguments. I may not have slain the giant, but apparently I at least held my own. Some suspected that McCrone was not in this just for discovering the truth about the Shroud. One article states:

> He runs his own outfit, McCrone Associates, Inc. up in Chicago, and there's a strong suspicion around the Sitea *[hotel in Turin]* that his interest in the shroud may not be selflessly scientific. McCrone is the man who blew the Vinland Map at Yale. This was the map that proved America was discovered by the Vikings, long before Columbus. Till McCrone spied anatase in the ink—which is a synthesized pigment not developed until the Twenties. He got a mile and a half of lucrative publicity out of that and there are grave doubts

around the Team about his priorities. He's not their type (Thomas 1978:82).

[Excerpt reprinted with permission from Rolling Stone.]

Another author writes, "'It's enough to make you want to reopen the case of the Vinland Map,' says Jumper, with perhaps more pique than some among the STURP rank and file might betray. McCrone for his part, is unmoved: I am very sure of the data I have" (Murphy 1981:55). Jumper's wish came true. Other researchers, including independent groups, have contested McCrone's Vinland Map findings. See for example, Cahill 1987, Olin 2003 and "Vinland Map of America no forgery, expert says" (2009).

I tracked down another newspaper account of the *Associated Press* story about the Elizabethtown conference and discovered that the St. Louis version had been edited. Portions that had discussed the evidence presented by the non-skeptics at the conference had been taken out. I discussed it over the phone with an editor, who agreed that the editing had changed the story considerably, and my letter to the editor was published.

In the spring, I graduated from St. Louis University with a B.A. in Theological Studies. One of the requirements for graduation was to write a "senior thesis." To no one's surprise, I wrote my paper on the Shroud. I worked on it for months, and after it was completed, my professor said it was good enough to get published. I was pleasantly surprised and decided to see if I could, in fact, *get* it published. I sent it out to several Shroud scholars, including the most prominent author on the Shroud in the world, Ian Wilson, whose 1978 book, The Shroud of Turin, was many people's first scholarly exposure to the cloth. One publisher was interested in it, but wanted me to add an index. I didn't have the time to do that, so I didn't pursue that lead. Eventually, a private individual in California volunteered to produce copies of it as a monograph and did so. I really enjoyed having written it, which set me on a path to author additional works in the future.

In the summer of 1986, I was able to visit Father Peter Rinaldi, stationed at Corpus Christi parish in Port Chester, New York, and one of the co-founders of the Holy Shroud Guild. Port Chester is a quaint town, known mainly for Father Rinaldi's presence there, and for the parish church as a Shroud shrine. Turin was Father Rinaldi's birthplace, and he saw the Shroud when he was an altar boy. He became extremely interested in it and knew some of the famous Shroud researchers of the early 1900s, who had started studying the Shroud after the first photographs were taken of it in 1898. As mentioned previously, when Secondo Pia took a picture of the indistinct image, the resulting negative yielded a positive result, meaning that the Shroud image has characteristics similar to a photographic negative. This was rather startling, given the fact that photography wasn't invented until about the 1860s, and the Shroud had existed centuries before that time. Father Rinaldi, a saint of a man, was eventually sent to the United States and became a dual citizen. He actually had a great-uncle who has been officially beatified (the last step on the way to sainthood) by the Catholic Church. Father Rinaldi was the liaison between the Church and STURP and was one of the key people to arrange for the Shroud to be studied by STURP. Father Rinaldi would often say, "Those who take up the Shroud take up the cross." He would also say that the "best of the Shroud is still to come." I was so glad that I was able to meet him in person.

While visiting Father Rinaldi, I also was able to visit Father Adam Otterbein, another priest of the Holy Shroud Guild, who worked with Father Rinaldi in many Shroud matters. Father Otterbein was stationed in Esopus, New York, where the Holy Shroud Guild collection of Shroud materials, including many rare items such as correspondence from one of the first significant Shroud researchers, Paul Vignon, was kept. Vignon was a French biologist and one of the famous early twentieth century sindonologists. It was a thrill to see and peruse all the marvelous materials that had been collected since the late 1890s.

By now I had been in the monastery for over six years, but because of my commitment to mentor Greg until he was 18, I had not been able to enter the initial, official trial period that monks normally undergo. This one-year trial period is called a "novitiate," and entails intensive studies related to the monastic life and a restricting of most personal freedoms. Greg had recently turned 18, so I was now free to go that route. In my case, the restrictions included an almost complete blackout of anything Shroud-related. That was going to be difficult, as I had become used to keeping up-to-the-minute with everything going on in sindonology. I entered the novitiate in the fall of

Chapter Three: "Are You Going to the Shroud Conference?" 45

1986. It was during this time that a large planning meeting was held in Turin to discuss the protocol for performing a C-14 test on the Shroud. (See Appendix D for various documents related to this meeting.) This test could supposedly date the age of the cloth within a 50-year range. Both proponents and opponents of the Shroud's authenticity look forward in excitement to the test. One of the participants, William Meacham, an archaeologist warned against placing too much emphasis on just one test, pointing out that C-14 test results were often wildly inaccurate, sometimes for reasons unknown. Many people don't realize that the C-14 test is not a stand-alone test, as inaccuracies in the media often lead people to believe. Radiocarbon dating is always used in conjunction with other scientific tests. If the results corroborate other data, it is considered a confirmatory test. If they don't match with the other data, they are routinely discarded—and the unknown reasons that contribute to inaccurate dating are often never discovered. Sometimes the reasons are later understood. But the test is often very problematical. Meacham wrote that for both scientists and laymen:

> There appears to be an unhealthy consensus approaching the level of dogma among both scientific and lay commentators that C-14 will settle the issue once and for all time. This attitude sharply contradicts the general perspective of field archaeologists and geologists, who view possible contamination as very serious problem in interpreting the results of radiocarbon measurement (Meacham 1986a:15).
> *[Excerpt reprinted with permission of William Meacham.]*

Meacham, who had quite a bit of experience using C-14, made some very accurate predictions pertaining to the 1988 dating. Recounting events at the planning meeting, he also wrote:

> The discussion turned to the question of statistical analysis again, and I began to realize that what the labs were most concerned about was obtaining matching results from each lab, or if not, then at least the one outlier could be easily identified and rejected before calculating the radiocarbon age. This concern seemed to me misplaced: what was **much** more important was insuring that a rogue sample was not chosen. It would be a tragedy if every lab got the same result but it was wrong because there was something inherently

wrong with the particular sample chosen. Adler agreed that this was the biggest worry . . . . (Meacham, 2005b:75).
[Excerpt reprinted with permission of William Meacham.]

(For an online source to see Meacham's predictions, see Meacham 1986b.)

Meacham actually was not the only one that foresaw significant problems if the tests weren't done properly. Archaeologist Paul Maloney, who learned of important information related to the protocol, wrote a letter in late November to Father Rinaldi shortly before the priest was to meet with the late Professor Luigi Gonella, the scientific advisor to the Cardinal of Turin. Maloney discovered that the original protocol was going to be changed. Backed up by a textile expert, he stated in this letter why the original protocol should be kept and what the problems would be if the new protocol was followed. His predictions, like Meacham's were stunningly accurate. (See Appendix E for the text of Maloney's letter.)

Meanwhile Dr. Harry Gove, inventor of the particular type of C-14 method used on Shroud ("AMS" for Accelerator Mass Spectrometry), who played a major role in the meeting, was upset at some aspects of the planning. He and Dr. Garman Harbottle of the Brookhaven C-14 laboratory in Upton, New York, held a press conference to try to get the Turin authorities, who had made some changes to the original protocol, to reconsider. In a Shroud history found at:

http://www.shroud.com/history.htm, one finds:

> **January 15, 1988:** In a press release Gove and Dr. Harbottle conclude, 'The Archbishop's plan, disregarding the protocol, does not seem capable of producing a result that will meet the test of credibility and scientific rigor' and that 'it is probably better to do nothing than to proceed with a scaled-down experiment'.
> *[Excerpt reprinted with permission of STERA, Inc.]*

When I emerged from the novitiate during the fall of 1987, the day for the actual taking of the Shroud samples for the vaunted C-14 test—April 21, 1988—was not far off.

CHAPTER FOUR

THE C-14 TEST: "1260-1390!"

When samples from the Shroud of Turin were taken in the spring of 1988, results of the C-14 test were expected to be announced some time that fall. One of the controversies in the planning (and there had been many) was the choice between the older method of C-14, known as "proportional counting," and the more recent method called "AMS" (Accelerator Mass Spectrometry), which required less material than the former. Despite the fact that the results could be rechecked with proportional counting but not with AMS and despite the fact that AMS was seldom used at the time for dating cloths, it was selected as the method to be used. For some basic details regarding the two methods, see:

http://www.shroudofturin4journalists.com/Details/c14b.htm.

The samples were cut from one single spot, believed by some researchers to be the worst possible area. Adler wrote:

> Only a single sample was taken in the lower corner of the main cloth of the frontal image below the so-called sidestrip from the selvage edge in an obviously water-stained area....The selvage edge was trimmed off before portions of the sample were divided among the participating laboratories. Whether such an obviously contaminated sample is truly representative of the rest of the cloth is clearly questionable . . . .
>
> [Reprinted with permission from "Updating Recent Studies on the Shroud of Turin," [in] Archaeological Chemistry: Organic, Inorganic, and Biochemical Analyses, American Chemical Society: 223-228, ACS Symposium Series 625. Copyright 1996 American Chemical Society.]

This section was chosen even though the 1986 planning meeting decreed that several areas on the cloth should be used. Nevertheless, the samples, all from only one controversial area, were given to Oxford University, the

University of Zurich, and the University of Arizona. The labs agreed, in principal, not to confer with one another before the results were to be tabulated by the British Museum, the institution which oversaw the project.

In mid-May, an article about the dating process at the University of Arizona was published in the *St. Louis Post-Dispatch*. The author, Bill McClellan, was a columnist, who just happened to be the son-in-law of Dr. Doug Donahue, one of main Arizona scientists involved in the test. McClellan was to use his connection to obtain information as the process there unfolded. I felt fortunate to be in St. Louis, as it was a local story only and didn't go out on the wire where it could be carried elsewhere. This was during the pre-Internet days when most of the information disseminated about the Shroud was still done by paper and snail mail. Naturally, I tried to glean any information that would indicate something about the results. Unfortunately, McClellan did not disclose enough for any results to be discernible. (See Appendix F for the text of the full article.)

By July, I had completed my novitiate and was once again able to attend the informal gathering held at Dorothy Crispino's house in Indiana. That summer, our group included a transplanted Englishman from Australia, Rex Morgan, who published *"Shroud News,"* a wonderful little periodical that kept people all over the world up-to-date on various Shroud matters. The fact that Rex flew over 15 hours just to join this informal gathering gives one an idea to what lengths (literally) sindonologists will go to learn more about the cloth.

During the course of the weekend, Dorothy received a call from Father Rinaldi, who said rumors were circulating that the tests had produced medieval results. He seemed genuinely concerned the rumors might be true. Around late August, a story was published in *USA Today* quoting Dr. Richard Luckett of the University of Cambridge, England, that the results of the C-14 test indicated a medieval date. Nobody familiar with the Shroud had ever even heard of him. But after Father Rinaldi's phone call to Dorothy in July, I began to suspect that the tests would, in fact, date to the Middle Ages. I had also heard another story, possibly more than just rumor, that Dr. Paul Damon of the University of Arizona, one of Donahue's colleagues, had presented Shroud lectures during the summer, and reportedly told someone,

"You will be pleased with the results." But since that person's position regarding authenticity of the Shroud was not known, the statement didn't help determine one way or another what the test results might have been. As speculation about a medieval date became more and more prevalent, the late Professor Luigi Gonella, the scientific advisor to the Cardinal of Turin, told the media that the rumors were just that—rumors only. Nonetheless, the suspense continued to build.

In early October, I received a call from Bill McClellan of the *St. Louis Post-Dispatch*, who had written the aforementioned article about the Shroud dating in Arizona. He was aware of the rumors about the supposed medieval dating, and wanted to interview me. I received the required permission to do it, and McClellan drove to the monastery one afternoon. I showed him my very large Shroud collection in my very small room, called a "cell" in monastic terms. I assured him that if the dating results were determined to be medieval, it wouldn't be the final word. On October 10, his column came out and was titled "Science and Faith Head For Collision." (See Appendix G for the full text of the column.)

The "Collision" occurred three days later. On October 13, 1988, the results were officially released. Michael Tite of the British Museum, Edward Hall, director of the Oxford lab, and Robert Hedges, also of the Oxford lab, announced the results with a blackboard behind them on which were written the numbers: "1260-1390!" The added exclamation point has been criticized ever since for being unscientific. Many people have seen this famous picture in Shroud books or on the Internet. Fewer people have seen the picture taken shortly after that in Britain's newspaper *The Independent*, showing Tite, Hall and Hedges, all with their arms folded across their chests, in the manner reminiscent of the television program trailers about smug detectives who solve every mystery in one hour or less. (A photocopy of the picture from *The Independent* can be seen in Wilson and Schwortz, 2000:94.) The headline of the article trumpeted "Turin Shroud shown to be fake." The article referred to rumors that had been circulating for months that the date would be medieval. One thing was clear—the labs had agreed in principle that they would not confer with one another and would not reveal the results except to the British Museum. The circulating rumors proved there had been leaks, which certainly didn't reflect well on the labs' scientific integrity.

Hall opined, "There was a multi-million pound business in making forgeries during the fourteenth century. Someone just got a bit of linen, faked it up, and flogged it." Simple as that! Hall added "that some people would probably continue to regard it as genuine, 'just as there is a Flat Earth Society'." *[Excerpts reprinted with permission of The Independent.]* The article concluded with mention of other Catholic "relics" such as a feather from the Archangel Gabriel and a vial containing the last breath of St. Joseph, as if to suggest that if those are accepted as relics, nothing can be accepted as authentic, no matter what the evidence showed.

Cardinal Ballestrero, the archbishop of Turin, made the following declaration:

> With a dispatch delivered to the Pontifical Custodian of the Holy Shroud on September 28, 1988, through Dr. Tite of the British Museum, the coordinator of the project, the laboratories of the University of Arizona, Oxford University, and Zurich Polytechnic which carried out the radiocarbon measurements of the fabric of the Holy Shroud, have finally communicated the results of their operations.
>
> For his part, Prof. Bray of the G. Colonnetti Metrological Institute of Turin, who was entrusted with the revision of the resume presented by Dr Tite, has confirmed the compatibility of the results of the three laboratories, whose certainty falls with the limits of the method employed.
>
> After having informed the Holy See, the proprietor of the Holy Shroud, I am announcing what has been communicated to me.
>
> While submitting to science the evaluation of these results, the Church confirms its respect and veneration for this venerable icon of Christ, which remains a cult object for the faithful in accordance with the attitude that has always been demonstrated towards the Holy Shroud, in which the value of the image is preeminent with respect to its possible value as a historical object—an attitude that refutes the gratuitous inferences of a theological character that were put forward within the sphere of an inquiry that had been presented as solely and rigorously scientific.
>
> At the same time, the problems of the origin of the image and of its conservation still remain mostly unsolved and will demand further

research and further study, towards which the Church will manifest the same openness, inspired by its love for truth which It has shown in permitting the radiocarbon test as soon as a reasonable working programme for this is submitted.

The unpleasant fact that many news items relative to the scientific investigation have been anticipated in the press, especially that in the English language, is a cause of my personal regret because it has even favoured the insinuation, certainly not an unbiased one, that the Church was afraid of science by concealing the results, an accusation which is in flagrant contradiction to the attitude which the Church, also in this case, has firmly maintained (Petrosillo and Marinelli 1996:97-98).

A journalist asked Cardinal Ballestrero if the Shroud could still be called a relic. The Cardinal replied:

> Without going into very complicated arguments, because even the concept of a relic is today generally accepted to be a pluralistic one, the image, I think, could be called an icon. It is an image, that is a revealing sign of a face, a face with a religious and a spiritual significance, and I would say that the right word to refer to it might be "image" or "icon" of the face of Christ, of the person of Christ. By using this word we somehow enter in the logic of icons as being an interesting argument concerning the cult of the Church, and there, I do not see any difficulty. I remember quite well that in 1978, during the last public exposition of the Shroud, having had to deliver the homily at almost all the evening masses. I never once used the word "relic." And to whoever asked me the reason why, I used to say: "for me the icon is the real value; to say whether it is a relic I would have to know with certainty things that I do not know." Today, however, I do have to reason somewhat differently, because even the word "relic" has been subjected to an extensive evolution by liturgists, theologians, and historians; but never mind: for me it is an icon (Petrosillo and Marinelli 1996:103).

Newspapers around the world ran headlines like "Turin Shroud a Forgery Catholic Church Says," "Shroud of Turin Mystery Solved," and "Tests Show Shroud Not Linked to Christ." Sindonologists, for the most part, were totally stunned, and the critics went about handing out their best "I told you so" pronouncements. A few months later, a journalist asked Pope John Paul II a question along the lines of what the Cardinal had been asked. The Pope answered, "A relic it certainly is!" To the question: "Do you think it is genuine?" he replied, "If you are referring to the relic, I think it is. If many think it is, their conviction that they see in it the body of Christ is not without foundation" (Petrosillo and Marinelli 1996:104). In an article pertaining to this interview in the Vatican newspaper, *Osservatore Romano*, these two questions and answers about the Shroud were omitted. Could it have been because Cardinal Ballestrero had said it wasn't a relic and the Pope contradicted him with his own answer? If so, the "love of truth" that the Cardinal had referred to was compromised.

Meanwhile, the Cardinal's scientific advisor, Luigi Gonella, referring to a spate of problems with the laboratories, stated, "We are not at all satisfied with the way the laboratories conducted their study of the Shroud" (Petrosillo and Marinelli 1996:115). For one thing, the labs had insisted that their representatives be present during the taking of the samples because they didn't trust the Church officials; on the other hand, they didn't reciprocate in allowing Church officials to be present during their testing. "Since when," Gonella asked, "has a dating laboratory wanted to be present during an excavation because it did not trust the archaeologist who was excavating the specimens? Since when have laboratories refused to collaborate?" (Petrosillo and Marinelli 1996:115).

The laboratories, which wanted to do the test separately and not in conjunction with multidisciplinary studies, refused to release the raw data of their results, something which is never done in archaeological datings (Petrosillo and Marinelli 1996:112). This refusal is suspicious to say the least. Some suspect that the data actually indicated an average date of the fifteenth century. Since it is known that the first documented appearance of the Shroud (i.e., that we know for sure is the Shroud of Turin) was in the 1350s, many surmise that the labs would not have admitted to that date, which would have indicated their results were not correct. To this day, the raw data from the tests still have not been officially released, which is nothing less than a scientific scandal.

Gonella didn't mince any words when he talked about the conduct of the labs. "It was blackmail. Either we accepted the Carbon 14 test with the conditions imposed by the laboratories or they would unleash a campaign of accusations against the Church saying It was afraid of truth and that It was the enemy of science" (Petrosillo and Marinelli 1996:116). He added, "They behaved like dogs. I protest against their complete lack of professionalism in the field of deontology. I protest against the infamous method they followed. I told them to their faces that they were mafiosi" (Petrosillo and Marinelli 1996:117).

Knowing what I did about the Shroud, I knew that *something* was wrong with those results. There was plenty of indications in both art and history that the Shroud was known long before the date assigned by the C-14 test, including the "Hungarian Pray Manuscript," reliably dated to AD 1192, about 70 years before the beginning range of AD 1260. The manuscript has an illustration of Jesus' burial shroud, which shows a herringbone pattern as well as L-shaped poker holes, two prominent features found on the Shroud of Turin. It is not within the scope of this book to go into more detail about the Hungarian Pray Manuscript or many aspects; the reader is encouraged to google and/or research these topics more at www.shroud.com, via the search function. One of the local television stations in town wanted to interview me about the dating announcement, but I was recovering from minor surgery and was unable to do it. They interviewed instead, one of the Jesuits from St. Louis University. I and other sindonologists, in the meantime, went about the business of trying to figure out why the C-14 results were medieval, when practically all of the other evidence pointed to a probable first-century origin.

When Cardinal Ballestrero resigned shortly after the dating results, Turin had a new archbishop. Gonella, after his rants about the labs, expressed some hope:

> On May 4, the new archbishop of Turin, Monsignor Giovanni Saldarini, while celebrating Mass in honour of the Shroud, stated plainly that the investigations would continue and that this time they would be entrusted to people who are more open intellectually. Also because it is not enough to say that the cloth is a medieval object; the problem is to understand how it originated. Surely it is not the last word. The best is coming (Petrosillo and Marinelli 1996:120-121).

Additional evidence continued to mount showing how the C-14 dating was marred by politics, skullduggery, maniacal egotism, and ineptitude. The sizes and weights of the samples differed, depending on which participant one talked to. If they couldn't even keep that straight, it's frankly difficult to put much confidence in their other measurements. The laboratories didn't even perform a chemical analysis of the samples, which would later become a critical issue vis-à-vis various theories later put forth regarding why the results might not have been valid. Meacham would write a book, graphically titled <u>The Rape of the Shroud</u> (Meacham 2005b), which, among other things, detailed much of the intrigue and behind-the-scenes happenings. Another participant, the late Dr. Harry Gove, inventor of the C-14 method used on the Shroud, also wrote another book <u>Relic, Icon or Hoax? Carbon Dating the Turin Shroud,</u> about the infamous test (Gove 1996). (Gove was mentioned by Dinegar in his notes reproduced in Appendix A pertaining to the 1985 Trondheim C-14 conference.) Meacham summarizes his view on Gove's book:

> In 1996, he wrote a book about the dating of the Shroud; it is an incredible and offensive mélange of fact, fiction, rant and self-trumpeting, liberally peppered with arrogance and ad hominem attacks on just about everyone involved who did not agree with him" (Meacham 2005b:62).
> *[Excerpt reprinted with permission of William Meacham.]*

To be frank, I wouldn't disagree with Meacham. The book is a good illustration of how finding the truth about the Shroud became a secondary consideration. Gove admits in his book that he tried to keep STURP, which was supposed to have done new tests in conjunction with the C-14 test, out of the picture. STURP was actually going to be given a full two weeks to perform multi-disciplinary testing. At one point, it appeared that Gove's lab was going to be one of the choices to take part in the dating. When they were dropped, no doubt at least in part because of politics and personality clashes, Gove angrily wrote a letter to the British Museum, in which he called the C-14 dating "a somewhat shoddy enterprise" (Meacham 2005:95). The excerpt reproduced in Chapter Three pertaining to the Gove/Harbottle press release and also Gove's letter to the British Museum gives one an idea how volatile the politics were in the whole enterprise. Another significant account of the intrigue related to the dating can be found in the book titled <u>The Jesus Conspiracy: The Turin Shroud & The Truth About The Resurrection</u> (Kersten and Gruber 1994). It is also interesting to note that Gove had exhibited his opposition to STURP even before the latter had begun their testing. According to STURP spokesman, Kenneth Stevenson, shortly after STURP arrived in Turin in 1978, he "was practically accosted" by Gove, who interrupted a press conference to ask what made Stevenson an "expert" in C-14 dating. Stevenson relates that he never claimed to be an expert. He merely was addressing the C-14 issue as part of the overall picture, especially because the media had been claiming that the authorities were not allowing the test because it had something to hide (Stevenson and Habermas 1990:47). As it was, the C-14 test was not performed until ten years later.

One of the changes from the original protocol for the 1988 testing had to do with the involvement of the Pope's advisers on scientific matters, the Pontifical Academy of Sciences. They were to have been one of the groups to scientifically evaluate the data from the testing. Shortly before the testing, a representative from the Academy announced that they would not be taking part. It was obvious that some political machinations had taken place, although the specific details were never known. Years later, I was informed by reliable sources that the Academy was still actually "calling the shots" after the dating. One can only wonder what was going on behind the scenes if the Academy scientists made a point to announce they would not be involved but were still exerting control.

After the dating, Hall, who was a member of the council of administration of the British Museum (Sox 1988:115), and his Oxford lab were given a donation of one million pounds (equivalent to approximately two million U.S. dollars) by what has been described as "rich businessmen." Suspicion arose that was payoff for "proving" the Shroud a fake. The donation was made on Good Friday, 1989. One cannot fail to see the irony of the timing. This action enabled the lab to establish a permanent professorship, which was filled by none other than Dr. Michael Tite of the British Museum (Wilson and Schwortz 2000:89). Clearly, there was a conflict of interest here. The question has to be asked: When did the labs learn that one million pounds would be donated if the Shroud were "proven" to be a fake? In February, 1989, the official report of the dating results was published, and it claimed with 95 per cent certainty that the Shroud was of medieval origin (Damon et al. 1989:611). Considering that, as recounted previously, in 1983 six labs had all dated a sample incorrectly. while Zurich was off by one thousand years on another sample, and (as documented in the next chapter) in 1989, only seven out 38 labs performed satisfactorily in an intercomparison test, one must view that 95 per cent certainty figure for the Shroud dating with an arched eyebrow. Gonella fired another salvo: "Actually the laboratories were more interested in press publicity than in scientific truth" (Petrosillo and Marinelli 1996:125).

On October 23, 1988, I called Dr. Paul Damon, the head of the University of Tucson laboratory, which took part in the dating. Because of the leaks that had occurred, I asked him if the three laboratories had discussed their results among themselves, something that was prohibited by the protocol. He replied, "No, not between the three labs at all. There were a lot of rumors attributed to various people but they all seemed to come from one source—one person" (Personal communication, 1988, from the late Dr. Paul Damon). I had to wonder how he was so sure that it was only one person who leaked the information. He then asked me if I knew who might have spread rumors. I thought it was interesting that he was asking me such a question. It was known by many that Damon's lab had invited Harry Gove to witness their testing. It was also generally known that Reverend David Sox, who had been General Secretary of the British Society for the Turin Shroud before accepting McCrone's painting theory and subsequently resigning, was privy to the Zurich findings. His book The Shroud Unmasked (Sox 1988) was printed two weeks *before* the official announcement of the results. Sox relates that Gove placed a bet with a co-worker about the outcome of the test and won himself a pair of cowboy boots! Damon, however, insisted to me that it was not Gove who had spread the leaks. Damon's response that the three labs had not discussed their results before the official announcement didn't tally with some information I received that month in the October issue of *Shroud News*, which stated:

Dr Michael Tite of the British Museum and supervisor of the test collation programme said on 27 August, "Results from each testing centre have been circulated to the others with a proposal for a co-ordinated date on the Shroud from the samples, but I haven't heard from anyone yet" (as cited in Morgan 1988:7).
[Excerpt reprinted with permission from Rex Morgan.]

Amazingly, the project coordinator admitted that the laboratories *had* consulted with one another. Given that fact, Damon's claim is troublesome for obvious reasons. One other troubling situation was soon revealed. The Oxford lab stated that they had found cotton fibers in their sample, "a fine, dark yellow strand, possibly of Egyptian origin, and quite old." The Shroud is linen. Peter South of a laboratory in Derbyshire said "It may have been used for repairs at some time in the past... ("Rogue Fibres found in the Shroud" 1988:13, back issue of *Textile Horizons*). This observation, for some reason, didn't raise many red flags with anyone at the time. Later developments would raise this matter again. But much damage had been done—at least in the short term.

CHAPTER FIVE

SINDONOLOGISTS STRIKE BACK

Not long after McClellan's column about his visit to me was published, a worker at KFUO, one of the local radio stations in St. Louis, called me and said he had seen the article. He wanted to have me on one of their programs. I once again received permission from the monastic superior and discussed the various details of the Shroud controversy. Antonacci and I also appeared together on a KMOX radio program, the "At Your Service" program I had hoped to get on. Shortly after, Antonacci (who was still at work on his book despite the medieval results of the C-14 test) called me with a request. He was in constant contact with Dr. John Jackson of STURP and told me that Jackson was trying to raise money for more research, which was especially critical given the C-14 results. Mark asked if I knew anyone who might be willing to donate. I told him I didn't but that I would keep my eyes and ears open. I really meant it, but part of me wanted to say to Mark, "Where in the world am I going to find someone like that, especially since the C-14 dating convinced most people the Shroud was a hoax?"

A few days after Mark called, I received a call from Dick Nieman, a St. Louisan who had heard me on the radio program. Dick said he knew a fair amount about the Shroud but wanted to learn more, so I invited him to come to the monastery to discuss the Shroud further. At the end of our discussion that night, he offered, "If there is anyway I can help, let me know." It was a prime "now-that-you-mention-it" moment. I told him that Jackson was trying to raise money for research, and Dick generously agreed to donate to Jackson's cause. Another improbable event related to the Shroud had just occurred.

After the Carbon 14 testing, many people around the world now believed the Shroud to be nothing more than a fantastic, medieval forgery. Even

Church authorities first said there was no reason to doubt the results. Three qualified labs in three different parts of the world had all produced the same outcome—the samples had all produced a medieval date. On the other hand, those samples had been taken from only one section of the cloth, an area that was handled whenever the Shroud was exhibited, and from which a small section had previously been taken for analysis. Because of this, various researchers proposed that this suspicious area might have been repaired. Others proposed that the effects of a fire in 1532, which left striking burn marks all over the cloth, might have thrown the date off. That fire occurred in Chambery, France, and was put out thanks to the heroism of a local blacksmith. People throughout the centuries owe him a debt of gratitude for having rescued the Shroud from destruction. (Ironically, I write this on a Thanksgiving Day holiday celebrated in the United States.) The Shroud would consequently show the resultant patches put on in 1534 until they were removed in 2002 during a controversial restoration. Jackson and others would study the possible effects of that fire on the C-14 results, and many others would explore other avenues to try to better understand the C-14 results in light of the Shroud's history.

In December, *Shroud News* published "The 50th Issue" special, which contained a short article I had written under a pseudonym (so that I wouldn't overdo asking from Father Prior permissions related to the Shroud). My article (see full text in Appendix H), was written before the C-14 results were released, but much of this 50th issue dealt with the AD 1260-1390 dates.

Immediately after the C-14 tests had been announced, I decided I would like to write an article about the whole affair. I had received permission from Father Prior to do so, and in the February, 1989, issue of the Catholic periodical *Fidelity,* my article, "The Shroud of Turin and the C-14 Controversy," was published. It brought out the many suspicious facts surrounding the test, which were cause for great doubt about the validity of the results.

My conclusion was as follows:

> To summarize: problems of contamination, especially those dealing with the fire of 1532, possible unknown factors of radiation, poor procedures including lack of blind controls, lack of agreement

between the 1988 C-14 test and other pertinent data, and various conflicts among those involved in the testing make the stated results of the Shroud C-14 test highly questionable. The C-14 test should be performed again, and it should be performed under a peer-reviewed protocol with the most stringent scientific conditions possible. Given the impact the Shroud has on millions, the world deserves nothing less. Since the Shroud is known to contain real blood, perhaps the new technology that has enabled blood to be carbon dated can eventually be used on the Shroud. There should be no objections to another C-14 test; if another test is done showing that it really is a fourteenth-century cloth, all that would be lost would be a few more milligrams of the cloth. If, however, another test is done and it comes out considerably earlier than fourteenth century, then the extra test will have been justified. Even Cardinal Ballestrero admitted, "This is but another chapter in the Shroud's story, or, as some would say, in the mystery of the Shroud." After all this research, we do not have any plausible answers to explain how the image of Christ was created. In the meantime, we would do well to remember Meacham's remark, "Regardless of the C-14 result, evidence from other sources would of course remain of considerable importance in the overall evaluation of the age and origin of the relic."

Some of my friends who gave Shroud lectures made photocopies of my article and passed them out, although the demand for Shroud presentations essentially dried up for everyone.

In the meantime, life went on. I was still involved in the monastery school and in the summer of 1989, a strange thing happened pertaining to the Shroud. I had lost a small booklet called <u>The Holy Shroud and Four Visions</u>, which compared the scientific evidence on the Shroud with the visions that four nuns, in different times and places, had about the crucifixion. The booklet was excerpted from a larger work, which I had on order, so I wasn't concerned that I could not find it. I had in my possession what I thought was an authentic relic of the Shroud (it later turned out that Adler and Jackson both looked at it and determined it was actually from the backing cloth). A nephew of mine suffered from a brain tumor at the time, so one day I planned to take the relic and touch it to his head. (My nephew eventually did recover.) Regarding Shroud miracles, one that many people acknowledge is the cure in the 1950s of a young English girl, Josie Woolam, who was not expected to live until her teens, but was cured after the Shroud was laid upon her lap. (See <u>Pilgrimage to the Shroud</u>, by G.L. Cheshire, London: Hutchinson, 1956.)

As I started to think about the theology of relics effecting cures, the lost booklet, which also dealt with the mystical, came to mind. The *very second* that my thought about the lost booklet came into my mind, I heard a noise behind me. When I turned around I saw that the booklet had hit the floor in the center of the room!! It could not have fallen from a bookcase or anything else, and it certainly hadn't been stuck on the ceiling! There was *no* rational explanation for that book appearing and hitting on the floor. As it hit at the exact moment I had thought of it and thinking about the mystical, I think it was God's way of saying, "Yes, the mystical exists."

A very significant Shroud conference was held in Paris in early September, 1989. Many of the people involved in the C-14 dating were there to make presentations. I was not able to attend the conference, but Mark Antonacci arranged to videotape everything, and I was able to see all of the lectures. One unplanned presentation occurred when Dr. Alan Whanger, a long-time Shroud researcher, asked the organizers if he could show a video of the sample-taking from 1988. Whanger claimed that close-ups of the sample showed what appeared to be foreign fibers. The audience in attendance wanted to hear what he had to say, and he was allowed to present the video. One of the scientists involved in the dating, the late Jacques Evin from France, was asked about the possibility that the sample might have had fibers not original to the Shroud. Evin said, "I quite agree that the labs did not take the weaving techniques into account and they did not date the threads *per se* . . . thus, if the weave was rewoven with threads from modern restoration, this would be reflected in more modern results" (Mark Antonnaci's personal video library; author has duplicate of tape). This was quite an admission! It seemed more and more plausible that repairs in the area of the C-14 sample could have been responsible for why the dating did not turn out to be first century, as most people expected.

During the very same month as the Paris Shroud symposium, another C-14 intercomparison trial among 38 labs took place in Scotland to gauge the general accuracy of carbon dating. The organizers of the trial concluded that the margin of error for the test was two to three times greater than previously claimed. They indicated that of the 38 labs involved, only seven produced satisfactory results (Coghlan 1989:26). These results gave added weight to many shroudies' convictions that something was probably suspect with the Shroud C-14 results.

The Vatican itself eventually began to have doubts about the validity of the results. In 1990, the Turin authorities announced that they were accepting proposals for new tests on the Shroud. Many individuals and groups submitted proposals, but another disappointment ensued when no follow-up action was taken by the authorities.

In the meantime, sindonologists continued their research. A conference was held at Columbia University (New York) in March, 1991. I was unable to attend that one and was actually busy planning a conference myself—*History, Science, Theology and the Shroud of Turin*—to be held at St. Louis University in June. I even invited an official from the *Centro Internazionale Di Sindonologia*, which includes members of the Turinese authorities who controlled the Shroud. The Columbia University conference was being sponsored by a group called "American Shroud of Turin Association" (ASTA, not to be confused with a later group called AMSTAR, which will be discussed later in this chapter.) For one main reason detailed below, many sindonologists were very much opposed to this group. They circulated a letter to publicize their stand and boycotted the ASTA conference. The opposition was virulent—I received a letter from a Turinese official stating that someone had signed his name to the petition without his permission!

There had been some pressure from Father Otterbein of the Holy Shroud Guild on the Columbia University organizers as well as me to not hold the conferences, as it was believed that these conferences might somehow be detrimental for the Shroud. In a letter dated February 9, 1990, Father Otterbein wrote me:

> We are trying to organize new tests, but want to avoid more bad Press. Hence try to keep scientists interested. Don't hesitate to say that we still think evidence favors authenticity. We are seeking scientific response to C-14, but for present avoid big Press Conferences, Public Conferences, etc.
>
> *[Excerpt reprinted with permission from Father Fred Brinkmann of the Holy Shroud Guild.]*

I also received a letter on November 28, 1990, from a lawyer from Texas. He also expressed his concern to me that the ASTA New York conference "could quite literally ruin it for us all." He was, however, more open than Father Otterbein was about the conference I was planning to organize, saying: "At the same time we all realize your Symposium is altogether different." Clearly politics were front and center of various efforts made regarding the Shroud—and matters were not getting better because of it. Although the lawyer was cordial and did not try to dissuade me from holding the St. Louis conference, the next encounter I had with him, about a decade later, was a horse of a different color. (There will be more on that in Chapter Nine.) I only recently learned from one of the organizers of the ASTA symposium that this lawyer actually was able to convince some speakers to withdraw. In the end, however, both conferences forged ahead, and many excellent papers were presented. More importantly, much face-to-face discussion between sindonologists took place. The belief that something was wrong with those 1988 C-14 results was gathering momentum.

While planning the St. Louis conference, I discovered that a Shroud group from Amarillo, Texas, called "The Man in the Shroud Committee" was also making plans to put on a conference. If they held a separate one, that would have been three separate conferences in 1991, which would be too many, especially for sindonologists' wallets! I suggested that they join forces with us, and the late Father Aram Berard, S.J., who headed the Amarillo group, agreed. The conference was held in June, 1991. People came from as far as Australia, Spain and France. The language of the conference was English only and one speaker from France, who spoke no English, was accompanied by a companion who read the paper for him. I felt sorry for the French speaker and for a priest from Spain, who also understood no English, but still was present for all the lectures. Hopefully both of then enjoyed all the visuals!

One of the speakers I invited to the conference was John Jackson. Eric Jumper seemed to have lost interest after the C-14 results. I contacted him recently for information for one of the appendices, and he told me he now thinks the Shroud is not authentic. However, Jackson continued his research and does to this day. He and his fiancée (and later his wife), Rebecca, who had converted to Protestant Christianity and then to Catholicism from Judaism, were planning to start a Shroud Center in Colorado Springs where Jackson lived after having been stationed there in the Air Force Academy.

After the conference, Jackson invited me to come out and visit him and Rebecca. "Yes, maybe I can come one summer," I said. "What about this summer?" he replied. I actually did have two weeks off for vacation (yes, some able-bodied monks go on vacation) and had only planned to spend them at my mother's house with no real activities planned. He encouraged me to see if I could get permission, since vacations, like being interviewed by the media, needed to be pre-approved by the Prior of the monastery. I was granted permission, so I was able to observe first-hand how John and Rebecca got their Shroud Center off the ground. As it turned out, I made the visit to Colorado Springs annually through 1997, even going there twice one summer to help with preparing some proposals for the Turin authorities. I enjoyed immensely the surroundings, especially the view of Pikes Peak, the famous mountain in Colorado Springs that could be seen from practically any point in the city. Once, Jackson and I hiked it. I think I set a record—for slowness. It took me nine-and-one-half hours to reach the summit.

Around 1991, I had another mystical experience. One night, just before I fell asleep, I had another locution. In my mind's eye, the word "priesthood" kept flashing in my mind, and I immediately knew that God was asking me to become a priest. It startled me so much that I literally exclaimed out loud, "What?!" I immediately protested that I didn't have the preaching skills, that I was too weak, but before I could get any additional reasons out, I heard an inaudible voice say, "It's not your own strength that will help you; it is my strength that will assist you." I immediately felt a sense of calm and acquiesced to this perceived request for me to become a priest. After consultation with Father Prior, I started my seminary studies in the fall of 1992.

In June 1993, the French Shroud association that had sponsored the Paris symposium in 1989 held another conference, this one in Rome, which I was able to attend. Two papers in particular received a great deal of attention. One was by a physician, Leoncio Garza-Valdes from San Antonio, Texas. Garza-Valdes had been given access to some actual Shroud fibers and asserted that they contained something called a "bioplastic coating," essentially, a microbial film that forms over time on many objects. He believed that it not only changed the C-14 dates, but actually played a part in the image-formation process. He was later to publish a book titled <u>The DNA of God?</u> (Garza-Valdes 1998). Most scientists, however, do not believe his theory is plausible.

The second paper that garnered much notice was by Dmitri Kouznetsov, a Russian. He claimed that experiments in his lab in Moscow showed that the 1532 fire may have caused a change in the amount of carbon in the Shroud and affected the final C-14 results. Others had also surmised that the fire could have produced this effect but here, apparently, was some scientific proof.

A similar situation existed with the theory that repairs to the Shroud may have caused the dates to be skewed. Several people had postulated this shortly after the results of 1988 had been released and some had even mentioned the possibility even before the results had been released. A paper on this topic was presented by the Swiss archaeologist Maria Grazia Siliato; the main difference was that her paper hardly caused a ripple compared to the papers by Garza-Valdes and Kouznetsov. Although I had heard the paper in person, I had forgotten about it, and as with many other sources proposing a repair hypothesis, I only rediscovered it after combing all of my materials when Sue Benford and I started working on the hypothesis, which will be described later in the book.

Also noteworthy was the fact that this conference was the most "heated" one I have ever attended. The high temperatures in the hall were uncomfortable in the extreme, but it was, after all, summer in Rome. At least the attendees left the conference full of hope that there were several reasonable explanations for why the C-14 dating results were medieval.

In June 1994, I was ordained a priest. Several of my friends from the "Shroud crowd" came to the ceremony. John Jackson did one of the readings, which was from 2 Corinthians 4:6: "For God, who said, 'Let light shine out of darkness,' has shone in our hearts, that we in turn might make known the glory of God shining on the *face of Christ*." In subsequent years, I assisted the priests at the Jacksons' parish when I would visit them every summer.

One of the jobs I had in the monastery before I was ordained was "kitchen master," which entailed overseeing the kitchen whenever the hired cook was not on duty. Given my kitchen skills, "master" is an overstatement. The job was very frustrating at times, especially when others would just leave things around, which I would have to clean up. Being kitchen master was not supposed to mean that others were not obligated to help out, but inside a monastery as well as outside, there's the ideal world and the real world. After I was ordained, I didn't expect to be assigned back to the job as no priest had previously held the position. However, the job was given back to me. As the phrase goes, "I didn't see that one coming." During that time I was seeing my old friend Father Tom Santen for spiritual direction. With him I could, among other things, vent some of my frustrations about the kitchen. My Shroud research, fortunately, helped me cope with such matters.

There were still articles as well as radio and television programs coming out about the Shroud in the mid-1990s, despite the medieval results of the 1988 C-14 dating. Around 1995, I was talking to STURP photographer Barrie Schwortz about an upcoming Shroud documentary. He said that the producer called him for an interview, but Barrie wasn't sure he wanted to participate. He was reluctant, but I told him, "If you don't do it, they will interview someone who knows a lot less about the Shroud than you do." I tried to convince him that his expertise was needed to spread accurate information about the Shroud. Thankfully, he agreed to be interviewed for that documentary, and he has done numerous ones over the years since then.

Around that period, a personal, and potentially legal problem related to the Shroud arose. In one issue of the newsletter that I disseminated, I reproduced a review of a Shroud book written by a skeptic. When citing a source on an historical point, he used a book written by a fellow skeptic. In my editorial comment added to the review, I said something to the effect that the author of the review cited this other skeptic instead of citing a bona fide historian. That was enough for this reviewer to contact me and threaten to sue! My lawyer friend Mark Antonacci wrote a letter on my behalf to the skeptic. Apparently realizing he had no legal recourse, the whole situation died down.

In April of 1996, a momentous event in sindonology occurred. Barrie Schwortz published on the Internet a new website, *www.shroud.com*. This was, still is, and promises to continue to be one of the most reliable and factual sources for information on the Shroud available. As Barrie told me, the website came about mainly because a friend of his had seen a tabloid article at the grocery store proclaiming that Leonardo da Vinci had produced the Shroud. Despite the fact that the provenance of the Shroud was known one for about one hundred years before da Vinci was born, many people might and did believe such misinformation. When Barrie heard this story, he made a note to himself to consider building a site. He realized that he had a lot of valuable information to share and that much of the information people were being fed was inaccurate. Once it was established, Barrie found out from reliable sources that Pope John Paul II had visited the site. Sindonology had entered cyberspace, and it changed the whole face of research. However, it certainly didn't eliminate the need for such events as conferences, which continued to be convened, or Shroud Centers, which continued to multiply around the world.

In the summer of 1996, Los Angeles physician August Accetta opened the Shroud Center of Southern California. I was first introduced to Dr. Accetta when he came out to Colorado Springs to meet with the Jacksons at their Center while I was there. Dr. Accetta invited me to the opening, and I was allowed to say some ceremonial words. Dr. Accetta had been an agnostic and says that the Shroud was instrumental in leading him back to his Catholicism.

Later that year, a Shroud symposium in Esopus, New York was organized by the Holy Shroud Guild to honor Father Adam Otterbein, who had spent many decades promoting knowledge of the Shroud. Father Rinaldi had passed away in 1993, so we were starting to lose some of the major old-guards in the Shroud world.

When I heard about the conference, I had an idea for a paper to present. I received the required permission from the monastic superior and submitted it to the organizers, who accepted it for presentation. This was my first paper to be delivered at a bona fide Shroud conference. It was titled "The Disciples on the Road to Turin," inspired by the story of the "Disciples on the Road to

Emmaus" in the 24th chapter of Luke. In the paper, I set forth some similarities between the Gospel stories of the Passion and Resurrection of Jesus and the history of the Shroud. (This paper is accessible via the Internet and is listed in Appendix I, which has a compilation of Shroud material authored by my late wife Sue and myself.) One attendee came up to me after the talk and thanked me for presenting something that was so easily understood. Obviously, some of the science involved in the study of the Shroud can be complicated at times, but for most people, all they have to do to "get it" is to just look at the face on the Shroud and accept that the Shroud dovetails well with the Gospels.

One sad aspect of the conference was to see prominent researchers who had contributed so much as a team to sindonology barely speak to one another. Only they themselves know all the reasons for this, but suffice it to say that personal and scientific differences between researchers were not, and are not, uncommon. That year also saw the formation of a new United States-based organization called the American Shroud of Turin Association for Research (AMSTAR). Many hoped that this organization would be an impetus for new testing on the Shroud. Sadly, the group eventually seemed only to cause additional divisions in sindonology, especially in 1998, 2001 and 2005, when they organized Shroud conferences. (See more on this in later chapters.) As 1996 drew to a close, I had no idea that the following year would be marked by three of the most significant events of my life.

CHAPTER SIX

A FIRE AND TWO PHONE CALLS

In February 1997, I received a call from Dr. John Jackson. He and Rebecca planned to visit the Holy Land, and wanted to know if I would be able to accompany them. It was an unbelievable, unexpected and welcome surprise! I received the required permission of the Abbot (we had progressed from being a "Priory" to an "Abbey"). What a thrill it would be to visit the land where Jesus walked and where the Shroud, if authentic, originated.

We, like most tourists, hired a local guide to take us to various prominent sites. On one particular day, I was taken aback by a very simple observation. As I sat in the back seat of the car, I could constantly see the guide's eyes through his rear-view mirror. What struck me was how much his eyes looked like the eyes of the man in the Shroud, even though the latter's are closed. It almost mesmerized me in a way comparable to the time when I first saw a picture of the Shroud on the book I had seen in 1977. Needless to say, the trip, which included visits to Jerusalem and Bethlehem and the opportunity to see sites such as the Sea of Galilee and the Jordan River, was most memorable, and I had the Jacksons to thank for it.

In April, I received another unexpected surprise, but this one was far from pleasant. Friday, April 11, 1997, was a typical day at the monastery. I walked into the faculty room of the school where one of the other monks casually said to me, "Did you hear about the Shroud fire?" "FIRE!" I exclaimed, "WHAT FIRE?!" He said, "The Shroud has been in a fire, but I think it's been saved." I immediately jumped on the Internet and began to search for information. I quickly discovered that the Shroud had been rescued and was unharmed, thanks to the heroics of a Turinese fireman, Mario Trematore. Although he had actually been off-duty that night, Trematore heard about the fire, rushed to the Cathedral and feverishly broke through thick, bullet-proof glass to get the casket containing the valuable piece of linen out of danger. I then heard through my grapevine that Barrie Schwortz was posting information and updates at *www.shroud.com*, so I periodically would visit his site to keep abreast of the situation.

I often recall that if it had not been for the blacksmith in Chambery, France, in 1532 and if not for the Turinese fireman in 1997, the Shroud would have been destroyed. It's hard even to imagine what my life would be like without the Shroud. I'm fairly certain that I would have never joined the monastery had I not encountered the Shroud. I certainly wouldn't be writing this book. Obviously, something as significant as a fire can easily alter one's existence, but sometimes something as commonplace as a phone call can also alter lives.

It was July 23, 1997. The monastery school was on summer break. Getting through the hot and muggy St. Louis summers was always a challenge. In the evenings, I would usually go to my air-conditioned office in the school library to work on Shroud research. One of the main tasks was to keep an up-to-date bibliography of all known English-language sources on the Shroud, including books, articles and videos. As I walked into my office, I noticed a voice mail message waiting for me. I listened to my answering machine and heard a voice say, "My name is Sue Benford. I'm from Columbus, Ohio. I was given your number by the Jacksons. I had some questions about the Shroud. You can call me collect." I received a lot of calls about the Shroud, and I didn't expect anything out of the ordinary with this one. Little did I know that I was about to step into the religious version of the "Twilight Zone" and enter a realm where my involvement with the Shroud would take a most unexpected turn.

I called the number and Sue introduced herself again. She said that she had originally called the Jacksons, who suggested that she contact me. Sue told me that she had only recently learned about the Shroud through some "revelations." She also said that she hadn't even been a Christian when she started to receive revelations. Although the Shroud attracts many balanced and intelligent people, it also attracts many unbalanced and unorthodox people. When someone tells me they've had a revelation, I'm automatically wary and cautious, but I also don't necessarily dismiss them out of hand. I had experienced the mystical several times myself, so I knew that those sorts of experiences were possible. She didn't come across to me as the least bit strange.

Sue said that she had written two papers and would like me to read them. They weren't specifically on the Shroud but had some related material. The papers were titled "The Two Faces of Adam: When Creation Meets Evolution" and "Understanding God." I agreed to read them, and she said she would send them. One of my suggestions was for Sue to contact Barrie, who had a "Research Registry" section on the website, to see if she could post something there in order to get feedback about her papers. I asked her if she had Internet access, and she replied she had just been connected but hadn't even sent an email yet. I sent her an email to test out her online access, and she later responded saying she had received the message. Sue, who wasn't a Catholic, also informed me that she had written a book (including a screenplay version) about her life and the revelations she said she had been receiving.

A few days later, I received a letter in the mail dated July 23, 1997, and copies of the two papers. Below is the text of the cover letter:

Dear Father Joe:

Thank you for returning my call and agreeing to review my papers. I am anxious to receive your feedback. I have been searching for a group who might be interested in pursuing my insights regarding the existence of the spirit within the human soul for which part of the proof of concept comes via the Shroud.

As I mentioned, I am neither a theologian, philosopher, physicist, and, by some people's definition, barely a Christian. However, for some unknown reason, for the past year I have been receiving some extremely interesting "revelations" regarding spiritual existence and operations if you will.

I have written a book, entitled <u>Strong Woman</u>, that has been accepted for publication which describes this astounding "transformation" that has taken place in my life and how the physical world often mirrors the spiritual world. You see, I am the strongest woman in the world (three-time World Powerlifting Champion, holder of all world records in the 97 lb. weight class) despite numerous handicaps resulting from radiation treatments to cure a childhood cancer.

I believe God raised me from the weakest of the weak to the strongest of the strong not only physically but now spiritually as well. This strength is now being demonstrated in form of documentable visions and insights that are well beyond my actual level of understanding. My entire life has changed as a result.

Part of what I have been learning has to do with the connection between science, especially physics, and the invisible world of the spirit. Although I have included some of these understandings in my book, there is a certain one that was omitted. These understandings could, quite possibly, prove the existence of the spirit.

Please excuse the lack of introduction on "how all this occurred." Should you question this aspect, I would be happy to forward more documentation to you. Suffice it to say that Rudolf Steiner adequately explained this occurrence when he stated " . . . in the course of the next three thousand years, there will be many new examples of the event at Damascus . . . Human beings will develop capacities so that they will be able to perceive the Christ on the astral plane as an etheric figure, as Paul did at Damascus. This experience of perceiving Christ through higher capacities—which will develop more and more among human beings in the course of the next three millennia, will begin in our twentieth century. From this time onward these capacities will gradually emerge, and over the next millennia they will be cultivated by a great number of human beings. That is, many people will come to know that Christ is a reality—that he lives—*by looking into higher worlds*. They will be acquainted with him, as he lives now." (Spiritual Hierarchies, page 245)

I have enclosed two of my recent works that I think you will find interesting. Please share them sparingly. Should you have any ideas for a publication venue I am open to suggestions. I look forward to receiving your feedback.

In Christ,
[signed] M. Sue Benford

Chapter Six: A Fire and Two Phone Calls

It seemed a strange combination: a handicapped Powerlifting champion. I read both papers. Both had a mixture of theology and science and both were quite erudite. I sent copies of both papers to other sindonologists for them to read. So far, nothing about Sue suggested that she wasn't a normal, sane person. We started corresponding regularly by email. At the end of July, she said that she had also contacted the late Father Kim Dreisbach *[deceased 2006]*, who ran a Shroud Center in Atlanta. He referred her to Kevin Moran, an optical engineer, who was also willing to read her papers.

In an email of August 6, Sue described a revelation she said she received from Jesus about the Shroud. She wrote:

> He told me that the Shroud was like a fingerprint left behind for us to discover when we were ready. I didn't know anything about a "Shroud" until he told me. When I first saw the image I could barely breathe. The only words that would come to me (and remember how unusual these words were to me at the time) was "my Savior." Still to this day I can't look at the Shroud without having that exact same emotional response. Plus, the Shroud image looks exactly like the being I had been talking to for months. I know it's him.

On August 8, I emailed Sue about a woman I read about in a book I found in the monastery library. I told her the book was:

> about some messages from Jesus that a woman named "Vassuala" has been getting. She was born in Egypt of Greek parents and is Greek Orthodox, I believe. Several of the messages mention the Shroud (Jesus tells her to get "my pictures" to give to a priest). One of her difficulties is that one Catholic who believes her messages at first stops believing when he finds out she's not Catholic. Although I'm committed to being a Catholic, I don't think God has to be a "Catholic." That's the sort of reason the Jews ran into problems. They believed they were the Chosen People, which they were, but they didn't leave room for God to do what he wanted for the Gentiles. God can communicate through whomever he wants. As you know from experience, you will run into people who won't even consider what you're saying.

Sue emailed me August 11 that she had met with a publisher about her book. She also heard that day from a movie producer in Hollywood who had read the synopsis of her screenplay. He asked her if he could forward it to a friend of his at CBS for a possible *Movie of the Week*. On August 12, she contacted a physicist at Fermi Lab in Chicago regarding questions she had about "antimatter," something she had discussed in one of her papers.

On August 13 she sent me a poem (author unknown) pertaining to a theological discussion we had how weaknesses make us strong.

> **I Asked God**
> I asked God for strength, that I might achieve.
> I was made weak, that I might learn to obey.
> I asked for health, that I might do greater things.
> I was given infirmity, that I might do better things.
> I asked for riches, that I might be happy.
> I was given poverty, that I might be wise.
> I asked for power, that I might have the praise of men.
> I was given weakness, that I might feel the need of God.
> I asked for all things, that I might enjoy life.
> I was given life, that I might enjoy all things.
> I got nothing that I asked for – but everything I hoped for.
> Almost despite myself, my unspoken prayers were answered.
> I am, among all people, most richly blessed.

In addition to emails, we talked on the phone periodically, and I found myself intellectually and spiritually attracted to her. Given her overradiation from her childhood cancer and the fact that she was a Powerlifter, I surmised she likely wasn't, from the world's point of view, attractive physically, but she seemed like a wonderful person on the inside, where it really mattered. I had no idea how old she was. My birthday was coming in two days. Sue sent me an email describing a paper she had mailed:

> I've been working on for several months but last night received more guidance on it related to the Shroud....
> Should my insights and visions on all this pan out to be in any way valid, remind me that I need to tell you something about the significance of today's date and the connection to it being your birthday. I won't get into it unless everything else appears to be true. But if it does, then there's something important you need to know about a vision I received nearly a year ago about today's date as a birthday.

Chapter Six: A Fire and Two Phone Calls

Here is how Sue relates the story in her book (Benford 2002:177-180; 2011:177-180). ("John" is the Apostle John; "guys" refers to the collective spiritual sources she said she had):

> Throughout my numerous discourses with my spiritual sources, I repeatedly requested (more like begged) for another soul mate to share the remainder of my spiritual journey. I wanted him to be a spiritual person in line with my own understandings and path. One night in a conversation with John, I became frustrated that my answers to these personal questions and requests had gone seemingly unanswered. Although they had assured me months earlier that, indeed, my ultimate spiritual partner would soon arrive, I had not received any more information. I badgered John to tell me more about this soul mate. Finally, after a great deal of badgering, John provided a birthday—August 15. It was not a lot to go on, but at least it was something . . . .
>
> During one of our conversations, Father Joseph mentioned an upcoming celebration at his mother's house to honor his birthday. Innocently I inquired exactly when his birthday was. His answer stopped me cold—August 15. My chest tightened and I could not breathe as I recalled my insight from John about my soul mate's birthday. What would I do with this information? Certainly I could not tell this to Father Joseph. Was this the guy's idea of some cosmic joke—"Have you hear the one about the priest and the heretic?"
>
> That night in my meditation I confronted Jesus and John with my dilemma. They verified that, yes, Father Joseph was indeed my soul mate and would be my partner in uncovering the spiritual mysteries at hand. If this was true, I asked, then why he was not getting divine signs and signals about the new spiritual direction of his life? Jesus said that he was receiving numerous signs but that I should tell him that he needed to, "Put the umbrella down. Truth is raining all around you like raindrops." This was insane and totally out of the question. How could I possibly relay such a "message" to this priest/monk who I had never met and had just begun to know? Not to mention that although I knew his birthday was the same as my future soul mate's, he had no such knowledge and at that point our relationship merely consisted of long phone conversations, mostly about the Shroud of Turin. I reasoned that there were only two ways to pull off a band-aid; slow or fast. Either way—they both hurt. I opted for the slow route first.
>
> In our next phone conversation I approached the whole subject of "miraculous signs" quite gingerly at first, but to no avail. He just was not getting it. The best I was accomplishing was to garner a

lecture on the Pope's beliefs and the "church's stance" on such things. Men! Clueless, no matter what collar they're wearing!

I decided to take the plunge so I just blurted it out, "Jesus said for you to take the umbrella down and you'll start seeing signs that you and I are soul mates and your mission is with me. Do you have any idea what he's talking about? Have you perhaps been missing some unusual happenings and passing them off as coincidences?" My heart nearly stopped during what seemed like an eternal pause after my last question. The answer was devastating, "No, I do not have any idea what you're talking about. I do not think I've been missing anything and I do not even understand what he means by 'put the umbrella down.'"

I could not believe his naiveté and lack of mystical understandings. This would certainly be some miracle for Jesus and John to pull off if they intended for this sweet, charming, and completely sheltered monk to join in the spiritual fray for which I was headed. I decided to simply exit the conversation as gracefully as possible by saying, "Well, just do me a favor and pay attention to possible signs they might be sending. Do not stretch to interpret anything but, if something gives you that 'Ah ha!' feeling, then do not discard it as a mere coincidence—think about it." Then I thought to myself, "Okay, guys, it's up to you! I really want to see you pull this one off."

That night in meditation it was me who was doing all the laughing instead of John. It was now my turn to sit back and let them do all the work. Could they possibly provide enough tangible, miraculous signs for this innocent and devout monk to understand he had a new life's mission that would mean rebuking his solemn priestly vows and leaving his beloved monastery and Church? After all, I had failed miserably with my job of relaying Jesus' message. Now it was entirely up to them. I asked them, and they seemed quite confident that, indeed, they would succeed. It was meant to be. I inquired of Jesus exactly how long he thought this miraculous feat would take and he confidently proclaimed, "One year." I marked my calendar for July 23, 1998—exactly one year from when Father Joseph and I first made contact. What a year it would turn out to be!

The next night, after our "umbrella" discussion, I received a somewhat panicked phone call from Father Joseph. Apparently, he had toiled the night before, distressed over the thought that I might be right and he might have to leave his secure, comfortable life and beliefs. He could not seem to shake the obsessive thoughts that lasted well into his morning routine. As he stated, his main concern was,

"What would other people think?" He feared disdain and retribution from family, friends, and the Church.

The next morning during the monks' usual contemplative reading, the book chosen was one by the famous American Trappist monk, Thomas Merton. A particular passage rang out from the solemn silence that encompassed the proceedings, "Too often in the spiritual life we are too concerned about what other people will think about us and not about what God's will actually is for us." A chill ran down his spine as he took note of the very first "raindrop" to sink in now that the proverbial umbrella was down, "It's almost like they knew exactly what I was thinking and feeling and that passage was specifically to answer my nagging fears. We've never read anything from that particular book before!"

Knowing what I already knew about the impact of miraculous signs, all I could do was smile to myself and reassure him that this was just the beginning. I recommended that he document everything that he believed was a sign and record its particular significance to him. Every "sign" should be put in writing and evaluated for its own merit. Over the course of the next several weeks, Father Joseph's journal became heavy laden with sign after sign, spiritual message after message, irony after irony. The guys were busy at work and it was becoming impossible to deny their influence any longer . . . .

I did start to document all of the signs that I received. I don't believe it was just a matter of me seeing signs where there were none. I can't prove to anyone's satisfaction that these so-called synchronicities were anything out of the ordinary. But strange things happened almost every day for a full year after I first met Sue, and sometimes we would independently get on the same day synchronicities on the same subject. I mention just a few of them below and in the next chapter. Another way I describe it is that events feel "orchestrated"—one senses a greater power is guiding all events. Make of them what you will, but I know they were meaningful for me, and I firmly believe they were part of the "plan" that brought Sue and me together.

On August 16, the monks began their week-long annual retreat. One of my self-imposed practices during retreat was to refrain from listening to my favorite music. At that particular point in time, I constantly listened to a solo CD by Justin Hayward of the Moody Blues, a group I had been listening to since the 1970s. There was one particularly beautiful song called "Broken Dream," which I played repeatedly. It would be a long week in the retreat without it. On that day, I received a birthday card from Sue, the paper she promised, and a copy of an article on her from the *Columbus Dispatch* about one of her research projects. The birthday card encouraged me to "listen to the sounds you enjoy" and to "speak to people who warm your heart." The article had a picture of her at home with her two young daughters. Due to her cancer treatment and because she was a Powerlifter, I had an image of her in my mind as a handicapped "tomboy." I was totally amazed to see a photo of a young-looking, vivacious, and attractive woman. Instinctively, I reacted with an emphatic: "UH-OH!" I was stunned. Although I had been attracted to her on other levels, I knew the fact that she was physically attractive, added to the other levels of attraction I already had for her, could definitely mean trouble. The combination of her inner beauty along with outer beauty that shone from this picture was almost overwhelming. If the reader looks at this photo on the back cover, he or she can understand why I was physically attracted to her. One of my friends commented to me that in the picture Sue looks "radiant." I would wholeheartedly agree. Even without having known Sue, a person can likely detect from this visible radiance some of the inner beauty she possessed. It is easily my favorite picture of her.

I'm quite aware that traditional theology says that I should have broken off communication with her at that point, so as not to open myself up to temptation. However, while I sensed that traditional theology was the safe, black-and-white path, the answer was not so simple—real life is sometimes very gray. (See Appendix J for more communications between Sue and me recounting some of the amazing phenomena that occurred with both of us.) As the first day of the retreat progressed, I thought of the card from Sue that advised "listen to the sounds you enjoy" and started to wonder if *not* listening to my favorite music was any more beneficial that listening to something I considered a window to an aspect of God's beauty. I recalled an experience I had some years earlier when I was in the seminary and living at an Abbey in Washington, D.C. The monks there owned a house in rural Virginia, similar to the house in rural Missouri that my own monastery owned. Brother Dunstan from the Washington Abbey and I went to their rural house on a cool spring night. We had a fire going and played a tape of the famous classical piece, "Pachebel's Canon in D," which he had received from a friend who worked in the mental health field. He said that many of his friend's patients told her that the piece "reminded them of God." I had heard the piece before, but listening to it that night by a fire in a relaxed setting practically sent me into an ecstasy. I decided to listen to "Broken Dream" during retreat week, and doing so lifted my spirits immensely. The song is hypnotically beautiful and practically takes me to another dimension—one step closer to God. It was a wonderful reminder that I did not have to be so set in my ways, including in spirituality.

The Shroud continued to be prominent in my life. I worked together with a monastery parish member interested in the Shroud to bring another Shroud photo exhibition to St. Louis in conjunction with the Jacksons giving seminars. Both were great successes, and it was very rewarding to see so many people attend.

In the meantime, Sue had sent me many questions via email and was concerned that she was overwhelming me. I emailed her on August 16:

> No, you haven't overwhelmed me with all your recent inquiries. I really enjoy talking with and corresponding with people about the Shroud. So that fulfills the part of the card where it says, "Speak to people who warm your heart." I really would like to work on the Shroud full-time. I pray for that. I don't know if it will ever happen, but I hope it does. I never feel closer to the Lord than when I work on the Shroud. On the other hand, I do believe it can be a danger if one gets everything one wants. I'm working on the assumption that if the Lord wants it, he will open doors for me, as has done in similar situations. One huge obstacle is that, as a Benedictine monk, I've taken a vow of stability to this monastery, which means I cannot be transferred anywhere else. Jackson would like me to be working with him full-time in Colorado Springs. There are exceptions to the vow. In the meantime, I will do as much as I can from here. Having email & the Internet helps me "get around."

Being curious about the details of her revelations, I asked her some very specific questions, which she answered in good time. (As there are many questions and she replies with long answers, I have reproduced the exchange in Appendix J.)

After the retreat, I shared with anyone near earshot the "Broken Dream" song simply because I thought it was so haunting and beautiful. I sent Sue a tape of it. She emailed on August 22, "I love that song!!" and added, "The words are ironic don't you think? 'Out of the dark I stumbled into the Light. Only my fear has tumbled. I think I always knew that I would run to you.' I know why I love this song so much but why do you? Do the words have special meaning to you?" I emailed her that I never pay that much attention to words in a song; I just loved the velvet-like sound of the singer's voice, the soaring, beautiful melody and lush orchestration. She emailed me on August 27, saying "I just put 'Broken Dream' on again. Something about that song touches the very deepest part of my soul. It's almost like being transcended." She was experiencing the same "other dimensional" sensation that I was from the song. I didn't try to suggest anything to her by the words, but the song was nonetheless increasing the bond between us.

It was around this time that Sue told me over the phone that it was revealed to her that science would soon discover new particles. It seemed strange that she claimed that she received scientific revelations as well as religious ones. I wasn't sure what to make of it. A few days after she told me this, on September 1, I read in the *St. Louis Post-Dispatch* a short article with the headline, "Physicists Discover Important Particle" (page 6A). It read:

> Physicists at Brookhaven National Laboratory on Long Island have found evidence of an "exotic" meson, a subatomic particle that has eluded discovery for 30 years and may help explain how matter holds together.
>
> In the currently accepted version of quantum theory, the branch of the discipline dealing with subatomic particles, mesons are composed of a combination of even more fundamental units called quarks.
>
> The existence of exotic mesons has been hypothesized as a special type of meson, necessary to support the rest of quantum theory.
>
> If the observation is confirmed, physicists said, the study of exotic mesons could reveal details of how quarks—and eventually everything in the universe—are stuck together. Exotic mesons are difficult to observe, however, because of their rarity and the fact that they can only exist for about a trillionth of a trillionth of a second.
>
> [*Article reprinted with permission of St. Louis Post-Dispatch.*]

I didn't suspect for a second that Sue had known of the story before it officially broke and that she was trying to con me into thinking she had received the information in the way she said. Although I had been communicating with her just over a month, I had already experienced enough strange things to convince me I could not dismiss what she was telling me. I soon read a letter to the editor in a national Catholic newspaper, which said, "Anyone can suppress one's feelings and live a lie for a long time, but it doesn't work in the long run." Was I, in fact, beginning to feel that my life in the monastery was somehow now becoming a lie?

One of the activities at the monastery school was a "prayer assembly," in which the boys were given a spiritual message by one of the school staff. It was while all these other things were going on in my life that a faculty member gave a talk with the theme: "be a risk-taker." That was something I definitely was not. She talked about how we often take the safe road and stay with the tried and true. She also noted that certain opportunities might not come along again. The message seemed so pertinent to me.

It seemed everywhere I turned, there were messages about going beyond boundaries. While preparing a homily during that period, I consulted a biblical commentary. It said:

> We must identify what keeps us in our world of isolation and illusion, what keeps us from looking at our own issues, and what keeps us from pursuing single-mindedly our own healing. Then we must take action. We must change. What stops us from going to any length to be whole? The greatest obstacle to human growth is fear . . . .

The theme of science and religion also came up during this time in an article in a local religious newspaper. The article asked the question, "Do you ever feel as if a series of events is sending you a message?" Given the events of the last month, I had to say "yes"—and wondered where I was headed.

CHAPTER SEVEN

WHERE ARE WE HEADED?

About six weeks after we first started communicating, Sue visited me in St. Louis on a Sunday afternoon in early September. Fortunately, Columbus was only about an hour away by air. I asked a good friend of mine, Margot, a social worker who is very spiritual and someone in whom we could easily confide, to accompany me to the airport to pick up Sue. I was somewhat nervous as we waited for Sue to deplane. I anxiously wondered how our first meeting in person would go. Finally, Sue appeared, easily recognizable since I had already seen that picture of her from the *Columbus Dispatch* article. What I first noticed was her beaming facial expression. She flashed what I later called her "million-dollar smile." It matched exactly to what I had seen in the "UH-OH" picture. I was also surprised at how tiny she was. She was barely five feet tall, and I already knew from conversation with her that she was under 100 pounds because her Powerlifting records were in the 97-pound weight class.

The afternoon at Margot's house went quickly, and I took her back to the airport for her return to Columbus. Although the visit was short, Sue and I both recognized that there was already an incredibly strong bond between us. Was this really happening so soon? I continued to individually consult with Margot and Father Tom about my situation with Sue.

After Sue returned to Columbus and while I tried to sort out in my head what was happening, she mentioned she had seen a write-up about a new television show that fall called "Nothing Sacred," which was generating a lot of fanfare. The show was about a Catholic priest, Father Ray, dealing with real-life issues, one of which was whether or not to pursue a relationship with a woman he loved. I wasn't in that position yet, but I knew that it wouldn't be impossible given the way things were going.

Sue emailed me on September 17:

> I did have some thoughts that might be helpful for both of us. It does seem that things are moving very quickly. I would like to suggest that we agree that no big major changes will be made (unless we get a super huge sign from God) for a minimum of one year. That will give each of us time to sort all of this out without any pressure of having to make a decision that will affect our entire lives. It should especially relieve you and give you time to grow into your feelings and evolving spirituality. Sound good?

The next morning, while at work in the library, I noticed that the Jesuit weekly, *America,* had a cover story about "Nothing Sacred." It concerned Father Ray's struggle with celibacy and another character, Father Eric, who had a desire to go to a monastery, where the vocation director asks "But is that what God wants?" Father Eric walks through the aisles of the Abbey church praying earnestly, "Please God, *want* this for me." The article struck a chord with me. Walking down a hall of one of the school buildings the next day, I heard two monks discussing "Nothing Sacred." I had an appointment scheduled with Father Santen for spiritual direction but called him to try to move it up, because my situation with Sue weighed heavily on my mind.

Sue, meanwhile, was involved in a Bible study group in her church (Reformed Presbyterian) and was also a "Stephen Minister," whose task was to help people in various sorts of crises. Sue emailed me on September 19:

> I know we agreed to slow things down as far as our relationship goes but I have to share with you a very interesting and poignant sign I just received. One of my fellow Stephen Ministers called me up out of the blue and asked me to go to lunch with her today. She is also in my Bible Study group so knew about you on a very superficial level. I have always considered her a very intuitive and extremely spiritually guided person—probably the most of anyone in our group.
>
> Soon after the chit chat ended, she told me that she wanted to share a "vision" she had about you and me that was also shared by one of the other Stephen Ministers who happens to be married to [a] former Benedictine Monk. She said that you and I would be married. I nearly passed out. She explained that she has had a strong intuition ever since I first talked with you and so has Carol. She wanted to see

what we had decided this weekend and to lend her support. She asked me if I loved you and I had to honestly tell her that I think I do.

I just got your email about the "Nothing Sacred" signs. I saw that show last night and it was very powerful. In fact, considering my recent position on slowing things down, it was almost uncomfortable for me to watch. I agree that you should push up your meeting with your Spiritual Director. I thought this might happen—that the signs would begin escalating as soon as we pulled back . . . .

Even with all that I've been through these past two years related to signs and miracles, I am left stunned by what's going on now between us. The harder I try to rationalize and push it away as mere "coincidence," . . . the more pervasive and outlandish they become, e.g. someone who's not even a good friend of mine saying she had visions we would be married! I'm not sure what to say at this point except God's will be done.

Sue also filled in a few details via a phone conversation: Carol apparently described (presumably known via some spiritual intuition) to Sue my struggles with freedom and celibacy. She told Sue that she was connected to me spiritually, emotionally, and physically. She also said that one can't get much more connected than that. Sue, however, was experiencing some guilt for the difficult position she had put me in. She knew that a person in Columbus named "Dale" was interested in her and hoped he would call—but no calls were coming—from Dale or from anyone. In addition, she was getting support from various sources, including her conservative 71-year-old mother.

I met with Father Santen on September 29 for spiritual direction. He advised that Sue should consult some wise and competent person about her revelations so that she wasn't "feeding off of herself." Sue had, in fact, been doing just that. Father Santen commented that while I seemed to get along with my community exteriorly, he didn't get the feeling that I was doing so much on an interior level. I told him that I struggled with the question of whether the direction I was going was just something I wanted to do and I rationalized that it was God's will or, whether it really was God's will, and I was trying to avoid it by not being willing to get out of my "comfort and security" zone. He said, "That's a sign that you're on the right track as far as the discernment process goes." He counseled me not to rush into judgment.

When I expressed worries about hurting various people if I left, he reminded me, "You can't be concerned with social approval," and added "the truth will set you free." The next morning at prayers, the last line of a reading was "I will listen to what the Lord God says within me."

Two days later at morning prayer, the theme of one of the readings was that our peace is in doing God's will—in believing what he wants us to be. A few hours later at the school's prayer assembly, a faculty member who had been a teacher at my high school when I attended, gave a talk about life lessons. She said we learn lessons, that learning lessons do not end and lessons are repeated until learned. What we make of our life is up to us—the answers to life's questions lie inside us: look, listen and trust. The message was for the students—but another one I could take to heart as well.

On September 26, I received the following message from Sue:

1. Yes, there is a purpose for our being brought together that has still not fully been discovered.

2. The path will become clearer as time passes (especially over the next year)

3. We are worrying about things that are up to God to resolve, not us.

4. The signs we are receiving are not meant to cause worry about the future but simply to affirm that there is a purpose and higher reason for our "joining."

5. The attraction and comfort level we have for each other is the most distinct "sign" we have received which should assure us we are on the right path and pursuing God's will.

6. They said to tell you Margot was right when she said as the truth becomes more apparent the fear will subside. (I guess I need to take a lesson from that too.)

All of this just seemed surreal, but I knew it was very real. Sue never pressured me—she continually told me that the path I took was my own

Chapter Seven: Where Are We Headed? 89

decision. I was very anxious to meet with Father Santen again to get his input.

In the meantime, I sent an email to Sue in which I mentioned something I saw in a Catholic periodical that dealt with how the Holy Spirit operates in the world. On September 29, Sue emailed:

> From your last email about the irony of the Catholic source referring to the Spirit at work outside the Catholic church, it sounds as if you're becoming more aware of the many incongruencies and inflexibilities in the Orthodox doctrine. Are you getting frustrated with these types of restrictions and elementary interpretations? Perhaps another sign?

Sue emphasized in another email the next day that spiritually we are all at different levels of understanding. (See Appendix J for full text of the email.) I couldn't help but wonder just where exactly I was at that time.

In October, Sue again came to St. Louis. I *really* enjoyed seeing her again. Her presence was like a breath of fresh air in my life. We went together to meet with Father Santen. Sue told him about information from her revelations she had been given concerning the apostles. Father Santen, who was in a program of studies on Church History, listened patiently to everything she said. I sensed that he was taking the same approach I did when I first encountered Sue: cautious but not outright dismissive. He later told me he was overwhelmed by all the data she gave. He also found it amazing that she hadn't even been a Christian very long but was so involved in her church, was a Stephen Minister, and studied biblical and scientific research. I commented to him that she was a "whirlwind." When Sue had to depart for the day again, it was abundantly clear that we would be missing each other greatly. As Sue was leaving on a plane, I felt like I was on a runaway train. Even though not much time had passed since we had met, I already knew that I deeply loved Sue on every level possible.

In a meeting in November that I had alone with Father Santen, he said he had concerns regarding how life in the monastery de-energized me. He noticed how excited I got whenever I talked about the Shroud. He thought it was a plus that I had been working on the Shroud for 20 years at that point while I had "only" been at the monastery for 18. He said it would be a different story if the Shroud passion had only surfaced in the last three years, for example. It was his opinion that I had made a significant contribution to sindonology and that the monastery should encourage it since it energized me so much. He was concerned about the monastery trying to limit my involvement. To be fair, I felt that although I wasn't able to do everything I wanted pertaining to the Shroud, I was given permissions to engage in many activities. A huge one was actually on the horizon.

In one of the last emails for 1997, Sue wrote:

> Jesus told me something interesting the other night when I asked why he's giving me all this knowledge about the universe, etc. He said it's there for everyone to partake of, but like a library full of books, the third grader can't read beyond his capacity; thus, only chooses books he's able to comprehend. He said they never have intended any truth to be hidden from mankind—it's available for check out at your local library!!! That also dovetails with him telling you to "put the umbrella down" in order to feel the rain. As he said, the signs were always there, you just were closed to them!

As 1998 began, my thoughts began to focus on the upcoming exhibition of the Shroud in Turin for the first time since 1978, when 3.5 million people saw it (see *http://www.shroud.com/history.htm*). I did receive permission to go, and I excitedly waited for the time to arrive. On May 24, Pope John Paul II visited St. John the Baptist Cathedral, where the Shroud is housed. He delivered a long homily about the Shroud, saying that it was an image of sin and salvation, a mirror of the Gospel accounts of Jesus' passion, and a challenge to scientific research. He encouraged experts to continue to seek answers about its mysteries, but cautioned that they should approach studies with an open mind and that "preconceived positions" could affect results of research. He undoubtedly was referring to the 1988 C-14 results. It was nice to hear that the Catholic Church's highest official seemed to seriously question the pronouncement that the Shroud was medieval. Certainly the Vatican would not have even allowed the exhibition if the evidence was convincing that the cloth was, in fact, from the Middle Ages.

Sindonologists also learned that year that Dmitri Kouznetsov, who had been held in high esteem after his 1993 presentation in Rome regarding the possibility that the C-14 date could have been skewed by the 1532 fire, was arrested in Connecticut for fraud as the result of a bad check. Other negative information about him would periodically surface in the upcoming years, including the accusation that he falsified references in some of his papers. All of this was a bit of a black eye on sindonology.

In June 1998, I arrived in Turin and was about to fulfill my dream of actually seeing the Shroud. While waiting to see the Shroud, attendees were shown a video called "Man of Pain." It managed to give a history of the Shroud without mentioning STURP. That would be on the same level with a documentary about rock music in the 1960s not mentioning the Beatles. If you prefer a religious analogy, it would be like writing about the history of Christianity and never mentioning the 12 apostles. It's no secret that the Italians, at least many Turinese, did not take a liking to STURP obtaining access to the Shroud in 1978 and thus receive a great amount of publicity, as well. When STURP's equipment (over four tons) needed for the 1978 testing came to Italy, it was held up in customs; the intervention of Cardinal Ballestrero was needed to get it released in time for the examination!

It was so exciting to actually be seeing the cloth I had been studying for 21 years. I was within ten feet of it! I didn't experience anything otherworldly, but it was still a powerful experience that was beyond the ability of any words to be able to express. It seemed as if none of the approximately one million people that attended the exhibition believed that the 1988 C-14 results had proved the Shroud to be a fake.

I also was able to attend a Shroud conference in Turin held in conjunction with the 1998 exhibition. The conference was chaotic, to say the least. Some speakers who had submitted abstracts still hadn't heard when they arrived in Turin if their papers had been accepted. Many speakers were given a maximum of seven minutes. I couldn't help but think, "How in the world can anybody present a decent paper in only seven minutes?" People had traveled thousands of miles at great expense, only to be dealing with great uncertainty and a lack of communication, in the Internet age, no less.

Multiple talks went on simultaneously, so if there were two papers at the same time that one wanted to hear, one of the talks simply had to be missed. There were numerous room changes, which made it even harder to figure out where one wanted to be. It was later discovered that every single abstract that was submitted was accepted. Everyone there felt that many should have been eliminated and that there shouldn't have had to be choices to be made among many presentations.

One of the highlights of the exhibition was a wonderful dinner for the attendees. We were served as an appetizer the absolute best ravioli I've ever had in my life. Truth be told, I would have been content just to eat those all night! Even though the conference was a disappointment, the whole trip was a wonderful experience, but I was somewhat distracted by the situation going on with Sue.

Sue and I both had come to strongly believe that God called us to be together to do Shroud research. I believed our joining was the culmination of the longtime feeling of my sense of destiny with the Shroud. A philosopher, the late Joseph Campbell, was known for his saying, "follow your bliss." He maintained that if one did that, "doors would open." I had found that to be true since I had met Sue and seemed to move toward the difficult decision of leaving the monastery. Following one's bliss is not a license to do whatever one pleases without regard for how it affects others, but a path decided on at the deepest level of being. There may be consequences for sure in terms of it affecting others, but those cannot be the final factor—determining the destination and goal, to which God is directing, as doors open, must be the guiding factor. A perceived call from God, albeit filtered through our human experiences and intellect, as it necessarily must, is always a mystery.

After returning from the exhibition, I knew I would soon have to make a cut-and-dried decision. Despite my strong feeling that Sue and I were supposed to be together, I was still troubled. Should I really alter my whole life over it? Do I stay or do I leave? When I saw Father Santen in a spiritual direction session, he didn't offer any concrete reasons for my staying. Knowing that leaving would be an upheaval for everyone concerned, I found myself wishing he would come up with a rock-solid reason that I should stay. Fear of what other people will say or think is often more powerful than the knowledge that a specific action is the correct one to take. When Father Santen—or I—didn't come up with a convincing reason for me to stay, I made the difficult decision to leave the monastery.

I starkly realized I had to plan to go through the very unpleasant experience of informing my community and my dyed-in-the-wool Catholic mother. Before I did the latter, I asked all of my brothers and sisters that resided in St. Louis to get together so I could give them a heads-up and get their input for telling my mother. All of them were very supportive of my decision. My non-St. Louis sibling was kept abreast of the situation by phone. While the decision was very difficult on one level, it was actually very easy on another. Every fiber of my being was telling me I needed to do this.

I had no prospects for a job in Columbus, but I was hoping that I would be able to latch onto something. But at this crucial time, something totally unexpected happened. After I had made my decision to leave the monastery and to join with Sue, she began to have second thoughts about me moving there. She explicitly told me she now didn't want me to come to Columbus. Although she had two small businesses, neither one was very lucrative and as she was raising two small children, she was worried that I possibly wouldn't be able to find a job, and she would find herself supporting me as well, without enough resources.

Was this a cosmic joke? Having gone out on a limb, I felt like I was now dropping off. Even with this unexpected situation, I would not consider remaining at the monastery. The decision to leave involved more than just wanting to join Sue—there were other spiritual considerations. I had no idea what I was going to do. The only action I could take was to trust that God would help me through this. Fortunately, Sue's second thoughts were short-lived, and our original plan was soon back on track. But it had been a very scary experience.

At the monastery, I informed each monk individually of my decision. Obviously, it was a difficult thing to do, especially since I had been there for over 18 years. Over the years I had seen several monks announce to the community that they were leaving—finding it hard to comprehend—and now I was taking the same action. I was probably as surprised as anyone. But my heart and my conscience told me I had to leave. The signs I had received related to my decision were so similar to all the ones I had received previously, including the ones that were the impetus for me joining the monastery in the first place. God had pierced my safe theological bubble that I had built up over the years, and I wasn't sure about everything that awaited me. I had some sense of how Saul of Tarsus felt as he was asked to become Paul of Tarsus. A call from God is always a mysterious experience, especially when it seems to contradict everything one had believed in.

Since I would be heading back out into the world with no job and no money, the Abbot was kind enough to give me $500. On July 12, 1998, one of my brothers and a friend came with their vehicles to the monastery to transport me and my belongings to my mother's house, where I would temporarily lodge. I stayed there until July 22, and on the next day, with a U-Haul rental truck containing various possessions, including my prized Shroud collection, I left for Columbus, Ohio. After about nine-and-one-half hours on the road, I pulled into Sue's driveway. It was one year to the day that we had first communicated. It had been a tumultuous year, but I was *completely* confident I had made the right decision, as improbable as everything had been. A whole new life lay ahead of me.

CHAPTER EIGHT

"IT WAS A REPAIR!"

After unpacking my belongings, I began to settle into my new life, no longer a monk and priest. As Sue's friend, Carol, had predicted, Sue and I eventually married. By the grace of God, it was, if you'll pardon the pun, a marriage made in heaven. We always had a tremendous love and respect for each other. Knowing that so many marriages, including those performed in churches, fail, we felt very fortunate to have the relationship we did. One of the affectionate things I would say constantly to her was: "If I weren't married to you, I'd ask you to marry me." It was wonderful knowing I would be seeing that "million-dollar smile" every single day and knowing I wouldn't have to be making trips to the airport to be able to see her and see her leaving again after a short time. It was wonderful knowing that I wouldn't have to depend on mainly email and phone to communicate with her. Sue told me that coming to be with her and her two daughters would be like going to the "Russian Front." It wasn't quite that bad. It was nice having to deal with only two children instead of the 350 boys in the monastery school. Fortunately for me, Sue, with all of her talents, was also a very good mother, which helped to make up for my deficiencies as a stepdad. It was as good as marriage gets.

Soon after I arrived, I looked for a paying job, something I hadn't had since the early 1980s. At one employment fair, I met a company representative who happened to be an uncle of a boy I had taught and coached at the Priory school. I hoped the connection would help land me at least an interview, but no calls came from that company—or any of the other companies to which I applied. Sue mentioned to a friend of hers, who knew an employee at Ohio State University Libraries, that I was looking for a job and had experience working in a library, which I had done at the monastery school. That connection led me to apply for a job at OSU. I applied for two different openings, one in the "Science and Engineering library" and one in the main library. I received a call from Human Resources that I did not get the job in the Science and Engineering Library and shortly after was informed that someone else had been chosen for the job in the main library. I soon learned, however, that the person chosen for the position in the main library did not show up for orientation and so, I was hired. The fact that I had been the second choice didn't bother me. I was just happy to get a job, and it ended up as long-term employment. It definitely made up for the disappointments of the recent job fair I had attended. One of the benefits of working in a library was, and still is, the access I get to any book or journal in the world, which I can utilize in my research and also share with other sindonologists. Rather than continue to mail a paper Shroud newsletter, I took advantage of the ease of emails and began to send news to other shroudies electronically. Not only was it faster, I saved a ton on postage!

In early November, 1998, an invitation-only conference sponsored by AMSTAR was held in Dallas, Texas. It was to be the first of three conferences they would go on to organize—and each would involve controversies. Although some commented on the wonderful spirit of cooperation that attendees had at the 1998 meeting, others felt slighted, since one had to be specifically invited. One can understand why the Turin authorities had an invitation-only conference such as the one they held in March, 2000, (see more on that further below) but it's harder to understand why a new group could not open up its first big event to the general public.

When the media had hounded STURP for information between 1978 and 1981, the group's somewhat secretive behavior led to some public-relations issues. By holding an invitation-only conference, AMSTAR refueled that problem.

Sue and I got busy writing our first Shroud article together. We submitted "The Shroud of Turin: Bridge Between Heaven and Earth?" to the *Journal of Religion and Psychical Research* (JRPR). On of my correspondents, Frank Tribbe, who had shared with me the information about his book being read by Elvis as recounted in Chapter One, was on the publications committee of JRPR.

Tribbe had read some of the articles that Sue had written previously and was not particularly open to them. The new *JRPR* editor, Donald Morse, who was Jewish, had only taken over a few months earlier. Even though he had suffered greatly at the hands of fundamentalist Christians, he was very open-minded and was willing to have the article reviewed. He had planned to let Tribbe review it, but Tribbe was out of town for an extended time, so the editor looked for another reviewer. It's very possible that Tribbe would have recommended against publishing it. The subsequent reviewer gave our article a passing grade; at some point, it would be published. Morse had planned to run a certain article in the April, 1999 issue, but it turned out to be too long, and he decided to run our article instead. The events that led to our article's publication had one of those "it was meant to be" feelings about them.

Soon after, Sue and I heard that there was going to be a Shroud conference in Richmond, Virginia in June, 1999. Fortunately, this one was open to the public, and we made plans to attend. Even though I had only been at Ohio State University less than one year, I was able to get time off work to go to the conference. In the meantime, our article in the *Journal of Religion and Psychical Research* was published. When we arrived at the conference, it was somewhat awkward for me to see other sindonologists there, given that the last time I had seen each and every one of them, I had still been in the monastery. I didn't feel overly sensitive about it, however, and Sue and I enjoyed the conference and lectures. Dr. Adler was one of the speakers, and he presented additional data that the area from which the C-14 sample had been taken had different chemical characteristics from the main part of the cloth. Adler's findings clearly indicated that the C-14 sample was *not* the same as the main part of the Shroud. Why that was the case was not exactly clear, however, although if the area had been repaired, the findings would make sense. Despite such data, the general public, for the most part, still accepted the 1988 C-14 results without question.

Even though the Shroud had been publicly displayed in 1998, Pope John Paul II authorized another Shroud exhibition for the first year of the new millennium. In March, 2000, an invitation-only conference was held in Turin. Meacham wrote in his 2005 book, <u>The Rape of the Shroud</u>, "Following on from it there was going to be a coordination of research proposals, an international dialogue about those proposals and research directions in general, and discussion of a process to evaluate them" (Meacham 2005b:237).

[Excerpt reprinted with permission of William Meacham.]

At the closing of the conference, one of the attendees, Dr. Avionic Danni, a botanist from the Hebrew University in Jerusalem who asserts that there are floral images from Jerusalem visible on the Shroud, read out in the cloth's very presence in Hebrew a passage from Isaiah 53:

> Without beauty, without majesty we saw him...
> A thing despised and rejected by men
> A man of sorrows and familiar with suffering...
> We thought of him as someone punished,
> Struck by God and brought low.
> Yet he was pierced through for our faults
> Crushed for our sins
> On him lies a punishment that brings us peace
> And through his wounds we are healed...

Subsequently, the Turin authorities, as they had in 1990, requested researchers to submit proposals for new testing on the Shroud. Only a few days after the October 30, 2000 deadline, some researchers affiliated with the "Centro," (the group in Turin charged with care of the Shroud) performed some analysis of the underside of the cloth. More than one person suspected that the authorities might "examine the contents of all the international scientific proposals and borrow any useful bits" (Meacham, 2005b:237).

Sue and I soon learned that there was going to be yet another conference, open to the public, in late August, 2000. This one was to be held in the small Italian town called Orvieto, and since it would be so far to travel and very expensive, Sue and I didn't seriously consider attending. We did ponder the

Chapter Eight: "It was a Repair!"

fact that until it could be proved that the C-14 dating was faulty, very few people would consider that the Shroud could be authentic. Sue wrote in her book:

> One night in meditation I took my questions and concerns to the guys. They agreed that it was necessary for us to first explain why the carbon dating had resulted in a medieval date before we could successfully explain the image-formation process and its implications. There was only one big problem—some of the best scientists in the world had been struggling with this dilemma for twelve years and were unable to come up with an answer—how would we?
>
> Typically, Jesus and John did not simply hand over direct answers to my questions. As good teachers, they made me work for the answers via my own efforts and initiatives. Often it was only after I had really gotten off track that they would intercede and steer me back in the right direction. The carbon-dating question was no exception.
>
> I initially pursued the theory that when Jesus's body was resurrected, there had been a biological nuclear reaction that released neutrons. These neutrons are known to cause a rejuvenation of cloth such that it appears much younger than it actually is. This explanation seemed neat and tidy in that it killed two mysteries with one stone—how the body disappeared and how the cloth ended up dating to the Middle Ages. At this point, I figured my work here was done. But, as with all my revelations in the past, my conclusions were premature.
>
> One day while busy patting myself on the back for resolving this confounding dilemma, out of the blue, they said, *"You're wrong."* Me, wrong? Okay, maybe it was some other nuclear particle that I had overlooked—perhaps muons or pions or . . . *"You're wrong. The cloth was repaired."* What were they trying to tell me? I had worked very hard on my nuclear theory and, as such, I deserved to be right! I was devastated. How was this possible—did they mean that the small sample of the Shroud used to determine its age actually contained newer cloth used for repairs? Where was the evidence for such a claim? Certainly someone would have seen such an obvious flaw in the sample? After all, the repairs were not "invisible" were they? Then they said, *"Look and we'll show you."*
>
> I ran to find Joe to tell him about this insight and to get his help in finding a picture of the actual carbon-14 sample used in 1988. Sure enough, he found one and there it was. The threads and the opposite sides of the separating "seam" that ran down the middle of

the sample were noticeably different. The differences were subtle, and if you did not know what you were looking for, you certainly would not see it. We found a clear picture of one of the subsamples and sent it to several textile experts for blinded reviews. Sure enough, they all saw discernible differences in each of the two sides of the weave pattern. One of the most dramatic affirmations came in a blinded review by a "French tailor" who readily pointed out and described the "invisible" mending techniques that his European ancestors used to mend damaged linens. Nowadays the process is known as "inweaving," and it involves a skilled weaver using a patch of identical fabric and placing it over the damaged area, matching the fabric's pattern. The frayed edges are then hand woven into the material. Both the patch and the repair are invisible to the eye. In the Shroud's case, the interweave involved about ½ inch next to the original raw edge; exactly the amount of aberrant material noted in the C-14 sample. There was no doubt in the tailor's mind that, indeed, exactly this technique had been used on the linen sample I was showing him.

But how, why, did this type of repair occur in the first place? The story began to unfold and documentation miraculously appeared each day to support our theory that a major portion of the sample used to date the Shroud had come from sixteenth-century material. What we learned was that the reinforcement with sixteenth-century material occurred following the removal of the 5½ inch x 3½ inch section of cloth adjacent to the C-14 sample. This may have occurred as a result of the Will and Testament Bequeath, drawn up on February 20, 1508, by the Duchess of Savoy, Margaret of Austria, who wanted to leave a portion of the Shroud to her church. Margaret died around the beginning of 1531 (*BSTS Newsletter*, no. 51, June 2000, pg. 43), at which time her last will and testament was executed. It is likely that it included the excision of the 5½ inch x 3½ inch section. Supporting this timeline of events is empirical testing by the late chemist Dr. Alan Adler, which compelled him to conclude that the "missing panels were already missing at the time of the 1532 fire." Since this would have been prior to the addition of the backing cloth in 1534, a more sophisticated patch-type repair would have been necessary to prevent unraveling of the raw edges. This type of detail to repairs would be consistent with the wealth and devotion of the Savoy family, who owned the Shroud at the time. All the pieces to the puzzle fit perfectly and in August, 2000, Joe and I presented our findings at "Sindone 2000," an international Shroud conference held in Orvieto, Italy (Benford 2002:189-191; 2011:187-189).

As noted in Sue's account, we did decide the research we had gathered was important enough to present, so we did make the trip, after all. We spent a lot of time together there with the late Don Lynn, a STURP member, and his wife Patti. We had thirty minutes to deliver our paper. We had practiced it at home over and over and always were always able to get under that time limit. During the actual presentation, as I was nearing the end, the moderator announced something in Italian. Not knowing any Italian, I wasn't sure what he said, but my first thought was that he was saying my time was up. I found it hard to believe I could be over the limit given how many times we had practiced it. I launched into hyper-speed as I was determined to complete it. I was able to finish, but I later found out I hadn't needed to rush—the moderator had actually announced that I had two minutes left. At that point I regretted not having learned Italian, especially as I am surnamed "Marino"!

Before the Congress was over, we were approached by a producer from the National Geographic Channel, who was interested to talk to us because they were planning a Shroud documentary in the near future. We also learned that the authorities were accepting test proposals. Like those who had attended the conference in Turin in March, researchers at the Orvieto conference were invited to send to the authorities proposals for tests. Sue and I soon submitted one related to C-14 testing.

Following the conference, Sue and I and many other attendees made our way to Turin to see the Shroud again. I had seen it only two years earlier and I felt very fortunate to be able to view the cloth again, especially considering that it usually was exhibited only two to three times a century, and that there had already been expositions in 1931, 1933 and 1978. As in 1998, I didn't experience anything out of the ordinary when I viewed it, but it was unbelievably moving and meaningful.

Sue described in her book what transpired after the conference:

> Although our paper received rave reviews, little happened initially to forward our hypothesis into a bona fide fact. Then in the waning days of summer 2001, almost coincident with the world's thirst for spiritual affirmation following the horrific events of September 11th, a near miracle took place. Through a series of odd connections and seeming "coincidences," I found myself in contact

with one of the most renowned members of the former 1978 STURP team. Ray Rogers, a retired chemist from Los Alamos Labs, was interested in reading our Orvieto paper. Soon after, he became singularly focused on proving that we were right! For a gentleman in his mid-seventies, his energy and constant pursuit of this endpoint was amazing and a bit mystical in its origin. On several occasions, I would receive numerous email reports of his findings, which included key factors such as that there was significant cotton in the adjacent Raes sample, some threads were literally "spliced" together as we had argued. The Raes threads were typical of the medieval backing cloth on the Shroud and not like the main Shroud threads (Benford 2002:191; 2011:189).

The "Raes sample" was named for the Belgian textile expert Gilbert Raes, who was given a sample in 1973 to analyze.

One of the things that should be noted is the providential convergence that brought Sue and me together, as well as the arrival of Ray Rogers on the scene. Had Sue and I never met, the Orvieto paper would never have been written, and Rogers would not have done his studies. This was one of the reasons we felt we had been called together for our Shroud work. It was fortunate that Rogers was involved again. After STURP had wrapped up most of the research in 1981, Rogers dropped out of sindonology before reappearing on the scene in 2000 to contest the scientific findings presented in a Shroud book titled <u>Resurrection of the Shroud</u> that was published that year. Rogers was a stickler for thorough and experimental science and never had an "I-think-I-see" approach. He even wrote a full critique about the book (Rogers 2001).

After Sue and I presented our paper, an electronic version was published at *www.shroud.com*. We also planned to submit a revised version for publication in the journal *Radiocarbon*. Rogers previously had considered Sue and me to be part of the "lunatic fringe" and hadn't been shy about telling the media, including in an interview on a Discovery Channel documentary first broadcast in December 2008 called "Unwrapping the Shroud: New Evidence." (The DVD, which contains footage of five hours of interviews that Barrie filmed of Rogers shortly before his death, can be obtained at:

http://store.discovery.com/detail.php?p=107095&v=discovery.

Although it's unfortunately packaged with a Leonardo-produced-the-Shroud DVD, the cost is very reasonable.) In the "Unwrapping the Shroud" documentary, STURP photographer Barrie Schwortz recounts that Rogers called him after the article was published on Barrie's site and said "What the hell is this?" (Schwortz admitted to me the language might have been a little saltier!) Rogers told Schwortz that he could prove us wrong in five minutes. "Well Ray," Schwortz replied, "go for it." Schwortz goes on to say that in less than hour, Rogers called him back and said "I can't believe it—I think they're right." Rogers rolled up his chemist sleeves and started doing serious research on the Shroud again. Rogers began to contact Turin about new proposals. Unfortunately, he received no response to his initial communication. Within a short time, however, the Shroud began to show up more and more again on the world's radar. But more controversy was just around the corner.

CHAPTER NINE

CONTROVERSIES IN DALLAS

Politics is a chaotic and often dramatic area, especially in Dallas, Texas, best known as the city where President John F. Kennedy was assassinated on November 22, 1963. After a Shroud conference in the "Big D" in 1998, there were two more Shroud conferences held in Dallas, in 2001 and 2005, and both provided their share of chaos, drama and political intrigue.

Sue and I got word that a conference would be held in Dallas in late October, 2001, hosted by AMSTAR and another major Shroud group. We planned not only to attend, but to submit a paper for presentation. The subject matter was not C-14, but an out-of-the-box hypothesis regarding how the image may have been put onto the cloth. Hypotheses about image-formation are plentiful, ranging from multiple forgery scenarios to very advanced ideas about certain kinds of radiations emanating from the body which thereby cause the imprints. One of the most humorous passages I've seen in serious Shroud literature pertains to the image-formation process. The writer, Cullen Murphy, wrote an extremely informative and entertaining article. He interviewed many of the STURP members, described various experiments in a serious vein, conveyed how one mixture they worked with didn't produce an image similar to the Shroud, but concluded, "it made a remarkably fine Hollandaise sauce" (Murphy 1981:46).

A little humor is always a good tonic, and we would soon need some. Sue had done a great deal of research in medical and scientific areas and incorporated much of that into our paper. While working on the paper, we sent in our registrations but had various problems with one of the organizers, a lawyer (mentioned in Chapter Five), who was demanding that registrants sign a document regarding liability. Some of the other people who planned to attend refused to sign it. No one had ever seen such a document as part of a conference registration process. After some difficulties, we finally completed the registration and continued to work on the paper we intended to submit. We had been in communication with the late Dr. Adler and Donald Lynn, also a STURP member, (who unfortunately died just days before the Dallas conference was to begin) about some aspects of the paper. Adler and Lynn were both on the board of AMSTAR. The problems we encountered with the registration process were a harbinger of things to come.

AMSTAR had invited the British author Ian Wilson, one of the most prominent Shroud researchers in the world, to give the keynote address. However, politics reared its ugly head immediately. Wilson sent an email to about a dozen sindonologists explaining how AMSTAR wrongly accused him of improprieties and then tried to cover up their actions. He decided to withdraw from the conference. Sue and I were also falsely accused of improper behavior. Ironically, after several communications from the lawyer, we actually discovered questionable actions on his part, which are detailed in the long email that I sent out to selected individuals in November, 2001, and reproduced further below. When Sue and I decided to withdraw from the conference, we sent an email on August 2 to selected sindonologists, explaining the situation. The lawyer was copied on the email. He wrote in response that our email waived any privilege of confidentiality with AMSTAR regarding our paper. He provided to us "two of the milder, self-explanatory peer reviews of your referenced paper by independent scientists. He then "clarified" our "implication" that two deceased board members, Dr. Alan Adler and Donald Lynn, were involved in any way in our paper. He asserted that neither AMSTAR, Adler, nor Lynn collaborated on our paper, "either officially or unofficially." Finally, he stated that our paper was not suitable for their forum.

It boggled our minds that he believed he could state that his board members weren't even working unofficially with us! Notice that he couldn't even bring himself to say our "statement" or "assertion" that we had been collaborating with two AMSTAR members—for him it is only an "implication." I don't question that conference organizers can have certain parameters for the kind of papers they want to accept, but when they alienate their keynote speaker to the point where he withdraws and when they do the

Chapter Nine: Controversies in Dallas 107

kind of things that will be detailed below, I believe one will have to admit that our objections were warranted.

The easiest way to explain the specific details is to reproduce both our response to the organizers after the lawyer's reply to my August 2 email and an email I sent out to many of my Shroud contacts in November. Both are long and very detailed, but they give all of the pertinent details, so I have reproduced them in their entirety.

Here is our reply to the lawyer in response to his email sent after our August 2 email and copied to various shroudies:

> We are not worried about losing privilege of confidentiality, as our whole point has been to get this information out to others for their critical review. As many of the people receiving this missive are aware, we have always welcomed interested and informed evaluation of our work. That is also why we publish extensively in peer-reviewed forums. Consider this an open invitation to interested parties who would like to review, assess, critique, challenge or replicate any/all of our findings.
>
> Your e-mail was quite disturbing on a couple of critical issues. First, you state, "We also wish to clarify your implication that our two deceased board members, Dr. Alan Adler and Donald Lynn, were collaborating or assisting you with the aforementioned paper. Never at any time did AMSTAR or any of its members collaborate on your imaging paper, either officially or unofficially. If Dr. Adler provided a thread to you that fact does not constitute collaboration or approval of your imaging hypothesis." There is nothing further from the truth and, should any of those receiving this email want to either view Al's handwritten note on the plastic bag containing the approx. 4" by 5" piece (NOT THREAD) of linen he sent to us for testing, or see one of Don's several correspondences pertaining to our work, we would be happy to forward them. How incredible that you would claim, clearly unknowingly, that these two men were not interested and involved in our research! Don was sent a copy of the De La Warr book, which he returned after he read. Al asked for a copy of the De La Warr book, which we sent him, and he also asked that a complimentary copy be sent to Whanger, which was sent. We were actually planning to meet with Adler (per Adler's suggestion) at Whanger's laboratory, since he had a good microscope that Adler wanted to use to look at our experimental linen sample fibers.
>
> Second, although we appreciate finally receiving two genuine reviews (WHY WEREN'T WE SENT THESE WHEN WE FIRST

ASKED FOR THEM?), there are clearly many points of misunderstanding, faulty interpretation and just plain ignorance of the subject areas involved. However, a couple of suggestions were well taken, such as the fact that we should have used Al's linen also for the gamma control. This is a good point.

Third, much of the critique ignores the basic fact that we DID create nearly identical discolored fibers matching the Shroud's image fibers using our techniques and De La Warr's images HAVE been independently verified as actual representations of the internal conditions of subjects in a 400-patient medical trial (results confirmed by surgery and autopsy). Further, the recent discovery that these images contain spatially-encoded 3-D information, similar to the Shroud's, has been confirmed by a noted MRI expert and astronaut Dr. Edgar Mitchell, as well as Dr. Peter Moscow, Dr. Peter Marcer, along with numerous other scientists.

Our paper attempts to show the similarity of our hypothesis to other previously little-understood scientific phenomena that are now being better explained due to the recent theory of Quantum Holography. If this connection is correctly understood, it can help to actually take the Shroud out of the category of "paranormal." Dr. Thad Trenn, who has extensively reviewed our work for over a year, had this to say regarding our paper:

"The truly novel feature of their research, however, involves the capacity of mind to act as an instrument of coherence. The brain seems to be able to engage the non-local signaling as a type of coherer. While this research is not totally new in the literature, their special application seems to be quite novel and pregnant with potential for the Turin Shroud. This is what excited Adler. Essential to the brain-coherer function vis-à-vis engaging, receiving and modulating non-local resonance states is the physiological ability to project this information forward, as it were, so as to capture the results in a type of holistic imaging. Extensive research was already done on this phenomenon during the 1950s in the area of medical technology, by De La Warr and colleagues. Ample photographic documents are available. Yet overall acceptance of the phenomenon languished for lack of an acceptable scientific basis of explanation. With the rise of quantum holography in more recent times, this complex phenomenon has begun to be taken quite seriously indeed." (via fax to a committee member and email copy to us 4/20/01)

It was clear from the very beginning that our paper was not going to be reviewed with an open mind as one committee member tried to encourage us from the very beginning to present instead the

Chapter Nine: Controversies in Dallas

much-lauded C-14 paper that we had given at Orvieto. We declined because we felt our image-formation paper was as significant and should be presented. After our image-formation paper was rejected, we agreed to be on standby to give the C-14 paper but after all these other events unfolded, we were then told that we couldn't present it on the flimsy pretext that it had been presented before.

I cannot help but recall Yves Delage, the French agnostic, who, in 1902, at the beginning of the last century, was admonished not to mention "Christ" in his Shroud paper read before the "free-thinkers" of the French Academy of Sciences. This ultimately led him to leave Shroud research. Another of the great Shroud researchers has been driven at least partly away because of a similar situation. As far as our situation goes, we have submitted our paper to several websites, and Sue has included it in her upcoming book.

It is worth relating a similar incident that Sue went through on one of her previous papers. When she submitted a paper to *Medical Hypotheses*, the most prestigious medical theory journal in the world, the editor had trouble with the referees. According to the editor, Dr. David Horrobin, "(I)n the end their criticisms boiled down to 'I do not believe it' rather than having any strong rational basis. I believe that the work should be published in order to provoke discussion irrespective of whether or not it finally turns out to be correct." Here is an example of the seeking of truth being the bottom line.

According to one speaker/attendee I talked with, at least two talks were given at Dallas for which people in the audience commented, "What did that have to do with the Shroud?" Despite having empirical evidence that has to be explained relating directly to the Shroud, despite the backing of many credible institutions and scientists, we were not allowed to present our paper. A former consultant to STURP who is also a board member of the Association of Scientists and Scholars International for the Shroud of Turin (ASSIST) emailed us that he was shocked and outraged that our paper was rejected. Some of our research has been posted on his website at www.gizapyramid.com/Turin/Sue%20Benford.htm. We were treated pretty poorly in this whole process. We were told that we weren't even working "unofficially" with people that we quite simply were working with, which is more than an implication that we were being untruthful about our research. Considering this came from people studying what is thought to be the image of the person who told us to treat others as we would like to be treated, it doesn't speak well for Shroud research.

A similar symposium had been held in Dallas in 1998. In the Proceedings of that conference, one of the committee members wrote, "Cooperation includes sharing information. The Shroud has no nationality or religion. It belongs to all mankind (and "womankind" too!) The Shroud is no one's fiefdom nor does anyone have a copyright on the data gleaned from the Shroud. Shared information on the Shroud generates more discoveries, which, in turn, translate into greater knowledge and understanding. As Father Peter Rinaldi was fond of saying, 'There is room on the Shroud for all.' Cooperation is the key to conserving the Shroud and unraveling its mysteries. Great and undreamed of discoveries await the development of new technology not now known or thought of . . . . [W]e must rise above our petty differences in the interest of future generations. We must remember the Shroud will be here after we are gone, and let it be our legacy that we leave it better than we found it . . . . I charge you to boldly approach the new century and millennium with a spirit of cooperation and collegiality. I strongly believe great Shroud discoveries lie ahead but they will be predicated on what we do today . . . . It is much more pleasant along the way if we cooperate and get along." (See <u>The Shroud of Turin: Unraveling the Mystery</u>. Alexander, NC: Alexander Books, 2002, pg. 353) Nice words—but you won't be surprised if we feel that these words ring hollow to us.

Sue and I received little support from other sindonologists, and we were quite disappointed. To be fair, I suppose there wasn't much they could do, but it would have been nice to receive more notes like the few supportive ones we did receive. (Another person's perspective on not receiving support from other Shroud researchers and the poisonous effect of Shroud politics can be found in Ian Wilson's comments in an editorial reproduced in Appendix K.)

In September, when we contacted the producer of the National Geographic Channel we had met in Orvieto and let her know the situation, she emailed: "You're kidding! They don't want you in Dallas? These people are nuts. They have no idea what they are doing." The lawyer, like most shroudies, was very passionate about the Shroud and was a great organizer, but was not usually too diplomatic in his dealings with others.

Below is the email that I sent in November to various Shroud contacts:

> I had planned to attend the Dallas Shroud conference held in late October. One person on my list suggested that I could report on it.

Chapter Nine: Controversies in Dallas

Unfortunately, Sue Benford and I withdrew due to farcical treatment we received from the main sponsor of the conference. Another group *[name intentionally omitted]* co-sponsored the conference, but seemed to have little or no input in the planning of the conference. They were never mentioned in our dealings with the main sponsor, and we never heard from any representative from the co-sponsor.

With that as initial background, I want to go into further detail about how the situation with Sue Benford and me unfolded, as our situation, like one outlined by Ian Wilson in the *British Society for the Turin Shroud Newsletter [#54, reprinted in Appendix K]*, is hurting the cause of the Shroud. It was Wilson who revealed that he was told by a main sponsor committee member, "We will neither invite nor accept papers from controversial people. No Walter McCrone, Emily Craig, no C14 maniacs, has-been STURP members who lost their faith, or anyone else who wants to bring outdated contact image ideas." By telling our story, I'm hoping that similar incidents can be avoided in the future and that the truth and the message of the Shroud can be disseminated to a world in need of it.

Sue and I presented a paper at the Worldwide Congress in Orvieto, Italy, in August, 2000 on the C-14 dating results. We presented compelling empirical evidence, supported by blinded reviews *[i.e., they were shown Shroud pictures but not told that it was the Shroud]* from textile experts, that the C-14 area of the Shroud contained a sixteenth-century patch. Many people commented that it was the best presentation at the Congress. We have had no significant, specific objections from anyone. Mechthild Flury-Lemberg, the Swiss textile expert, told us it was "technically impossible," but there have been institutions and individuals from the Middle Ages onward that have done invisible weaving for a living . . . thus making her comment simply wrong. Dr. Ray Rogers, an original STURP member, looked at our paper and has concluded that the C-14 samples were spurious. His unofficial report was sent out to this list. Since then, he has written a more official report and is submitting it to peer-review journals for publication.

We have also been working on a paper related to image-formation. We had been working with AMSTAR board members Dr. Alan Adler and Don Lynn on this paper before their untimely deaths. Adler actually supplied the linen we used in our experiments. Another supporter was physicist and former Apollo astronaut Dr. Edgar Mitchell, who told us that he thought our theory explained the Shroud image. Sue is the primary author of a paper related to our image-formation theory that was presented with Mitchell at the Fifth

International Conference on Computing Anticipatory Systems at Liege, Belgium, August 13-18, 2001
(see http://www.ulg.ac.be/mathgen/CHAOS/CASYS.html for the conference website and
http://www.homestead.com/newvistas/CASYS.html for the text of the article.

Sue also had an article related to aspects of our image-formation theory published in the *Journal of Theoretics* (http:llwww.journaloftheoretics.com/Articles/2-5/Benford.htm), but didn't actually mention the Shroud in the article. Much to our pleasant surprise, the editor of the journal, Dr. James P. Siepmann, wrote an editorial titled "Science Explains the Image on the Shroud of Turin":
(http://www.journaloftheoretics.com/Editorials/Editoria%202-5.html). He had figured out the connection without our even telling him.*[See note at end of chapter.] In addition, Canadian physicist and theologian Dr. Thaddeus Trenn, who once supported a "weak dematerialization" theory as the cause of the image, now completely supports our theory after having studied it for more than a year.

When we heard about the Dallas conference, we submitted a brief abstract for an image-formation paper that we wanted to present. As the committee was unfamiliar with some of the terms in the abstract, we were asked to submit a full draft of the paper, which we did immediately, along with a more elaborate abstract. Sue was also required to send in a curriculum vitae, which she did (was this required of anyone else?). You should know that Sue was a semifinalist in the 2000 *Discover Magazine* awards (top 100 out of 4000 entries) related to the spatial-encoding aspect of this research. She was also a semifinalist in the 1999 awards for an unrelated discovery. Sue has had ten (10!) peer-reviewed, scientifically based articles published since 1999 (see our website www.homestead.com/newvistas for a listing of articles, including full-text access to some of them). In all of her peer-reviewed papers, there has not been one question that she or her co-authors weren't able to satisfactorily address. (In fact, she was recently hired as Executive Director of the Ohio Scientific, Education and Research Association, which has as members representatives of all the top universities and corporations involved in biomedical science in Ohio.)

For our paper, we consulted and employed outside institutions such as NASA, Argonne Labs, The Ohio State University and the Rochester Institute of Technology. As in the Orvieto paper, the reviews were blinded. We ended up submitting 35 illustrations, graphs and tables, including a table showing over 20 matches between the Shroud and our experimental linen.

The paper was read by two committee members and three anonymous reviewers. Despite all the evidence presented and all of the aforementioned scientific backing, our paper was rejected. We were informed that the committee was unanimous in its rejection. I'm certain that if Al Adler and Don Lynn were alive, the committee would not have been unanimous. Letters of support from Dr. Trenn and also one from a Canadian professor of computer science, Dr. Robert Hadley, were to no avail. We were told in a phone conversation by one sponsor committee member that some committee members suggested that our paper could be presented informally after dinner, but the three anonymous reviewers totally rejected the suggestion. Besides the contradiction of committee members officially rejecting the paper but suggesting that it be allowed to be presented after dinner, one has to wonder why three anonymous reviewers have more power than the committee members. What exactly were the reviewers afraid of?

It is traditional in a peer-review process to get specific reasons from reviewers why a paper was rejected. When we asked to see the comments from the reviewers, we were told that the operations of one of the elements in our paper, something called the "De La Warr camera,"*[See note at end of chapter] "admittedly remain unknown." That didn't prevent STURP scientist, Dr. John Heller, from being supportive of De La Warr's work; we cited several references in our Orvieto C-14 paper published in the Proceedings. Just because something remains unknown doesn't mean it should be discounted. Scientists don't know exactly why aspirin works, but it doesn't keep us from using them. We were informed that "one cannot prove an unknown process with another unknown process." Wouldn't that eliminate any Shroud theory that posits some sort of radiation causing the Shroud image? After all, a dead body disappearing and emitting radiation enough to cause an imprint is an unknown. If this is posited, wouldn't that be an example of using an unknown to prove an unknown? Our paper incorporated the little-understood subject matter of quantum physics. Ironically, a paper also dealing with quantum mechanics was read by a main sponsor committee member (she read it for the absent Author), which according to one speaker/attendee I talked to, didn't even directly tie in the Shroud. So apparently quantum mechanics is okay to talk about, but as soon as a connection is established with the Shroud, it's using an unknown to prove an unknown. We, in fact, didn't try to prove anything. The title of our paper was "Empirical Findings Suggesting Comparability

Among the Turin Shroud, OuantaGraphic, and Magnetic Resonance Imaging (MRI)."

In our conclusion, we say: "Although an undeniable comparability exists between the OuantaGraphic image formation process and the TS, several questions still remain. First, is it possible to create a "quantum MRI," exactly like the Turin Shroud, without the assistance of an artificial imaging system? George De La Warr speculated that, indeed, it was and our preliminary research in this area is promising."

However, a major variable in the success of this venture is the "key component" of the conscious intention of the one seeking to create such an image. It is most likely that a being of highly evolved emotional, mental, and spiritual development, such as Jesus, would be capable of manifesting identical images without assistance of a device, regardless of "when" and "from where" the intention is originally projected. This leaves us to ponder whether or not others will achieve this remarkable feat, possibly shedding light on *why* the image was left in the first place. As a result, the Turin Shroud can be said, for now, to be a unique example of an unassisted OuantaGraphic process.

In accepting the possibility that the TS image may be more in keeping with Jesus' energetic body than his physical body, "scientists must be ready to overturn even their most hallowed principles if observation warrants . . . And let us keep in mind, that to date, no 'conventional' hypothesis has been advanced, which successfully explains the TS image" *[quote from "An Uncoventional Hypothesis to Explain All Image Characteristics Found on the Shroud Image," by Dr. John Jackson in paper presented at the 1991 St. Louis International Shroud Conference]*. Neither the title of our paper nor the conclusion indicates that we were proving anything. Our paper fits Jackson's observations, yet it has apparently been rejected precisely because it's too unconventional. But what is grossly overlooked is that ours is not merely a "theory." We have independently validated, replicated, empirical evidence, which puts it in a whole different category!

We were told that, "the paper reads . . . as a treatise on paranormal phenomena." Doesn't the Shroud qualify as being "paranormal?" Isn't the Resurrection of Jesus "paranormal?" One of the committee members emailed me that the reviewing members did not regard our paper as being suitable for their forum and do not regard the Shroud as a "paranormal" object. I emailed him back that the American Heritage Dictionary defines "paranormal" as "not within the range of normal experience or scientifically explainable phenomena." Considering that the Shroud is totally unique and still as yet unexplained scientifically, the Shroud is by definition "paranormal." In another ironic situation, one of the speakers allowed to speak at Dallas is described on one website as being known as "'Germany's most prolific UFO expert' and investigator of the great mysteries of our times" and publisher of "Europe's largest magazine on the paranormal." Sounds like he wouldn't be adverse to calling the Shroud "paranormal," and yet his papers (he gave two and was asked to write a third as an addendum to the Proceedings) were suitable and ours was not.

We quote John Jackson in our paper as saying "scientists must be ready to overturn even their most hallowed principles if observation warrants. And, let us keep in mind that, to date, no 'conventional' hypothesis has been advanced, which successfully explains the Shroud image."

The committee mentioned that there is a skepticism held by those in the broader scientific community about the qualifications and motivations of Shroud researchers and that we "must observe the most rigorous standards of scientific methods and reporting." When I started working with Sue about three years ago, she had the scientific background that complemented my theological background. I have been researching and disseminating information about the Shroud for nearly 25 years, and I think most people would agree that I am as interested as anyone to find out the truth behind the Shroud. I have read every major item in the English language on the subject (and countless minor items), have seen and heard numerous tapes, attended numerous conferences, and have voluminous correspondence with scientists and researchers. A Shroud scientist once complimented me because he said I always had the Shroud's best interests at heart. I believe our paper is truly significant and warranted presentation; our scientific methods and reporting are sound and valid, even if the data is not easily understood. Sue's scientific methodology and reporting has been good enough to enable her to publish 10 peer-reviewed scientific articles in the past two years and shows that she has a strong scientific background. We approached our proposed Dallas paper with this same scientific rigor that marks her articles and that marked our Orvieto paper. [Not one criticism raised by AMSTAR's review of our paper brought forth any argument with our scientific methodology or data.]

As Georges Salet said in *Revue Internationale Du Linceul De Turin*, no.10, pg. 20, "In all scientific matters, it is the experiment that has the last word." Unfortunately, in this conference, it is the committee that has the last word. We have been told that our paper does not fit the "general agenda and spirit" of the conference. Finding the truth of the Shroud should be the goal of any agenda and spirit of a Shroud conference, as opposed to preserving a predefined political and/or theological perspective. It should try to resolve the Shroud mystery, not perpetuate it.

The policies of the committee have been disturbing. We submitted a full abstract and a full draft long before the deadline. We then learned from the registration packet that some speakers had not submitted an abstract (they were given an extension to July 15) and yet were on the list of provisional speakers. Further, I learned via email from several persons on the speaker list that they didn't even have an idea for a paper yet. Another speaker from outside the U.S. made arrangements only several months in advance to attend the conference and was given a slot. If previous reputations played a role in awarding slots to speakers, I humbly say that we should have been given the benefit of the doubt based on our Orvieto paper and my nearly 25 years in sindonology. Perhaps, I, as a former priest and monk, was considered to be part of the "controversial people." After we submitted our paper, we received an email from a member of the committee asking us for permission to let anonymous reviewers read our paper. The same email requested "documentation for [our] footnotes." Since we didn't have any footnotes in the draft we sent, we asked for clarification. We were then told in a subsequent email that it had been a request of one of the reviewers but was no longer needed. So if a reviewer had already seen the paper, why were we even asked, in the previous email, for our permission to let them read it? Since we were uniquely required to submit a full, completed paper on our research by May 30 (well before we had originally planned to have all the experiments completed), we were criticized when we submitted our additional evidence in sequence as it became available.

After Wilson sent an email to about a dozen prominent Shroud researchers detailing his unpleasant experiences with committee members (and then related it in the *British Society for the Turn Shroud Newsletter*), I sent an email to the same group, spelling out details of our situation. One of the committee members sent us, as well as the others on this aforementioned list, an email with attachments of comments by several reviewers about our paper, saying we had "waived any privelege [sic] of confidentiality" concerning our paper. It was clearly an act designed to "put us in our place." One of the researchers later emailed me that he was "appalled" by the way we were treated.

The email also said that they wished to clarify our "implication that our two deceased board members, Dr. Alan Adler and Donald Lynn, were collaborating or assisting you with the aforementioned paper. Never at any time did AMSTAR or any of its members collaborate on your imaging paper, either officially or unofficially. If

Dr. Adler provided a thread to you that fact that does not constitute collaboration or approval of your imaging hypothesis." We also later realized from the reviewers' comments that they had only received the first draft and weren't even sent the updates that we sent because the questions they had proposed had been addressed in the updates.

I wrote a firm letter to someone in another major Shroud group that, even though his group was billed as a co-sponsor of the conference, no one from that group did nothing to object to the behavior toward us that could only be described as inconsiderate. I did receive an email back from a representative from the group, who said:

Dear Joe,
    I am sorry things worked out so poorly for you and Sue at the Dallas conference. Shortly after Orvieto, [the group] realized that Rochester, NY was not the best place for the conference, and [we] seemed to feed right in to the hidden desire of [name intentionally omitted] to host the conference in Dallas with *[names intentionally omitted]*. They were the editorial committee—I'm sure [the group] was just included for eye wash, to attempt to disguise the coup they were pulling off. I tried to do all I could to avoid this fight among people I thought were all friends. There are some hidden agenda in the shroud crowd, and I tried to pretend I didn't see it. I spoke to this in Dallas, saying that people were getting hurt in the shroud crowd, and shame on us when we let that happen....
    In closing I would like to say that I enjoy your work with the shroud very much. Your presentation at Orvieto was interesting, exciting and fresh. If I had anything to say about it at all, you would have presented in Dallas. In any case, I hope the wound caused isn't too deep that it can't heal, and will look forward to enjoying your and Sue's company again before too much time passes us by.

Here we have a representative of a co-sponsor being forthright enough to admit that AMSTAR attempted a coup and had an agenda. Coups are rarely painless; there's nothing wrong with an agenda if motives are good, but if it is a detriment to the cause of the Shroud and hurts people in the process, it needs to be made known. The New Testament, after all, does refer to the need for brotherly (and by extension, sisterly) correction (Matthew 18:15-18). The response I received from the co-sponsor group representative is the sort of thing that we definitely need more in sindonology! I hasten to add that I believe that the lawyer negatively influenced several of the other organizers in his group, who had always been and still are kind and wonderful people. I was able to reconcile with them, although the lawyer stayed in control of matters through the 2005 Dallas conference, which also would be fraught with problems.

In the meantime, Sue and I submitted to the journal *Radiocarbon* an updated version of the C-14 paper that we had presented at Orvieto. The journal sent us back some reviews in October. We alerted Rogers about the response we received from *Radiocarbon*. He made some educated guesses regarding who the reviewers were. He emailed us on October 20: "I am pretty offended that *Radiocarbon* would use the persons they did as referees. I almost sent a letter to them, but I hesitated. What do you think? This is the well-known way in which 'peer review' falls down and is counterproductive to science." *[Excerpt reprinted with permission of Joan Rogers.]* A few hours later, he emailed again, telling me who he thought three of the reviewers were. As I found out after the journal later revealed to me who the reviewers actually were, he was correct on two of the three. However, the reviewer he missed had, like the two he had guessed correctly, taken part in the 1988 dating and certainly would have had difficulty being totally objective as well.

The year 2001 will be remembered for the second Dallas conference but no one had an inkling that 2002, which included the continuation of the saga of our submission to *Radiocarbon*, would bring even a bigger controversy—this one from Turin itself.

---

*The British engineer George De La Warr invented in the 1950s a remote-imaging camera. Using only a "test object" provided from the subject such as a small blood or hair sample, this device imaged the subjects' internal conditions, with a high degree of accuracy. A unique feature of the De La Warr camera is that it is able to detect diseases at their earliest stages. In many instances, detection can occur before conventional images such as X-ray, CT, and MRI can resolve anatomical changes. Our theory was that there was a plausible connection between the image-formation processes of the Shroud and the De La Warr camera and provide a compelling comparison between both phenomena and MRI. De La Warr's camera was way ahead of its time—and apparently so was our theory.

CHAPTER TEN

CONTROVERSIES IN TURIN

Despite receiving no reply from Turin to his communication, Ray Rogers continued to explore the theory that the C-14 dating had been skewed by invisible reweaving and published various articles at *www.shroud.com*.

In a letter dated January 1, 2002, Dr. Timothy Jull, editor of the journal *Radiocarbon,* and one of the scientists from the University of Arizona laboratory that dated the Shroud in 1988, sent Sue and me a reply regarding the submission of our C-14 paper. For those not familiar with the process by which papers are published in scientific journals, the editor chooses various reviewers, usually anonymous to the author and supposedly objective, who then make suggestions to the author(s) on how to make the paper better. After changes are made, the reviewers read the paper again, and make their recommendations to the editor as to whether the paper should be published or not. However, the final decision is in the hands of the editor. The review of our paper was out of the ordinary insofar as the reviewers were revealed to us, something that normally doesn't occur. They were all originally directly involved in the specific topic of our paper, the 1988 Shroud C-14 dating. It was our contention that the C-14 dating was skewed due to the presence of a sixteenth century repair. Here is a list of the reviewers of our paper:

* Paul Damon, head of the Arizona laboratory that participated in the 1988 Shroud dating
* Jacques Evin, French C-14 expert present at the 1988 sample-taking
* The late Gabriel Vial, French textile expert present at the 1988 sample taking
* Franco Testore, Italian French textile expert present at the 1988 sample taking

* Harry Gove, inventor of the AMS radiocarbon dating method, who had literally bet a companion that the Shroud was medieval and was heavily involved in various aspects of the dating

What were the chances that any of these men, each of whom would publicly look bad if our theory were correct, would want to see our paper published? The answer was obvious. Needless to say, our paper was not accepted. Most interesting was a comment by Evin, who wrote in the review sent by the editor to Sue and me:

> The authors, who, for several reasons, are convinced that the shroud is authentic, want to publish an article in *Radiocarbon* only to introduce a doubt about the dating. All people involved in the sampling and in laboratory analyses, will be very angry with these suspicions turning on so an important mistake or a misconduct...
> [Evin 2002].

We certainly did want to introduce a doubt about the dating because we had compiled enough evidence to warrant questioning the results. I'm not sure if Evin was actually admitting that a mistake or misconduct took place, but he surely seemed open to the possibility that it very well could have happened! And given what Rogers and others found, it would seem that their analyses were not as thorough as they should have been.

Meanwhile, Rogers wrote a significant article with his findings up to that point, which was published at *www.shroud.com*. Many started to acknowledge that the C-14 results could not be accepted with the 95 per cent confidence level that the testers had bestowed upon it. As sindonologists' hopes about the authenticity of the Shroud reignited, news that sent shock waves broke from Turin on August 9. Orazio Petrosillo, a Vatican affairs reporter (now deceased) for *Il Messaggero*, released a story saying that a secret restoration of the Shroud took place during the summer. The text read as follows (all translations of following articles in Italian newspapers made by Emanuela Marinelli, co-founder of the influential Shroud group *Collegamento Pro Sindone* and member of the Internet "Shroud Science Group," of which I am also a member):

Chapter Ten: Controversies in Turin

IL MESSAGGERO —Friday, August 9, 2002, page 8
The 1534 'patches' and backing cloth eliminated
Sindone, a new mystery: 30 patches removed
The operation was led by the Swiss textile expert Flury-Lemberg between June and July. But the Commission for the relic preservation was not involved. Damages are feared.

At first sight, the news seems incredible. The Shroud of Turin is no longer the same one millions and millions of people have venerated and contemplated in the last 1978, 1998 and the Jubilee year of 2000. A month ago, in the utmost secrecy, changes were made altering its universally known aspect. The Shroud of Turin is no longer the one it has been for nearly five centuries, from April 1534 until some weeks ago. A restoration has altered changes made in 1534. In fact, the thirty patches of various sizes, which the Poor Clare nuns of Chambery had sewn on the Sheet in the restoration carried out after the fire of December 4, 1532, that had burnt it in various areas, have been removed. Moreover, the so-called "Holland cloth", then sewn on the back of the Shroud in order to better support it, has been replaced.

The most important antique relic of Christianity, of universal value because thought to be Jesus of Nazareth's burial sheet, with amazing confirmations from many scientific tests of various disciplines, has undergone an intervention certainly of no little conservative significance, with the elimination of a restoration of many centuries and remarkable risks for the Shroud Man's image itself. All of that was carried out in the utmost secrecy, without the scientific communities *[outside the circle of the Turin authorities]* having been informed and without ever they having been any suggestion to remove the patches and the Holland cloth in any of the eight international conferences on the Shroud in the last four years...

From the historical-documentary point of view, the damage is obvious. Even if they may have acted with precaution and professionalism, the unsewing of the patches on the burned parts of the cloth, above all the one nearest the side wound, cannot have happened without loss of small fragments. It seems amazing indeed that such a permission has been granted by the Custodian, Cardinal Severino Poletto, and granted (even if, as far as we know, with remarkable difficulty) by the Holy See, who is the relic owner. The "operation patches" took place from last June 20 to July 22. The Shroud was removed from the new case under the royal stand in the left transept of the Turin Cathedral, and brought into the new adjoining sacristy, and thus became inaccessible during all the proceedings. The patches were removed from the sheet, 4.37 m long and 1.11 m wide. Those patches, more or less triangular, are in parallel couples next to the frontal and dorsal images of the Man, naked, scourged, hit on the face, with marks of a helmet of thorns on the head and bruises of the horizontal beam of a cross on the shoulders, who was crucified with nails and pierced on the side after his death. In the fire of the night between December 3 and 4, 1532, in the "Sainte Chapelle" of Chambery, a corner of the Shroud (folded in 48 layers measuring 27 to 36 cm) was burnt, causing symmetrical burns to the longitudinal and cross-sectional lines of folding.

The operation in 2002 was led by a textile expert of international reputation, the Swiss Mechthild Flury-Lemberg who, after removing the patches and the Holland cloth, replaced the latter with a cloth of her property. The patches removed have been preserved in sealed containers, as well as the Holland cloth. It is alleged that one of the cloth foldings near the Man of the Shroud's face would have disappeared as a result of these unsewings, but another one would have remained. It seems that the two people in charge of the International Centre of Sindonology, the mathematician Bruno Barberis, its director, and Gian Maria Zaccone, director of the Museum, were behind this intervention, while Mgr. Giuseppe Ghiberti, the most important collaborator of the Cardinal as far as the Shroud is concerned, seems to have been reluctant. Moreover, the whole Commission for the Shroud preservation (where, nevertheless, the same Flury-Lemberg is the only textile expert) does not seem to have been involved, nor, least of all, was Pierluigi Baima Bollone, predecessor of Barberis and one of the most qualified scientist sindonologists. Sindonologists are clamorously asking why this "transformation" of the Shroud has been carried out. Granted, the photos taken by the present trusted photographer of the Centre, Giancarlo Durante, are worth millions of Euros and the next volume in which they will be published will obtain for this a worldwide resonance. Nevertheless, a lot of things are not clear regarding what happened.

In the very same edition, Petrosillo also published an article about Rogers' findings:

Chapter Ten: Controversies in Turin

IL MESSAGGERO —Friday, August 9, 2002, page 8
Other polemics —The 1988 dating is questioned
Two scholars: there are also invisible repairs on the linen cloth. The radiocarbon test may have been altered.

«According to the 14C test the cloth appeared Medieval. Perhaps only some threads were.»

ROME –The repair was medieval, not the Shroud. After 30 visible patches were removed, some scholars are now directing their attention to the invisible repairs on the Turinese Sheet. They were widely used in the Middle Ages for very precious cloths, just like the one venerated as the holiest of relics. Therefore, the result of the dating tests of the Shroud with the radiocarbon method (14C), carried out by the laboratories of Oxford, Tucson and Zurich in 1988 that dated the Shroud cloth between 1260 and 1390, has been altered by the presence, just in the area of the dating of the small linen samples, an invisible reweave dating back to the sixteenth century. Sue Benford and Joseph Marino, two American sindonologists, claim this. A series of pictures of one of the samples taken in 1988 for the radiocarbon dating and of the remaining part that was not used were submitted to three textile experts, independently and without being told the samples had been taken from the Shroud. All the three experts recognized a different weaving on one side of the samples. According to the calculations of Beta Analytic, the largest provider of radiocarbon dating in the world, a mixture of 60 per cent of material, from the sixteenth century, with 40 per cent of material from the first century would result in a thirteenth-century dating . . . .

Interesting observations were made by Ray Rogers, a chemist who was a member of STURP, the group of American scientists who examined the Shroud in 1978. Rogers had linen fibers of the Shroud, which had been cut by the Belgian expert Gilbert Raes in 1973 from the same area of the sample for the 14C analysis, as well as fibers from other areas of the Shroud. In only the Raes' corner, where the 1988 sampling had been carried out, the fibers appear coated and soaked by a yellow-brownish amorphous substance, whose color varies in intensity from one fiber to the other. On the other hand, the fibers coming from other parts of the Shroud do not have such a coating, which is almost certainly a yellow-rubberous vegetable, very likely the gum-arabic once used for textile applications. Moreover, Rogers observed a super-imposition (splice) in the center of a thread of the Raes sample: it is an invisible reweave, widely used in the sixteenth century . . . . This is an impetus for the Holy

See to plan a new 14C test with confidence but in a multidisciplinary context and with particular attention to the representativeness of the sample.

Petrosillo followed up the next day with another article that included some comments by the Turin authorities:

IL MESSAGGERO —Saturday, August 10, 2002, page 10

The removal of the patches has been confirmed.

The Curia: "But the Shroud cloth has not been damaged"

by ORAZIO PETROSILLO

ROME — The Curia of Turin has fully confirmed the controversial operation of removal of the Shroud patches, completed in great secrecy in the Turin Cathedral's new sacristy from June 20 to July 22, and revealed yesterday by our Newspaper. It was announced that in the first half of September a press conference will take place in order to document, including photographically, the results of the operation, consisting of the removal of thirty patches sewn by the Chambery Clare nuns in 1534 on the burns of the Sheet, caused by the December 4, 1532 fire, and of the substitution of the backing cloth, called "Holland cloth . . . . " However amazing it seems, according to someone the "burns move forward as time goes on" (but in five centuries they would have "eaten" a lot of cloth . . .), hence the idea to intervene, eliminating the carbonized parts. If so, last month's operation would have been "invasive". On the contrary, in yesterday's statement of the Turinese Curia spokesman, Marco Bonatti, who confirmed the intervention, there are references to new scientific "non invasive" tests, that is, which have not damaged the cloth. Obviously, this intervention, carried out by the textile expert Flury-Lemberg, was authorized by the Shroud papal Custodian, Cardinal Severino Poletto, after obtaining the consent of the Holy See, who owns othe precious Relic after the last Savoy family King Umberto II's testamentary donation in 1983. The news of this last "operation-Shroud" also surprised many Turinese clergymen themselves, both for the intervention weight—with the removal of the thirty sixteenth-century patches and the substitution of the "Holland cloth" below, completely stitched to the patches and to the Shroud (only the Face area was left out), and for "the furtive attitude, like Carbonari that surrounded the operation. *[Translator's note: the Carbonarist movement was a secret sect of the Italian nineteenth-century Risorgimento.]* In eight International Shroud Conferences, which had taken place in the last four years, no expert suggested such a challenging and risky intervention as necessary. The Curia has specified that the matter had been dealt with in the International Scientific Symposium, which had taken place behind closed doors in Villa Gualino (Turin) from March 2 to 5, 2000. When we asked them, some alleged participants confirmed they did not hear of it at all, nor is there any trace of it in the Proceedings of the March, 2000, conference. Perhaps the three textile experts who were there (Flury-Lemberg, Testore, Vercelli) discussed it in an informal way. More probably, the decision must have been made during the scanning of the Shroud back, carried out in November, 2000. Then, the experts may have realized there were dust and dirt between the Shroud and the Holland cloth, sewn in 1534.

On August 13, I received a personal email from Bill Meacham, who expressed surprise that the shocking news published in *Il Messaggero* had only been picked up by one non-Italian online newspaper. He also wrote,

> There is a growing feeling now that massive public outcry is needed to force [Cardinal] Poletto and/or the Vatican to change the system, and to take the heat off by some masterstroke such as inviting the scientists in to conduct research . . . and C14. I haven't heard back from my contact in the archdiocese of Turin, but he . . . is going to try and speak with Poletto as soon as possible. I have heard from someone who has contacts at the Vatican that international public outcry will send tremors through the Vatican. There is a movement among some in Italy to try to force the Vatican to move the Shroud to Rome . . . .
> *[Excerpt reprinted with permission of William Meacham.]*

Although the public outcry didn't develop at that time, the Vatican was eventually to exert more control over the Shroud, but it would take a few more years before that transpired.

The news about the Shroud restoration was finally picked up by non-Italian sources about a week later. Some of the articles only discussed the restoration and emphasized how Shroud researchers all over the world felt betrayed and were frustrated that none of them had been consulted, whereas other accounts included information about the invisible reweave theory. One example of the latter included a piece in *The Ottawa Citizen*, and contained material about Sue and me that would cause Rogers to label us part of the "lunatic fringe," despite his belief in our theory. The article, titled "A Fresh Attempt to Prove Shroud of Turin is No Fake," read:

> The Ohio woman who appears to have discovered a critical flaw in the 1988 carbon dating of cloth samples from the Shroud of Turin says her insights into the controversial Christian relic were communicated to her by Jesus Christ himself.
>
> Sue Benford, who co-authored a research paper in 2000 with her partner Joseph Marino, a respected shroud scholar, told the Citizen yesterday she's "excited" that their findings could help refute the 1988 tests that have led most experts to conclude the shroud was a medieval forgery and not the burial cloth of Christ.
>
> Roman Catholic officials in Italy have confirmed that new experiments are being performed by a Swiss textile expert, apparently to test the Benford-Marino theory that the cloth sample chosen in 1988—and which yielded a date of origin between 1260 and 1390 A.D—was actually a blend of original material almost 2,000 years old and newer threads woven into the shroud as recently as 400 years ago to repair damaged or pilfered portions of the sacred object.
>
> Ms. Benford, a former nurse who now runs a nonprofit educational organization near Columbus, said it was a "divine revelation" in March 1997—followed by months of arduous research with Mr. Marino—that produced their theory that the 1988 study was fundamentally flawed.
>
> "I was working at my computer when a voice told me to go watch TV," said Ms. Benford, 45, who began flipping channels until she happened upon a show about the Shroud of Turin.
>
> "I was just stunned," she said, because she instantly recognized that the face on the shroud belonged to the same man whose voice had instructed her to watch television, and which later explained to her why scientists had mistakenly concluded the shroud was a fake.
>
> "I don't want to sound like a nut case, but that's what happened," she said. "I was given the answer."
>
> The couple's theory was presented at a conference in Italy in August, 2000, around the same time the Vatican announced there would be no further testing on the age of the shroud in the immediate future.
>
> But members of the official Committee for the Conservation of the Holy Shroud have disclosed to the Italian newspaper *Il*

Messaggero that testing has begun again. *[It is not known what this testing referred to.]*

They said that the cloth's backing and about 30 triangular patches used to mend the shroud in the sixteenth century after it was damaged by fire have been removed in a "secret experiment." They added that the committee as a whole has not been consulted and instead the testing has been authorized by a small number of church "insiders."

Officials in Turin also confirmed that the shroud has been removed from its case and would not be on display while the experiment was in progress. They said the operation is being conducted by Swiss textile expert Mechthild Flury-Lemberg.

As startling as Ms. Benford's story might seem, the central argument she and Mr. Marino have advanced has also been embraced by a prominent U.S. scientist who first studied the shroud in 1978 and still possesses samples of the cloth.

Ray Rogers was part of an international team 20 years ago that performed a chemical analysis of shroud fibres and determined that the image on the cloth was not painted.

That finding ruled out an obvious hoax and left open the possibility that the shroud was authentic. But most of the scientific community—including Mr. Rogers himself—were later convinced by the 1988 carbon dating that the cloth was a fake after all.

Mr. Rogers, a retired chemist living in Los Alamos, New Mexico, told the Citizen yesterday that he dismisses Ms. Benford's story about speaking with Jesus.

But the observation itself—that old and new fibres had been mistakenly mixed in the 1988 experiments—is valid, he says.

"When I first saw Benford and Marino's study, I said they're full of it," recalls Mr. Rogers, who re-analyzed his shroud threads based on the Ohio couple's hypothesis. "But I have to agree with what they're proposing. The 1988 radio-carbon analysis was probably the very best ever done, but it was done on the worst, most stupidly selected sample of cloth."

The 1988 sample, explains Mr. Rogers, comes from the lower left corner of the shroud which, it appears, has been "cleverly rewoven" over the centuries to disguise the fact that cuttings have been taken from the outer edge of the cloth from time to time.

But several threads studied by Mr. Rogers in 1978 came from a section of the shroud slightly closer to the famous image of a crucified man that appears in the middle of the cloth. Some of those threads had been expertly "spliced" to connect older and newer fibres.

In 1982, says Mr. Rogers, one of the threads from his samples was carbon dated —unbeknownst to himself and against the wishes of Roman Catholic officials who had authorized the chemical analysis. Nevertheless, that test showed an age difference of more than 1,000 years between the newer and older fibers—and suggested the original portions of the shroud dated from around the year 200 A.D.

"I have not been able to find any information on the accuracy and precision for the dating method used," says Mr. Rogers. "However, the dates determined are so different that I could believe a real difference between the ends of the threads."

The shroud, preserved in Turin Cathedral, is held by many Christians to be the cloth in which Jesus Christ was wrapped after the Crucifixion. Venerated for centuries as the Holy Shroud, it preserves the image of a tall man with crucifixion marks which only came to light when the 4.37-metre-by-1.11-metre cloth was first photographed at the end of the nineteenth century (Boswell 2002).

[Excerpt reprinted with permission of Postmedia Network.]

Evidently Sue was correct in saying that when she claimed that she was given the answer by Jesus, she sounded like a nut case. Obviously, Sue's claims were impossible to prove scientifically. But it is what it is. Sue felt that she had to be honest on how she obtained the information, even if it did sound crazy. If she were a nut, I think I would have noticed in the decade plus that we were together! To this day, no one, friend or otherwise, has offered me a plausible alternative to Sue's assertion that she was actually receiving these revelations.

Stories about the restoration continued into the autumn. On September 21, a press conference was held in Turin regarding the restoration. Three documents were given out to those in attendance. (The text of those documents can be found in Appendix L.) Sue and I contacted a journalist from England who had been at the press conference and asked him for his impressions. He emailed:

The coverage was rather muted: basically all the Vatican correspondents (Italian) have accepted Cardinal Poletto's explanation (plus [Monsignor] Ghiberti et al) that the operation had the approval not only of the Pope but also of all Shroud scholars; that it was a necessary intervention to remove the patches carried out with the greatest delicacy; that no carbon dating tests are envisaged;

and that the secrecy was necessary because the Shroud was among post 9/11 potential targets for Muslim terrorists. Petrosillo in *Il Messaggero*—who of course made the story public in August—noted in his piece that most scholars have ceased to be alarmed, "although not all accept the need for urgency or the lack of consultation". . . .

The Turin authorities would continue to hear the criticism of sindonologists because of the restoration—and would also continue to hear more news about Rogers' findings.

CHAPTER ELEVEN

THE INVISIBLE REWEAVING HYPOTHESIS GATHERS STEAM

Several events occurred in 2002 that helped to spread the news about the growing evidence that the samples used for the C-14 dating of the Shroud were from an invisibly rewoven area. Sue's autobiography, <u>Strong Woman</u>, published that summer, contained some material about the hypothesis. In early September, Sue and I also appeared on one of the major Internet radio programs, The *Art Bell Show* (also known as *Coast to Coast AM*). Barbara Simpson, a substitute host, conducted the interview, in which we discussed the hypothesis as well as some of our beliefs regarding spirituality. Afterwards, we were sent some interesting emails. One person, clearly not pleased with my career change, put in the subject line "pope Joe" (he didn't even give me the courtesy of capitalizing "pope"!) and in his message he simply said, "BUNK BUNK BUNK." Another individual, for whom the Shroud and the divinity of Jesus are obviously worrisome, wrote:

> If you could prove the shroud came from the first century and it was in fact blood from a face, how does that link it to Jesus any more than to Santa Claus? I mean, I couldn't count all the people the Romans crucified on crosses. Also, lets [sic] pretend it was the shroud of the guy in the Bible. How does that prove that Jesus was divine and the Bible isn't a flat out collection of fairy tales with little truth and lots of stretching?

I can't remember if I responded to him, but I think I probably didn't, since he didn't seem too open to an honest intellectual exchange. Besides, we weren't trying to convince anyone of anything—we just presented the evidence to which listeners or readers could evaluate and make up their own minds.

We also received some emails that were not antagonistic, and were, in fact, supportive. One gentleman said:

> ...I am also a child of God. I listen to *Coast to Coast* almost nightly here in Lowell, Massachusetts. Unfortunately it is on from 1 to 5 am, but last night it didn't come on until 3:30 a.m. As I lay there turning off and on the ads from some other show, I started wondering why I just didn't turn it off and go to sleep. As I turned it on for one last time. Suddenly, Praise the Lord, you were there.
>
> The message you were giving is dead on with my beliefs and that is so rare I just had to listen. I am planning on writing you again, but I just had to get up to tell you now, that you are doing the Lord's work in these final Days. The only real spirituality is a personal relationship with God and the spiritual power of the Son and Spirit which is given by the grace by which we have been saved. As the Darkness approaches I have been feeling my spiritual powers increasing.
>
> I will leave off now, but there is so much more I want to talk to you about. I never gave the shroud much thought as I don't believe in idols and such. BUT, the fact that you say it is a holographic representation of the glorified Christ and therefore our own Spirits as well BLEW me away, simply brilliant. I will research your site and write again if you don't mind.

A policeman wrote this heartfelt email, with the subject line "Thank you":

> I am sure that you have been besieged by email since your appearance in *Coast to Coast* Live last evening. So I just hope that you have the chance to read this!!
>
> I am police officer in Indianapolis, IN. I listen to the show on patrol just to stay awake a lot of nights. But the Shroud has always been a subject of interest to me,
>
> So I was glad to hear a show topic that would keep my attention. But that is not what I am writing about today.
>
> For years now I have called myself an agnostic because since I was a child I felt that there was more to God than was being taught in church. I also saw the church itself as a business. Selling something that is already inside each and every one of us. As soon as I was old enough to say that I didn't want to go anymore, I stopped attending.
>
> Unfortunately, since that decision I have had pangs of guilt and trepidation that I might have made the wrong decision, that the "bible thumpers" may be right and that if I don't go to church, I am

away from God. Listening to you and Joseph last night helped open my eyes to the fact that I don't have to feel guilty about opting out of mainstream organized religion. As in many other things in life I have simply chosen my own path.

Sometimes I have caught myself feeling sad for or even, at times, disdainful of people who seem to need the guidance of a structured religious life in a formal church institution. You helped me realize that they are simply on their own spiritual journey. As in all things in life, we all do things at our own pace.

My question for you and Joseph is . . . Is it possible that even as a child I had a deeper knowledge of the nature of God? That assertion, to my own ears, sounds a little arrogant. Who am I to think that I know more than anyone else about God? But you are right about the fact that we are all at different levels of understanding.

The analogy of the bucket of ocean water was beautiful. It summed up everything I have not even been able to put into words myself about how I feel and think about the nature of God. I hope you won't mind me using your analogy to help explain my choice to my children, family and friends. ☺

Thank you both so much.

It was nice to know we received some positive responses. Up to that point, I spent a fair amount of time and effort electronically sending out various news and articles on the Shroud. I felt that the work Sue and I were doing, both on the Shroud and on matters of spirituality, was important, so in order to have more time to devote to it, I informed the 200-plus people on my email list that I would no longer be sending out the information bulletins. I received back various responses that all showed support for my decision, as well as their own deep passion for the Shroud. A retired newsman on the list wrote, "Although I may never write another piece on the Shroud, it has had a profound effect on my life. More correctly, Jesus produced the effect. Profound thanks for keeping this layman in touch with Shroud research." Reverend Albert "Kim" Dreisbach, emailed me: "A 'call' is a special phenomenon and only he or she who is its recipient can full understand same. I wish you well in yours and am thankful for the many years that yours served mine and those of many others in the field of sindonology. May God continue to watch over and bless you and Sue in the future."

I received several other supportive emails. One came from a STURP member:

> I do not think you do justice to what you have put out on e-mail. While I do not agree with everything you say, they are not—on the average—significantly WORSE than other supposedly "SCIENTIFIC" ruminations I receive!!! Your news bulletins are especially interesting. I hope you will reconsider, continue to do what you have been doing...

One of the members of the Turin "Centro" wrote:

> Many thanks to you and to Sue Benford for your work and for your news-letters. Unfortunately, I was not able to read them all but I am deeply convinced that you worked 'bona fide.' As everybody else I have had my own way to the Shroud and passing this way I learned to understand very well your somewhat resignative statement: "I have come to realize more and more that most people are not willing to look at data that conflict with their world-views." I hope that you will have the faith and the health to continue your work. Thank you again!

The following came from a Shroud author:

> Thank you. You have performed an excellent service and I want to commend you for it. I have picked up a great deal of information that I would have missed. I also think that the work you and Sue Benford are doing regarding the carbon dating and Raes area with invisible threads may provide the answer that could account for errors in the carbon date and concomitantly see how the dating labs could still save face. Good luck to you and Sue Benford in your endeavors and may the good Lord guide your endeavors. Please keep me informed of your work. I am doing a complete revision of my book and plan to include your work in it.

Sue and I felt the time was right to write to the Cardinal of Turin to update him about the progress on the work related to the invisible reweave hypotheses. On July 20, 2003, I sent the following long, detailed letter by "snail mail":

Chapter Eleven: The Invisible Reweaving Hypothesis Gathers Strength 135

Sua Eminenza Card. Severino Poletto
Via Dell'Archhivescovado 12
10121 Torino
Italy

Emanuela Marinelli, organizer of the Sindone 2000 Worldwide Congress held in Orvieto, Italy, on 27-29 August, 2000, had suggested that we should send you proposals regarding testing of the Shroud of Turin, which we had done in October 2000.

Along with my co-author, M. Sue Benford, I presented a paper at Orvieto titled "Evidence for the Skewing of the C-14 Dating of the Shroud of Turin Due to Repairs," which was very well received by sindonologists and media at the Congress.

You can find that paper at:
  http://www.shroud.com/pdfs/marben.pdf. Two follow-up papers were also published. You can find those at:
  http://www.shroud.com/pdfs/textevid.pdf and
  http://www.shroud.com/pdfs/histsupt.pdf.

I wanted to update you on significant events related to this hypothesis.

Our hypothesis was tested by former Shroud of Turin Research Project (STURP) chemist Ray Rogers, who has had access to Shroud samples/fibers. His extensive comparative testing led him to conclude that our hypothesis of a sixteenth-century patch skewing the C-14 dating was, in fact, correct. His findings were published at http://www.shroud.com.pdfs/rogers2.pdf. Also in 2002, a paper by another STURP team member, the late Dr. Alan Adler (who, as you know, was on the official Conservation Committee), was published. His findings also strongly support our theory.

I have taken the liberty of citing the key passages from both Drs. Adler and Rogers.

From "Further Spectroscopic Investigations of Samples of the Shroud of Turin," by Alan D. Adler, Russell Selzer and Frank DeBlase. Presented at 1998 Dallas Symposium.

A radiocarbon dating of samples taken from the Shroud reported a mid-fourteenth century date, seemingly settling the authenticity issue. However, it is now argued that since it was not old enough to be authentic, it must be a painting. Unfortunately, a detailed protocol for sampling the cloth to assure both precision and accuracy recommended by a convened meeting of consultants was not followed. Only a single sample was taken from a rewoven edge in a waterstained area a few inches from one of the burn marks incurred in the historically recorded 1532 fire. This location was near the bottom of the frontal body image on the edge where a large section of cloth is missing below the seamed so-called side strip. No historic record exists accounting for this missing material and how or when this damage occurred. The nature and/or extent of the repairs undertaken here are also unknown. Therefore, the possibility exists that this selvage edge might be linen not original to the Shroud.

The selection of this single suspicious sample site is a sufficient reason to doubt the accuracy of the radiodate. This spectroscopic investigation was therefore undertaken to determine whether any evidence can be obtained to support such doubts.

FTIR *[Fourier Transform Infrared Spectroscopy]*: Typical spectral absorption patterns for each fiber type and the blood samples are displayed in Figures 1 through 11 and clearly show distinctive differences indicating differences in their chemical makeup. It should be noted that there is more variation in the patterns of the radiocarbon samples representing an area of a few square centimeters than in those of the non-image samples taken from areas a whole body-image length apart.

Note this is specifically true for the radiocarbon fibers and the non-image fibers from the bulk of the cloth, thereby demonstrating that the area selected for the radiocarbon sampling is atypical and is not clearly representative of the rest of the Shroud.

Again, it should be noted that a great deal of variability was evidenced in the radiocarbon samples. Some of the patchy encrustations were so thick as to mask the underlying carbon of fibers whose continuity were clearly obvious in the microscope images.

There is clearly evident chemical compositional difference between this sample area and the non-image areas of the cloth. In fact, the FTIR data for the radiocarbon sample, in a sense confirming its inappropriate physical location, shows physical characteristics of both the waterstain and scorch regions of the cloth. To what extent this affects the observed date is not at all obvious. Nevertheless, the accuracy of the reported date is justifiably suspect. Further, comparison of the dorsal head wounds on the Shroud with a similar pattern of wounds on the seventh century Cloth of Oviedo confirms the inaccuracy of the reported radiocarbon date.

[Excerpt reprinted with permission of Dr. Russell Selzer and Dr. Frank DeBlase.]

Chapter Eleven: The Invisible Reweaving Hypothesis Gathers Strength

From "Scientific Method Applied to the Shroud of Turin: A Review" by Dr. Ray Rogers:
http://www.shroud.com/pdfs/rogers.pdf.

We have recently found that some plant gum, mordants, and dye(s) coat the yarn of the sample which was taken by Gilbert Raes in 1973 for textile analysis. These deposits are unique to the Raes sample; however, that area was in immediate contact with the radiocarbon sample that was removed for dating in 1988. This fact makes the validity of the radiocarbon sample questionable.

The 1988 radiocarbon age determinations were the best that could have been obtained anywhere in the world. Effects of sample-preparation methods were studied and careful statistical analyses were made. Damon, et al., reported that "The age of the shroud is obtained as AD 1260-1390, with at least 95 per cent confidence." Unfortunately, that date does not reflect the STURP observations on the linen-production technology and the chemistry of the fibers from the tape samples . . . .

Unfortunately, the sample was approved at the time of sampling by two textile experts, Franco Testore, professor of Textile Technology at the Turin Polytechnic, and Gabriel Vial, curator of the Ancient Textile Museum, Lyon, France. No chemical or microscopic investigations were made to characterize the sample. I believe that was a major disaster in the history of Shroud studies.

Samples from the main part of the cloth are significantly different from the Raes sample with regard to cotton content.

Differences between amounts of lignin on linen fibers in the Raes samples and on Shroud fibers are significant. There is probably a similar difference between the radiocarbon samples and the main part of the Shroud.

The outside of Raes thread #14 showed the heaviest encrustation and deepest color of any of the samples. The encrustation is heaviest on cotton fibers, it is the vehicle for the yellow-brown color, and it suggests that the cotton was added by wiping a viscous liquid on the outside of the yarn in order to match the color of new material to the old, sepia color of the Shroud . . . .

(T)he presence of a gum coating on retained 1988 radiocarbon-dating samples would prove that the samples were not representative of the main part of the relic's cloth. Such a lack of association would prove that the radiocarbon date is invalid.

Raes thread #1 shows distinct encrustation and color on one end, but the other end is nearly white . . . . [T]his section of yarn is obviously an end-to-end splice of two different batches of yarn. No splices of this type were observed in the main part of the Shroud.

The radiocarbon sample area is darker than normal, a fact that is not the result of image color or scorching. The cloth is much less fluorescent in that area, brightening into more normal fluorescence to the right. The photograph proves that the radiocarbon area has a different chemical composition than the main part of the cloth, and it is truly anomalous.

The combined evidence from chemistry, cotton content, technology, photography, and residual lignin proves that the material of the main part of the Shroud is significantly different from the radiocarbon sampling area. The validity of the radiocarbon sample must be questioned with regard to dating the production of the main part of the cloth. A rigorous application of the Scientific Method would demand a confirmation of the date with a better selection of samples.

Linen-production technology indicates that the Shroud of Turin is probably older than indicated by the dates obtained in 1988. There seems to be ample evidence that an anomalous area was sampled for the radiocarbon analysis; therefore, the reported age is almost certainly invalid for the date the cloth was produced.

[Excerpt reprinted with permission of STERA, Inc.]

I am also sending a copy of this letter to your advisor and to the Pope. I hope you will find the evidence compelling enough to allow the appropriate testing to further confirm these findings so that the real truth of this cloth can be made known to the world.

Sincerely,
Joseph Marino

I received back from Cardinal Poletto a letter on September 2. I reproduced the text in an email to Bill Meacham, who is fluent in Italian. Meacham's translation informed me that Cardinal Poletto acknowledged receiving my letter of July 20, 2003, in which I cited the Orvieto paper that Sue and I had published and had also mentioned pleas from Adler and Rogers for new testing. The Cardinal stated he was not in a position to make judgments on the scientific matters raised in my letter. He did say that proposals for new testing were being evaluated by a group of scientists chosen by the Turin Centro. When they had made a judgment, he would then refer it to Pope John Paul II.

Chapter Eleven: The Invisible Reweaving Hypothesis Gathers Strength

Meacham took the opportunity to comment to me regarding Cardinal Poletto's letter:

> He mentions the jury of scientists. [Monsignor] Ghiberti wrote me a few days ago saying that the proposals have *already* been sent to the jury for review. I am very suspicious of this, since I heard just a few weeks ago that none of the suggested international peer reviewers had been contacted yet. They could of course have gathered a bunch of local cronies, plus one or two non-Italian scientists who know little or nothing about the Shroud. This would be wide open to manipulation and facade, which I suspect is what this exercise is all about.
> My reply to Ghiberti is going to focus on remarks Poletto made at the press conference last September, as recalled by Anna Arnoldi, in which he made it clear that the dust and other bits removed from the Shroud were no longer considered as part of the relic and hence did not need to be treated like the relic itself.
> *[Excerpt reprinted with permission of William Meacham.]*

Ironically, around the time I received the reply from Cardinal Poletto, I was sent an official letter from the Benedictine order that I had been officially dismissed. Frankly, I was not upset by it at all. They had given me several years to reconsider, but that was never an option for me. After all the incredible experiences I had, there simply was no going back. I only saw the pronouncement in the letter as a natural progression of the events of the previous years.

It was clear that politics would continue to play a huge role in whether or not the Shroud would be tested again. I wrote an email to Ray Rogers, encouraging him to write a letter to Cardinal Poletto's scientific advisor, Piero Savarino, to emphasize the strength of the evidence that had been found regarding the invisible reweave. Hopefully, this in turn would help convince Turin and the Vatican to authorize new tests. Rogers emailed me on August 5:

> I have sent many, many messages and letters to Savarino. I sent him a copy of a report (about two years ago) I had bound that compiled much of the information on chemical analyses of the different samples, including the Raes sample. He teaches organic

chemistry, and I had assumed he would be interested enough to discuss the science . . . .

He stated that he did not have access to the STURP tape samples, and he did not even know where they are. He stated that he had trouble with English (I believe that) . . . .

What would you suggest?

I could write something that would approximate a technical paper on the radiocarbon sample. Do you think that would be enough?

Unfortunately, Shroud chemistry all fits together, and it is impossible to separate radiocarbon facts from a complete understanding of the main part of the cloth . . . .

I really do not know what would be the best approach toward clearing up the misunderstandings and negative reactions that separate us from Turin. They carefully avoided any communications with US researchers before the 1988 dating fiasco. It would have been so easy to avoid the problem, but they completely ignored all of the information we sent before the test.

I will do whatever you think would have a positive effect. Let me know.

[Personal communication, reprinted with permission of Joan Rogers.]

Armed with an "if-at-first-you-don't-succeed-try-try-again" attitude, I emailed Rogers that he should attempt once again to write to Savarino. Rogers agreed to do so. (For other personal correspondence between Rogers and Sue and me, see Appendix M.) Unbeknownst to me, Rogers had recently collaborated with Bill Meacham on a letter to Cardinal Poletto. I discovered this about three weeks later when Meacham emailed me a copy of the letter and asked if I would be willing to organize signatories from the recently-formed Internet "Shroud Science Group," composed of numerous scientists and researchers from around the world, who discussed various matters related to the cloth. Here is the text of the letter from Meacham and Rogers:

Chapter Eleven: The Invisible Reweaving Hypothesis Gathers Strength

August 5, 2003

His Eminence Severino Cardinal Poletto
Archbishop of Turin

Dear Cardinal Poletto,

In the light of the removal last summer of material from the Shroud, we are writing to you to request that a small portion of that material be released to us for C14 measurement. This is intended only as a data measurement to confirm, or otherwise, the previous C14 dating of the Shroud conducted in 1988.

From the reports that have been published about the intervention last summer, we learned that data and measurements of various kinds were obtained at that time. The material that was removed can serve the very basic yet highly important purpose of corroborating or contradicting the 1988 C14 result.

Re-testing and replicating results is an important part of science. It is not necessary to have a full understanding of all factors that could be involved or that could conceivably have had an influence on the previous C 14 result. The evidence does very strongly indicate, however, that the sample taken in 1988 was NOT representative of the cloth as a whole.

We believe that it is extremely important to move forward with this very simple and basic measurement, as the previous C 14 dating of the Shroud has generated much debate, dispute and consternation over the last 15 years. It led to the Shroud being universally considered a medieval fake. However, there are very good reasons (please see Appendix II) to believe that the result of 1988 does NOT indicate the true radiocarbon age of the cloth. Continued discussion of this issue on any level, popular or scientific, is useless, whereas testing of a very small amount of material will settle the basic question—was the sample taken in 1988 representative of the cloth as a whole? It will put an end to the debate that has raged in Shroud circles for years over the reliability of the 1988 sample.

We note that Mons. Ghiberti in the publication <u>Sindone le imagine 2002 Shroud images</u> stated the following:

"an unexpected amount of material for future examination was collected when the patches were removed and the burnholes cleaned."

A very small portion of this material, chiefly consisting of carbon dust and tiny fragments of burnt fiber, will be sufficient for this very important measurement. As no new access to the Shroud itself is required, and the proposed C14 measurement is quite straight-forward, we do not see any need for peer review of this proposal. The measurement we are proposing is similar to other measurements that were made without peer review during the intervention last summer.

The following assumptions are made:
1. that the requested material has been kept under tight security and that its provenance from the Shroud can be assured;
2. that it was collected with due diligence to avoid mixing with any fragments of stitches from the 1534 repairs.

The Shroud has languished under an almost universal cloud of dismissal ever since the C 14 results were announced in 1988. Most people wrongly believe that science has now proven the precious relic to be a medieval forgery. The measurement that we are proposing COULD have an enormous and positive impact on the public perception of the Turin Shroud around the world, if it contradicts the earlier date. In that case, a more thorough and comprehensive program of study and testing of fresh samples, as proposed already in the paper submitted by Meacham, Cardamone, Raes, Rogers and Schwalbe, will be required before any firm conclusion can be drawn about the radiocarbon age of the cloth.

Alternatively, if the result is the same as that of 1988, it will have virtually no impact in the public arena; for scientists and Shroud researchers it would eliminate the possibility of an anomaly or aberration in the original C 14 sample, and focus attention instead on theoretical issues.

Cardinal Poletto, we trust that this proposal will gain your support, and that we may soon take a very important step in discovering the truth about the age of the Shroud.

Sincerely,

William Meacham
Hon. Research Fellow
Centre of Asian Studies
University of Hong Kong

Raymond N. Rogers, Fellow
University of California,
Los Alamos National Laboratory, USA

cc: Prof Savarino, Scientific Advisor to the Archbishop

Chapter Eleven: The Invisible Reweaving Hypothesis Gathers Strength

(For Appendix II referred to in the letter, as well as another appendix they sent, see Appendix N.)
[Reproduced with Meacham's permission.]

On August 10, I emailed Rogers, curious to know about any progress in his letter to the Cardinal's scientific advisor. He wrote back:

> You asked how I was doing in preparing a letter to Savarino. The following is the current version, composed of a few disjointed thoughts that might be used. All this represents is my judgment on what is important. One thing I learned from the military establishments of the world is that the biggest gun won't fire a shell of the wrong size or shape. If our letter doesn't "fire," it won't hit the target. I have no idea what "ammunition" can reach Savarino. I have been notably unsuccessful in the past, and I really can not decide what the most productive approach would be. I would, however, be extremely careful that "far-out" "theories" not be included.
>
> My first approach to Savarino was as a scientist. That got nowhere at all, not even a response. My next approach was to a person I assumed cared about the Shroud. That got nowhere at all. My most recent approach has included statements on how most of the world (certainly main-stream scientists) put the Shroud in the same category as UFOs, ghosts, and cold fusion. That got nowhere. I can't even make him mad.
>
> If I write a technical paper, it will get nowhere with the Cardinal (or Savarino.) What do you think I can do to be helpful? I'm stuck.

Ray also reproduced in his email to me the text of the letter he sent to Professor Savarino:

Dear Professor Savarino:
    Communications among the Shroud Science e-mail-list participants have brought a few serious problems into sharp focus. The group can not help correct them without cooperation with the officials in Turin. Can you help us establish communications with the proper persons?
    The foremost problem is the world's perception that the Shroud of Turin was proved to have been produced during medieval times. The radiocarbon age is not the only piece of evidence for the age of the Shroud; however, it is the only evidence that has appeared in the popular literature.

All of the other scientific analyses conflict with the conclusions of the published radiocarbon age. This is a common occurrence in archaeology, where other evidence often results in a repeated radiocarbon analysis with a different sample. The most common reason for disagreement between a radiocarbon date and other observations is a lack of association between the radiocarbon sample and the event being dated. Many independent scientific observations suggest that this is the case with the Shroud.

It is impossible to present all of the contrary evidence in a single letter, and this fact makes it difficult to argue against the single, authoritative, 1989 statement about the radiocarbon age. Another problem is the prevalence of "theories" about the "error" in the date that absolutely defy scientific principles. Many of these have helped destroy the credibility of the science that has been applied to studies on the Shroud. We believe that it is imperative to open discussions in an honest attempt to find the truth.

In support of our statements, we offer you a few confirmed observations that do not fit the medieval age claim.

1) Ultraviolet-fluorescence photography shows that the area cut for the radiocarbon sample was anomalous: it exhibited a very different fluorescence than the main part of the cloth. Since fluorescence is a result of chemical structures, the chemical composition of the radiocarbon sample was not representative of the Shroud.

2) Chemical analyses of retained samples of both the Raes sample and the radiocarbon sample show outstanding anomalies. Both areas are observed to be coated with a significant layer of gum. The gum is easily soluble in water. The gum is so thick that it obscured both visible-light-microscopy and scanning-electron-microscopy (SEM) views of the cloth's surface. The composition of the gum proved that it was not a "bioplastic polymer." The gum contains Madder root dye (alizarin and purpurin) and a mixture of hydrous-metal-oxide mordants to adjust the color presented. The SEM analyses of the radiocarbon area showed extremely high concentrations of aluminum, a fact that agrees with the observation of mordants on Raes fibers.

3) The main part of the linen shows significant deposits of lignin at its growth nodes; however, the lignin does not give the sensitive, characteristic vanillin test for lignin. Both the Holland cloth and Raes sample give the test: linen from the Dead Sea scrolls does not.

The vanillin content of lignin decreases slowly with time, and we have made measurements of the chemical kinetics constants for the

Chapter Eleven: The Invisible Reweaving Hypothesis Gathers Strength 145

rate of vanillin loss. The observations and measurements prove that the Shroud's linen is much older than the Medieval Holland cloth.

4) Absolutely no thick gum coating can be observed on any part of the Shroud outside the Raes and radiocarbon sampling areas.

5) Elemental analyses of the Shroud are much different from those of the Raes and radiocarbon sampling areas. There is much more iron than aluminum in the Shroud: there is very much more aluminum in the radiocarbon sample than in the Shroud.

6) The gum does not give any of the sensitive tests for protein: it can not contain bacterial or fungal cells.

We realize that textile experts have declared the radiocarbon sample to be valid; however, we have not seen any chemical analyses or photomicrographs that support their claims. We believe that there should be sufficient evidence to support doubts about the experts' opinions.

We strongly urge you to propose a new radiocarbon analysis of the Shroud. The carbonized material removed from the burns can be cleaned much more thoroughly than can cellulose. It could even be heated in nitric acid. Heating does not cause a significant amount of isotope fractionation; therefore, the samples should be valid. Careful heating in nitric acid should remove any adsorbed or reacted thymol, and it would nitrate and decompose all residual polysaccharides, including "bioplastic polymers."

We are anxious to discuss the scientific aspects of ethical studies on the Shroud. We have no desire whatever to attack any person's religious beliefs, indeed we may be able to support some. At the very least, we can reject the unfortunate radiocarbon age determination.

Sincerely,
Raymond N. Rogers, Fellow
University of California,
Los Alamos National Laboratory-Los Alamos, NM, USA
And as many credible Shroud researchers as will join us
   [Personal communication, reprinted with permission of Joan Rogers.]

Rogers' humor shines through brightly in his last line.

On September 5, Meacham sent an email to the Shroud Science Group mentioning the letter of August 3 that he and Rogers had sent to Cardinal Poletto. Meacham was trying to garner support for his and Rogers' proposal; he had also written to various Shroud organizations from around the world.

He asked those on the Shroud Science Group who supported the proposal to send me their names. I would then send on a letter with those names to Cardinal Poletto. Meacham ended his email to the group by saying, "Virtually everyone who cares about the Shroud wants to see the C14 test redone, and there is absolutely nothing controversial about it. Either it will not change anything, or it will change EVERYTHING!"

[Excerpt reprinted with permission of William Meacham]

On September 29, hoping to have a positive effect, I sent the following letter to Cardinal Poletto:

Sua Eminenza Cardinal Severino Poletto
Via Arcivescovado 12
10121 Torino
Italy

Your Eminence,

First of all, I want to thank you for taking the time to send me your gracious letter of 2 September in response to my letter of 20 July regarding findings pertaining to research presented at a Shroud conference in Orvieto, Italy, in 2000 regarding a patch in the C-14 sample area and scientific support for this theory provided by researches of Drs. Alan Adler and Ray Rogers.

Dr. Rogers and I are part of an Internet Shroud Science discussion group that includes scientists and researchers from all over the world. Dr. Rogers and William Meacham, who is also part of the group, submitted to you last month a proposal for new carbon dating on the Shroud based on various findings, including the aforementioned theory and other compelling evidence that indicate that the Raes/C-14 area is clearly anomalous when compared to the main part of the Shroud.

This letter is to inform you of those on this Shroud Science group that want to express their support for the Meacham/Rogers proposal. I have printed copies of their expression of support but only include their names here.

Please note that the authors of the proposal and some of the signatories, many of whom hold a Ph.D., have had key positions in Shroud research. Dr. Rogers is from the 1978 Shroud of Turin Research Project (STURP) team. He is co-author of one of the main summary papers by STURP, "Physics and Chemistry of the Shroud of Turin," published in *Analytical Chimica Acta* 135, 1982, pp. 3-49. Bill Meacham was involved in the 1986 planning meeting in Turin

Chapter Eleven: The Invisible Reweaving Hypothesis Gathers Strength

held in preparation for the 1988 C-14 testing. Dr. Robert Dinegar was a member of the STURP team and was the author of the C-14 proposal that STURP had submitted to the authorities. Barrie Schwortz was the documenting photographer for STURP and is the publisher of the renowned website www.shroud.com. Dr. Kenneth Stevenson was spokesman for STURP. Dr. Frederick Zugibe is a physician and Professor at Columbia University who has studied crucifixion for over 50 years and has written books and articles about the Shroud. Giulio Fanti is Associate Professor of Mechanical and Thermic Measurements at Padua University and since 1997 has authored or co-authored two books, one journal article and 17 conference presentations on the Shroud.

We hope that this proposal will be the first step to allow further investigations and a rigorous C-14 dating that takes into account data that has been discovered since 1988. As stated in the proposal: "The measurement that we are proposing COULD have an enormous and positive impact on the public perception of the Turin Shroud around the world, if it contradicts the earlier date . . . . Alternatively, if the result is the same as that of 1988, it will have virtually no impact in the public arena . . . . "

[Note: the proposal referred to in this letter refers to Meacham's letter of August 5, 2003, to Cardinal Poletto, reproduced earlier in the chapter.]

Sincerely,
Joseph Marino

Listing of Shroud Science discussion group members who support this proposal:
[Nineteen researchers' names from original letter were listed.]

When 2003 ended, I had not yet received a reply from Cardinal Poletto to my letter. However, during the spring of 2004, I learned that something momentous did occur at the end of the 2003.

CHAPTER TWELVE

RETESTING THE 1988 C-14 SAMPLE

As Easter, 2004, approached, there was only silence from Turin regarding my letter. A posting on the Shroud Science Group alerted Sue and me to an article on the National Geographic Channel website (Trivedi 2004). The article revealed that in December, 2003, Rogers had been given a leftover portion of the sample that had been used in the 1988 dating. He had done all of his previous work on the "Raes sample," (named after the Belgian textile expert Gilbert Raes, who had been given a sample in 1973 to study). This Raes sample had been right next to the actual sample cut for the 1988 C-14 dating. He had been reluctant to say that what he had found on the former would definitely be found on the latter. But now that he had an actual C-14 sample, he could compare the two. To no one's surprise, everything that he found on the Raes sample was present on the C-14 sample. This was HUGE news—it greatly solidified his theory that the C-14 sample was anomalous. The article also stated that his findings were being submitted to a peer-reviewed scientific journal, which meant that other scientists would be reviewing his research, and if it was accepted, there would be a solid scientific basis for the theory.

An article on the history of radiocarbon dating by a member of the prestigious National Institute of Standards and Technology in Maryland was published in spring, 2004. The author had a section on the Shroud and noted regarding the controversy surrounding the sample-taking that the samples were taken from a corner that had undergone a fire and repairs and undoubtedly had extra carbon due to contamination (Currie 2004:202, fn 10). On December 18, I sent Rogers an email and said, "Thanks for all your great work on this article and your other Shroud work. It is having and will continue to have much influence and significance." He replied the same day, "Thanks for the message. I was feeling very discouraged about work on the Shroud."

[Personal communication, reprinted with permission of Joan Rogers.]

Sindonologists eagerly awaited the publication of Rogers' paper. It was finally published on January 20 of the next year (Rogers 2005), but it was sandwiched between significant personal events in my life, the gravity of which would change me forever.

In January, Sue was diagnosed with breast cancer. It seemed so cruel. She had already been a childhood cancer survivor. She had beaten the first one, but she was now as an adult diagnosed with a second kind. Because she had been over-radiated with her childhood cancer, she didn't want to go the traditional path with treatment. She was an extremely knowledgeable researcher about alternative methods and decided to take that route. I supported her 100 per cent in her decision—how could I not? I felt confident that she could again overcome cancer as she had when she was a child. In retrospect, I wasn't as worried as I should have been.

In late February, my mother died of natural causes. No matter how old one is, it's never easy to lose one's mother. What made that event even more painful was the fact that on the day of burial, I decided to be with Sue as she underwent a cancer treatment in the Northeast. Although I was present for my mother's wake, not being present for the burial made a difficult situation even worse. Events like cancer and deaths of loved ones are part of life, and I tried to deal with them as best as I could, although it was hard not to be deeply distracted and greatly affected by both Sue's cancer diagnosis and my mother's death, especially since I was not there for the latter's burial. However, life doesn't stop just because one is having personal problems. But cancer and death are reminders of our mortality, something none of us want to dwell on.

Chapter Twelve: Retesting the 1988 C-14 Sample

One day before the publication of Rogers' paper, AMSTAR put out the following release:

Wednesday January 19, 2005, 8:32 am ET

DALLAS, Jan. 19 /PRNewswire/ — The American Shroud of Turin Association for Research (AMSTAR), a scientific organization dedicated to research on the enigmatic Shroud of Turin, thought by many to be the burial cloth of the crucified Jesus of Nazareth, announced today that the 1988 Carbon-14 test was not done on the original burial cloth, but rather on a rewoven shroud patch creating an erroneous date for the actual age of the Shroud.

The Shroud of Turin is a large piece of linen cloth that shows the faint full-body image of a blood-covered man on its surface. Because many believe it to be the burial cloth of Jesus, researchers have tried to determine its origin though numerous modern scientific methods, including Carbon-14 tests done at three radiocarbon labs which set the age of the artifact at between AD 1260 and 1390.

"Now conclusive evidence, gathered over the past two years, proves that the sample used to date the Shroud was actually taken from an expertly done rewoven patch," says AMSTAR President, Tom D'Muhala. "Chemical testing indicates that the linen Shroud is actually very old — much older than the published 1988 radiocarbon date."

"As unlikely as it seems, the sample used to test the age of the Shroud of Turin in 1988 was taken from a rewoven area of the Shroud," reports chemist Raymond Rogers, a fellow of the Los Alamos National Laboratory in New Mexico. Rogers' new findings are published in the current issue of *Thermochimica Acta*, a chemistry peer-reviewed scientific journal.

"Pyrolysis-mass-spectrometry results from the sample area coupled with microscopic and microchemical observations prove that the radiocarbon sample was not part of the original cloth of the Shroud of Turin which is currently housed at The Turin Cathedral in Italy," says Rogers.

"The radiocarbon sample has completely different chemical properties than the main part of the shroud relic," explains Rogers. "The sample tested was dyed using technology that began to appear in Italy about the time the Crusaders' last bastion fell to the Mamluk Turks in AD 1291. The radiocarbon sample cannot be older than about AD 1290, agreeing with the age determined in 1988. However, the Shroud itself is actually much older."

Rogers' new research clearly disproves the 1988 findings announced by British Museum spokesperson, Mike Tite, when he declared that the Shroud was of medieval origin and probably "a hoax." The British Museum coordinated the 1988 radiocarbon tests and acted as the official clearing house for all findings.

Almost immediately, Shroud analysts questioned the validity of the sample used for radiocarbon dating. Researchers using high-resolution photographs of the Shroud found indications of an "invisible" reweave in the area used for testing. However, belief tilted strongly toward the more "scientific" method of radiocarbon dating. Rogers' recent analysis of an authentic sample taken from the radiocarbon sample proves that the researchers were right to question the 1988 results.

As a result of his own research and chemical tests, Rogers concluded that the radiocarbon sample was cut from a medieval patch, and is totally different in composition from the main part of the Shroud of Turin.

[Reprinted with permission of AMSTAR.]

Amazingly, AMSTAR was giving the impression that they were somehow involved in the data that would be released. In fact, there was *no* connection between AMSTAR and Rogers, whose name is not even mentioned until the fourth paragraph!

Rogers wrote in his published paper that the chemical analysis of the C-14 sample strongly suggested a manipulation of the area:

> Specifically, the color and distribution of the coating implies that repairs were made at an unknown time with foreign linen dyed to match the older original material. Such repairs were suggested by Benford and Marino. The consequence of this conclusion is that the radiocarbon sample was not representative of the original cloth (Rogers 2005:192).
> *[Excerpt reprinted per Elsevier website on behalf of Thermochimica Acta.]*

The media started to carry stories about Rogers' paper. The Italian newspaper *Avvenir* quoted Monsignor Ghiberti, president of the Shroud Commission of the Archdiocese of Turin and part of the Turin "Centro," as saying that he was surprised that a specialist like Rogers could be so imprecise. Monsignor believed there could be an answer that would explain the medieval dating, but he didn't believe the answer was the patch hypothesis. Rogers, however, insisted that there was a clear difference between the main part of the Shroud and the 1988 C-14 samples. Rogers went on to say that although he wasn't a textile expert, he was an acknowledged and respected chemist and that his *Thermochimica Acta* article had been reviewed before publication by other experts. He said that few people believed the C-14 tests could be wrong and it was difficult to convince skeptics ("1988 Test on Shroud Disputed" 2005). Regarding whether the data he amassed proved the 1988 C-14 results to be in error, he posted one message to the Shroud Science Group in which he said, "How much evidence is needed?" *[Excerpt reprinted with permission of Joan Rogers.]* Rogers also said that "the people who cut the sample didn't do a very good job of characterizing the samples;" i.e., performing chemical tests on the samples to insure that they were representative of the main cloth. He also felt that the 2002 restoration would adversely affect any new chemical tests on the Shroud (D'Emilio 2005).

Many of the articles included his recounting of his first reaction to the reweaving hypothesis that Sue and I had proposed, one in a line of possible explanations as to why the C-14 results were wrong:

> "This one was the last straw," Rogers said, who was confident he could disprove their claim. So he got his archived thread samples out and began looking at them again, only to conclude that the idea of the patch that threw the carbon dating off might be correct. By god, these people might be right," he said about the moment of realization. "That's very hard for a scientist to agree with the lunatic fringe" (Snodgrass 2005).
> *[Excerpt reprinted with permission of lamonitor.com.]*

Another Italian newspaper, *Il Giornale*, wrote:

> Raymond Rogers from the Los Alamos National Laboratory and leader chemist of the team who, since 1977, have taken part in the project of dating the Holy Shroud, declared that he would have "proved Sue Benford and Joseph Marino wrong in five minutes"; five years ago they claimed the unreliability of the C-14 dating, carried out in 1988. Well, here is how the scientific method works: Rogers, who had started with the purpose of proving his colleagues

wrong, has had to recognize their reasons, or, at least, their conclusions (Battaglia 2005).

One has to recognize that some scientists with less integrity than Rogers might not have had the courage to admit they were wrong and agree with people they thought were lunatics. Most people and certainly most scientists don't like to admit publicly that an assessment that was made was wrong, especially when it involves giving credit to those toward whom one feels some animosity. To give one more example of how Rogers did not mince words, he said that there were some sindonologists, "who would have sold tickets to the crucifixion" ("Local Scientist Dates Cloth to Christ's Time" 2005).

Although Monsignor Ghiberti had at first questioned Rogers' findings, the official stance of the Turin authorities quickly changed. The January, 2005, issue of *Sindone News*, the Diocesan Commission for the Holy Shroud monthly newsletter, had this to say:

SOME REMARKS ABOUT THE RESULTS OF DR. RAYMOND N. ROGERS' RESEARCH

The paper recently published by Dr. Raymond N. Rogers [*Thermochimica Acta* 425 (2005) 189-194] makes some interesting observations. The work claims that the Shroud samples taken in 1988 for the radiocarbon dating and the samples taken in 1973, in contiguous areas, by Prof. G. Raes present anomalies in their composition. According to the author, on the cloth there are "plant gums" with a polysaccharide structure and coloured compounds deriving from interactions between Madder (alizarine) and aluminum ions. These coloured additives were apparently used after a reconstructive restoration of the cloth to make the colour of the new fibres the same as those of the Shroud.

Two remarks are necessary here:

1) The finding of the presence of extraneous coloured substances (pigments and real colouring agents which were used in the past for dyeing cloth), even though they are restricted to the site in question, is a new finding. Indeed Rogers himself proved the absence of any type of pigment and colouring agent on the fibre samples he took in 1978 from several different areas of the Shroud cloth. The observation is to some extent in line with the IR spectrometry findings obtained by Prof. Alan Adler. Indeed Prof. Adler stated that

Chapter Twelve: Retesting the 1988 C-14 Sample

the site where the samples had been taken for the radiocarbon dating might have been contaminated by extraneous substances.

2) The hypothesis that the site where the samples were taken might have been subject to repair work to reconstruct the cloth in mediaeval times, although strongly suggestive, has not been confirmed by the textile experts and researchers who have examined it. The most recent tests (made in 2002) were carried out to discover any possible traces of such work in the light of similar hypotheses already made several years ago. Consequently, caution is obligatory in order to avoid drawing rash conclusions that it is not possible to demonstrate scientifically.

In conclusion, Dr. Rogers' observations are very interesting and certainly provide a basis for further investigation and studies on the chemical characteristics of the cloth and its possible inhomogeneity.

[Reprinted with permission by Diocesan Commission of the Holy Shroud.]

Their remarks require some comment. They admit, based on the findings of both Rogers and Adler, that materials found on the cloth are suggestive of a repair. But because this "has not been confirmed by the textile experts and researchers who have examined it," they assert that to conclude that a repair exists would be a "rash conclusion." So under what circumstances would pigments and coloring agents for dyeing have been used without a repair of some kind? And how did they try to determine if a repair had taken place? Apparently it was just a visual inspection and a simplistic optical device, neither of which would reveal any detailed chemical composition. Rogers complained that the 1988 samples were not properly characterized chemically, and the inspection of the fibers for possible reweaving in 2002 apparently suffered from the same negligence.

One has to wonder whether the Turin authorities would have been willing to admit that a repair had been done, which would indicate that they had overlooked important evidence both in 1988 and 2002. Although the official reason for having done the 2002 restoration was for the conservation of the Shroud, it is interesting that it is not mentioned when they say, "The most recent tests (made in 2002) were carried out to discover any possible traces of such work in the light of similar hypotheses already made several years ago." They are, of course, referring to when Sue and I first presented the hypothesis in 2000. Their statement leaves one with the impression that looking for signs of a repair was more on their minds than the official reason of conservation.

On March 7, 2005, Ray Rogers sent an email to the Shroud Science Group to say that a scientist he admired had passed away. Ironically, we got word the next day that Ray himself had died. He lost his long battle with cancer. Sindonology had lost a giant. His output had been nothing less than gargantuan, all the more remarkable because of his illness. Barrie Schwortz told me in an email in December, 2002, that Ray had told him that about a year before that (i.e., late 2001), doctors had given him only 6 months to live. I really believe that Ray's passion for the truth and sense of mission with the Shroud kept him alive much longer than could have been expected. Although Rogers had tried time and again to get the Turin authorities to respond to his pleas regarding possible new testing, he hadn't even been given the courtesy of a response.

I am awed by the output of this man in his last years. He sent numerous, long and detailed messages to the Shroud Science Group, he carried on correspondence with many individual sindonologists; he performed experiments in his home lab; he wrote many papers, both individually and with co-authors, including the very significant one in *Thermochimica Acta*, and even managed to write a book called <u>A Chemist's Perspective on the Shroud of Turin</u> (available in print or as an e-book; see www.shroud.com).

Not long after Rogers died, his widow Joan (who also is a chemist and had also been a STURP member) received an email, purportedly from Cardinal Poletto, asking her to return Ray's leftover Shroud samples back to Turin. Joan shared the email with Barrie Schwortz, who was suspicious of the email, since normally a communication from a Cardinal would arrive by regular mail. She wondered if the communication really did come from Turin. Schwortz did some computer digging into the file signature that identifies the authors' computer/name and discovered that it had actually been composed, not in Cardinal Poletto's office, but in the office of the "lawyer" referred to in Chapter Nine, "Controversies in Dallas." Joan did not respond to "Cardinal Poletto" (Schwortz, 2005).

As we had received no direct responses from the Turin authorities to our letters, Meacham and I put together another letter, this one to be sent to

Cardinal Theodore McCarrick, Archbishop of Washington, D.C. A Shroud Science Group member, Father Kim Dreisbach, had a friend who the knew the Cardinal very well, so we decided to send a letter to him and see if he would be willing and able to raise some issues with Cardinal Poletto. On May 17, 2005, we sent the following letter:

Cardinal Theodore McCarrick Archdiocese of Washington DC
Dear Cardinal McCarrick,

We the undersigned are Americans from Catholic, Protestant and Jewish backgrounds who are deeply concerned over the future of the Turin Shroud. We are writing to you in the hope that you would be willing to raise certain issues with Cardinal Severino Poletto, Archbishop of Turin and Pontifical Custodian of the Shroud. We feel that much closer and more effective communication with Cardinal Poletto would transpire if conducted by a fellow cardinal.

The issues that we feel very strongly about are:

1) The need for a proper international commission of prominent scholars, whose names would be published, and the proceedings of which would be open. Currently, an "international jury" has supposedly been appointed to review proposals for scientific testing of the precious relic. The membership of this jury is not known, nor how it was selected, who appointed it, or what its terms of reference are. We fear that it could be subject to manipulation, that it may include unqualified persons, and that it may not be fair and objective. The international commission we would like to see was requested in a petition to the Pope signed by 52 Shroud researchers from around the world. It was suggested to have a much wider remit, not only to oversee future scientific testing but also conservation of the relic.

2) The need for C-14 dating, without further delay, of tiny samples from the Shroud as per the proposal submitted by Ray Rogers and William Meacham to Cardinal Poletto in 2003. This proposal has wide support in the community of Shroud researchers; a letter signed by 23 Shroud researchers was sent to Cardinal Poletto in October 2003, but there has been no reply. Much future scientific testing – both in research design and fund raising – would hinge on the outcome of this test, and the result, if significantly different from the medieval date announced in 1988 would have an electrifying effect on the world. Cardinal

Poletto's response has been that the decision of the "jury" must be awaited, then a recommendation to the Pope, and then a final decision must be awaited from the Vatican. The proposal of Rogers and Meacham is different from the other proposals, however, in that it does not require access to or direct testing of the Shroud itself, but rather makes use of the minute samples removed already. And, the late Pope John Paul II said on several occasions that he wished to see the scientific study of the Shroud continue.

Our deep concern arises from a number of issues, most notable of which is the disastrous "restoration" of the Shroud carried out in 2002. Irrevocable damage was unwittingly done by an aggressive conservation approach that was adopted by the parochial "Commission for Conservation" appointed by Cardinal Poletto (composed of seven Turinese, one German and one Swiss). There was considerable shock and dismay among Shroud researchers around the world at this "restoration." This could have been avoided if proper consultation among scholars and conservators had been carried out. Comments on this intervention can be seen at www.shroud.com/restored.htm.

Another source of concern is the inconsistent and unfair practice of allowing testing by certain selected researchers to proceed with no review. At an international congress convened in Turin in 2000, proposals were invited by Cardinal Poletto with a deadline of October 30 of that year. In the first week of November, Turinese researchers were allowed to conduct a scanning project on the Shroud for one week, and in 2002 a number of other Turinese researchers were allowed to conduct tests on the Shroud during the "restoration" work. None of these tests were submitted to the "jury" or to any peer-review process before being carried out. All other scientific proposals have been required to await the formation and consideration of the "jury" and approval from the Vatican. As the review process drags on, as it has for five years now, there is a very real possibility that it will get or has been swallowed up by events; this happened with a similar official invitation to submit proposals for testing of the Shroud in 1990. There was no outcome to that process and no proposal was ever approved or rejected.

In the light of the considerable media interest in the crucifixion of Christ generated by the movie by Mel Gibson, and the recent scientific publication by Ray Rogers casting doubts on the medieval C-14 dating, we feel that the time is ripe for a proper re-dating of the Shroud. All of us believe that the dating done in 1988 was not conducted properly, that the result of 1260-1390 A.D. is not the true age of the Shroud, and that the impact of a new dating could be tremendous. What is most compelling is that the amount of material required to find out the truth is minuscule—about the size of one's little fingernail, from a cloth that is 14 feet long and 3 feet wide!

We would be very grateful if you would raise these concerns with Cardinal Poletto. Please feel free to contact us for further information or copies of the documents mentioned in this letter.

Sincerely,

[Sixteen researchers' names were listed as co-signers in original letter.]

Joseph Marino

For email correspondence:
Jmarino240@aol.com

Not surprisingly, no response was ever received from this. The Shroud Science Group decided to try to send one more letter to Cardinal Poletto, which was sent in July:

Cardinal Severino Poletto
Archbishop of Turin

Your Eminence,

We the undersigned are part of an Internet Shroud Science discussion group that includes scientists and researchers from all over the world.

In 2003, Raymond Rogers and William Meacham submitted to you a proposal for new carbon dating of the Shroud, based on strong evidence that the sample dated in 1988 is unreliable and anomalous when compared to the main part of the cloth. We are writing to you to express our support for the Rogers/Meacham proposal.

The very important findings recently published by Rogers establish beyond reasonable doubt that the carbon dating sample is unrepresentative of the cloth as a whole, and cast grave doubt on the result obtained from it. We note with keen interest the recent statement in *SINDONE NEWS* that certain examinations and tests were conducted during the intervention of 2002 to investigate that possibility. However, we feel strongly that the proper and straightforward way to confirm or rebut Rogers' hypothesis regarding the inaccuracy of the 1988 result is to conduct further carbon dating on samples from different parts of the cloth.

After the publication of Rogers' article this year, there has been a great renewal of interest in the Shroud, especially the possibility that it is older than the carbon dating indicates. All the world now wants to know whether the 1988 carbon dating result is in fact erroneous. We urge you therefore to grant the very small amount of material requested in the Rogers/Meacham proposal, consisting of 60mg (about one spoonful) of carbon dust and fiber bits already removed from the Shroud. In addition, to secure general acceptance of the new dating, we urge that one very small sample (one square centimeter) be freshly taken from the Shroud with proper documentation, at the location indicated on the figure at
http://freepages.religions.rootsweb.com/~wmeacham!c14new.htm.

Removal of such a sample would in no way detract from the appearance or violate the integrity of the Shroud. Please note that the authors of the proposal and many of the signatories below have had key positions in Shroud research, come from many countries and represent the overwhelming view among Shroud researchers.

Finally, we note with great sadness the death of Ray Rogers earlier this year. He devoted much of his life to researching the Shroud, and his recent article on the C-14 sample has had a profound impact. We ask, in consideration of the enormous effort that Rogers made for the study of the Shroud, that you release the tiny amount of material that he had requested, so that Ray's hypothesis can be confirmed or rejected (true scientist that he was, he would be pleased either way!), and the true radiocarbon age of the Shroud can be known.

We hope that you will take this important step towards discovering the truth about the Shroud. The amount of material required is minuscule, the possible gain enormous. The case is simple and it is compelling, so compelling in fact that we cannot imagine any legitimate reason why the test should not be conducted forthwith. As stated in the proposal by Rogers and Meacham: "The measurement that we are proposing COULD have an enormous and positive impact on the public perception of the Turin Shroud around the world, if it contradicts the earlier date . . . . Alternatively, if the result is the same as that of 1988, it will have virtually no impact in the public arena . . . ."

Sincerely,

[Twenty-nine researchers' names in original letter were listed, including author's]

Once again, there was no response to the letter but there still was hope. Another conference was to be held in September in Dallas, and several members of the Turin Centro, including Monsignor Ghiberti, were scheduled to be there. Perhaps face-to-face communication would be able to advance the dialogue. Even so, no one expected immediate results. After all, the Turin authorities had not shown any tendencies to receive any advice from outside groups, and the conference was to be sponsored again by AMSTAR, which had been the real force behind the controversial 2001 Dallas conference. (As noted previously, the 2001 conference had supposedly been co-sponsored by another major Shroud group, but, in reality, they had no significant input.) Would the 2005 conference be any less controversial? We would soon find out.

CHAPTER THIRTEEN

DÉJÀ VU IN DALLAS

Despite our horrible 2001 experience with AMSTAR, Sue and I decided to attend the 2005 conference to be held at the Adolphus Hotel in downtown Dallas from September 8 to 11. We had also accumulated additional information in support of the invisible reweaving theory (upgraded from a hypothesis due to Rogers' work) and considered submitting a paper about it. However, AMSTAR was requiring speakers to submit the full text of their papers before the conference, and would not allow any changes to be made after submission. Few, if any, previous conferences ever had that restriction. It certainly appeared that "control" would be a major factor in the 2005 conference. Due to that fact and because of what we had learned about the email sent to Joan Rogers, ostensibly from Cardinal Poletto (as recounted in the last chapter), we decided not to submit the paper. On the small chance that we would be allowed to unofficially present the paper, we asked AMSTAR if that would be possible. Much to our surprise, we were given the okay to present it informally on the Friday night, when no official papers were being presented.

Shortly before going to Dallas, (which would be extra exciting for me as I would be able to visit Dealey Plaza, the scene of President Kennedy's 1963 assassination), I reread a small booklet that had been written by Professor Piero Savarino, scientific advisor to Cardinal Poletto. To my shock, Savarino stated that the 1988 C-14 testing might have been erroneous due to:

extraneous thread left over from 'invisible mending' routinely carried out in the past on parts of the cloth in poor repair" [italics added].

Savarino went on to emphasize:

[I]f the sample taken had been the subject of 'invisible mending' the carbon-dating results would not be reliable. What is more, the site from which the samples actually were taken does not preclude this hypothesis" (italics added) (Savarino 1998:21-22).

[Excerpts reprinted with permission of Piero Savarino.]

I immediately emailed several shroudies to let them know of this passage. While Savarino's use of the phrase "invisible mending" probably does not refer to the technical procedure as Sue and I had proposed it, these passages show that even the Cardinal's advisor acknowledged that numerous repairs have been made on the Shroud throughout the centuries, which made the invisible reweaving theory quite plausible. The reason I say that the phrase probably doesn't refer to the technical procedure as proposed by Sue and me is that a member of the Turin Centro later told me that "invisible mending" was an inaccurate translation of the original Italian.

While en route to the conference, I came down with the stomach flu. I managed to land without any problems, but unfortunately did not feel 100 per cent during the entire weekend. Sue and I did manage to get to Dealey Plaza before the start of the conference, and Sue took a picture of me standing at the spot where Abraham Zapruder had shot the famous home movie of the JFK assassination. It was exciting being in a place where a key moment in American history had played out.

Attendees to the conference were startled to learn that an armed guard would be on hand for the whole of the conference—yes, that's a security guard with a weapon. Why was an armed guard needed at a conference discussing the supposed burial cloth of Jesus, the "Prince of Peace"? It was no secret that it was because the outspoken archaeologist Bill Meacham would be in attendance. The organizers apparently felt that an extreme show of force was needed to keep Meacham in line. If that wasn't humorous (or sad?) enough, there was a real knee-slapper in a local newspaper report about the conference. A reporter had interviewed Barrie Schwortz before the start of the conference. At one point, Schwortz mentioned the belief by the late microscopist Dr. Walter McCrone that the Shroud was a painting. Schwortz specifically said that McCrone had died a few years previously, but when the story came out, the reporter wrote that "some scientists believe the Shroud was nothing more than a clever painting, a view originally put forth by Dr. Walter McCrone, who would not be at the conference. Had McCrone turned up at the conference, I'm fairly sure his resurrection would have made front-page news! (Rarely, if ever, do I find that newspaper reporters, local or otherwise, are 100 per cent accurate in their articles.)

During one of the conference presentations, Schwortz showed a 30-minute video that contained portions of five hours of interviews he had conducted with Ray Rogers before his death. Rogers was critical of the Turin authorities, although no one was specifically named in the clips shown. Schwortz added to the video the text of the 1998 statement by Savarino saying that the C-14 dating might have been erroneous due to "extraneous thread left over from 'invisible mending' routinely carried out in the past on parts of the cloth in poor repair." Several members of the Turin Centro who were present walked out of the hall before the video was finished.

On Friday night, Sue and I informally presented the paper we had decided not to officially submit. Eventually, it was published on Schwortz's website (Benford and Marino 2005). We received many compliments about it from those who attended. None of the Turin Centro members were present at the talk. However, the next morning at breakfast, by chance (or Providence perhaps), we ran into Susie Phillips, the translator for Turin Centro members who had difficulty with English. Sue gave a short synopsis of our paper, and Phillips seemed captivated by the story. She asked if she could have a copy of the paper to pass along to the various Centro members, which we gladly gave her.

Attendees to the conference were promised that a big announcement was going to be made at the banquet held on Saturday night. Much speculation ensued among those at the conference, but the announcement was only that the proposals that had been submitted in 2000 had been completed and recommendations would be made to the Vatican in the upcoming months. It was a total let-down for all the researchers who had been hoping for some major news. In addition to disappointment from the C-14 results from 1988, sindonologists had to endure false hope after test proposals were submitted in 1990 followed by no response, and a five-year delay after more proposals were submitted again in 2000, only to be told that the authorities were now just starting to go through them. The good news was that they were also allowing additional proposals to be made.

The conference concluded on September 11 with a question-and-answer session (with pre-submitted questions only), but there were some rather unpleasant moments. When one speaker, in response to a question, went on too long for the lawyer's liking, the latter gruffly said, "Give me the microphone" and did not let the speaker finish the answer. Meacham posted a scathing review of the conference on his website. He wrote:

> [R]equiring questions to be submitted in writing, only to be read out by the chair at the last session . . . [is] nothing more than blatant censorship. The reason given by AMSTAR, that there was no time for questions from the floor, is patent nonsense. The purpose of this show conference was to provide a safe environment for the Turin delegation to pontificate, with no possibility of being disputed or shown to be incorrect. Even the two-and-a-half hour final session labeled "discussion" was no such thing, but a veritable farce in which questions were sidestepped and official pronouncements were made. To cite one of the most blatant examples, one question asked how the two views on whether the C-14 sample area was re-woven could be resolved. Flury-Lemberg responded with this: "There is no re-weaving. There is no re-woven area on the Shroud." Someone dared to voice the comment that this did not answer the question. [The lawyer] responded: "The next question is . . . "
>
> And so it went. There was no discussion at the "discussion session", and 40 minutes ahead of the time given in the schedule, [the lawyer] announced that the last question had been dealt with and the conference was closed. No call for comments or questions from the floor, though there was time to spare. It could not have been more of a farce! These sorts of situations left a bad taste in everyone's mouths (Meacham 2005a).
>
> *[Excerpt reprinted with permission of William Meacham.]*

In the Turin Centro's version of events:

> Dr. Flury-Lemberg specifically addressed and responded to a number of unfounded rumors about the 2002 Restoration. In addition to addressing the rumors, Dr. Flury-Lemberg and Monsignor Ghiberti also frankly answered all written questions submitted by the attendees concerning the 2002 Restoration and candidly addressed the many unfounded rumors (*Sindone News*, No. 28, October 2005).

Chapter Thirteen: Déjà vu in Dallas

[Excerpt reprinted with permission of Susie Phillips.]

The reader can decide if Meacham's account or the Centro's account conforms more closely to reality. An interaction that Sue and I had, as attendees were leaving the conference, was telling. Sue, Meacham, and I were in the main part of the hotel when one of important Turin Centro officials got off the elevator, near where we were standing. We tried to engage him in conversation regarding several key Shroud issues. He gave us the "I'm-in-a-big-hurry-to-get-to-the-airport" song and dance, so the exchange never got off the ground. A short time later, Sue and I went to lobby to get ready to depart. Who do you suppose we saw standing around just killing time?

A few days after the conference ended, we sent Susie Phillips an updated version of the paper and asked her to keep it confidential. On September 13, she emailed us:

> Thank you very much for sending me your revised text so promptly. Please just confirm that you will authorize me to pass on the new version to Don Giuseppe [Ghiberti], Baima [Bollone], Karlheinz [Dietz], Mechthild [Flury-Lemberg] and also to Bruno [Barberis], Piero [Savarino], Nello [Balossino] and Gian Maria [Zaccone]. Karlheinz, Don Giuseppe and Baima read it on the aeroplane and they were very interested and asked me for a copy. Mechthild was not with us, but I know she would be interested too. I shall stress the confidential aspect of your paper and if you could include details of when and where it will be published we would very much appreciate it.
> Thank you again and I look forward to hearing from you.
> *[Reprinted with permission of Susie Phillips.]*

We emailed her back that the paper would be published on *www.shroud.com*, which would give it maximum exposure. Flury-Lemberg emailed us on September 22, saying:

> I got your paper and read it with great interest. I agree completely [with] your historical research. Unfortunately there is a great misunderstanding in the aspect of "reweaving". Your paper is based on "tapestry-reweaving"= tapestry – mending. This was of course very often done in the past, —until today. My students did it under my guidance over many years on the Burgundian Tapestries of

the Historical Museum in Berne. In the case of tapestries it is no problem to make "invisible mending". (Invisible from the surface but easily recognizable from the back!) But a linen or silk weaving, done on a shaft loom is a different matter!
[Reprinted with permission of Mechthild Flury-Lemberg.]

Nevertheless, the evidence that Rogers found does suggest that the C-14 sample area was rewoven. There's a saying: "Against the fact there is no argument." It was around this time that I learned of a book written in 1998 by a Swiss archaeologist Maria Grazia Siliato, titled <u>Contre-Enquête sur le Saint Suaire</u>. In it she stated that in 1976 Italian Riccardo Gervasio had published a detailed study of the repairs and restorations that the Shroud had undergone. He had found in the upper left and right corners some fabric incrustations with topstitches, as well as medieval seams, which were used to partially patch up and support the frayed original. (I was able to read an English translation of book excerpts from a restricted website I had access to.) I alerted Susie Phillips about this passage on November 10 and she responded that day thanking me and indicating that she had forwarded it on to various members of the Centro.

We also discovered in 2008 some information about invisible reweaving of linen—but more about that in the next chapter. Even as Flury-Lemberg continued to speak out against the invisible reweave theory, more evidence in its favor continued to mount. Rogers, a thorough scientist, had sent some of his samples to the late Professor John Brown, a microscopist, to see if his findings matched his own. Brown wrote a paper, specifically for *www.shroud.com*, in which he said:

> The author, as a microscopist, has had an opportunity to examine some of the Raes threads. Figure 1 shows a weft thread, R7, at an original magnification of 28X. The thread has a yellow-brown coating with the exception of indented regions which are white. These indented regions are at the intersection with the warp thread. The weave was tight enough that the application of a relatively

viscous gum/mordant/dye solution did not penetrate the intersection of the threads. *This would appear to be obvious evidence of a medieval artisan's attempt to dye a newly added repair region of fabric to match the aged appearance of the remainder of the Shroud (emphasis mine).* Figure 2 *[not shown here]* shows the same thread at 56X magnification. The coating and encrustations can be seen on individual fibers (Brown 2005).
[Excerpt reprinted with permission of STERA, Inc.]

Another writer noted:

Lupia *[author of the book* The Ancient Jewish Shroud at Turin, www.reginacaelipress.com, *2010]* mentions how Flury-Lemberg noticed no patching or mending when she examined the Shroud. That she thinks the entire side was mended in antiquity nevertheless shows the edge area may have been rewoven at various times (Salamone 2011:117, footnote 30).

Sue and I submitted via Susie Phillips another proposal for testing on the Shroud, this one having to do with the DNA that could possibly be extracted from the cloth. On January 6, 2006, we got an email from Susie saying:

Just a quick line to inform you that, from what Don Giuseppe tells me, the scientific committee has accepted for consideration both the first project you sent (by the correct deadline) and also the second (sent in later after deadline). Both will therefore be included in the overall report given to the Cardinal. At present it is not possible to predict what will happen after that.
[Reprinted with permission of Susie Phillips.]

If they had predicted we wouldn't hear anything for quite some time, they would have been correct. It's now been over five years since they sent that email, and I've never heard anything—a familiar situation. All we could do was to keep plugging away at our research and hope that, someday, new testing on the Shroud would really be done.

CHAPTER FOURTEEN

MOVING FORWARD—WITHOUT A KEY PLAYER

After Rogers died on March 8, 2005, his materials, including his computer, were given by Joan Rogers to Barrie Schwortz. While Schwortz was doing an inventory, he discovered that one of the important Shroud samples from the C-14 sample area that Rogers had been working on was missing. In the meantime, Sue received one of her "insights" and said that she thought someone named "Bob" at Los Alamos National Laboratories had been given the sample by Ray. After Schwortz did further checking, he discovered in Rogers' computer that the sample had indeed been given to someone named Robert Villarreal—at Los Alamos National Laboratories. Sue's insight was totally correct. Villarreal was then contacted by Schwortz, and Sue and I also started communicating with him.

During 2006, Sue and I heard of a conference that was being planned which would have papers presented on various relics but would include the Shroud. To our dismay, it was another invitation-only conference. We also learned that many strict rules would be in place. One of the most puzzling was that the speakers would not be allowed to congregate at the conference. As I began to recall the unpleasant aspects of the 2005 Dallas conference—and not liking at all what I was hearing about the upcoming conference—Sue and I began to discuss the possibility of organizing a conference ourselves. We quickly decided we wanted to proceed. One of the first things I considered was the fact that the organizers of the Dallas conference required Barrie to pay the conference fee and for his hotel room, even though they asked him to handle all the audio-visual aspects (which he graciously did). I decided that if Barrie was able to attend and handle all of the audio-visual aspects at our conference, he would not pay for the conference fee or his hotel room. We also resolved that there would not be any heavy-handed aspects like armed guards or strict rules prohibiting speakers from congregating.

We started to plan for the conference, to be held in the summer of 2008. That year would be the thirtieth anniversary of the STURP testing and the twentieth anniversary of the infamous C-14 dating of the Shroud. We opened it to discussion on the Shroud Science Group forum, and many seemed excited about having a conference. The chosen venue was the luxurious Blackwell Hotel on the grounds of Ohio State University. From the hotel, one can see the famous "Ohio Stadium," where OSU's football team plays. I tell people that in much of Ohio, especially Columbus, OSU football is practically the state religion. The hotel had only opened in 2002, so it was a state-of-the-art facility and a wonderful place to hold the conference. As I was an OSU employee, I was even able to get a discount on the costs for the attendees.

Barrie agreed to handle the audio-visual aspects of the conference, and I informed him that he would not have to pay for his conference fee or hotel room. I felt good about that, and I'm sure Barrie was glad to save some money! I hoped to get as many former STURP members as I could get to attend, although the best I could do financially for them was to offer a discount on the registration fee. I have to chuckle when Shroud skeptics accuse sindonologists of using the Shroud to make money. Some STURP members actually took out loans to attend Turin in 1978. Most people who work on the Shroud gladly spend much of their time and money to share knowledge about it. Besides Barrie, STURP members who committed to attending the Columbus conference were Joseph Accetta, Thomas D'Muhala, John German, and Kenneth Stevenson. Also planning to attend was Pete Shumacher, inventor of the famous VP-8 image analyzer that STURP members John Jackson, Eric Jumper and Bill Mottern used to show that the Shroud image had encoded three-dimensional information.

In the meantime, a professor of mathematical physics at Tulane University published a book called <u>The Physics of Christianity</u>. He discussed the Shroud and summarized Rogers' major findings:

Chapter Fourteen: Moving Forward—Without a Key Player

> Linen is made from flax, and flax contains a chemical substance called lignin. Over time, the lignin will lose its content of another chemical compound called vanillin. Thus, one can obtain an estimate of the age of a linen sample by comparing the relative amount of lignin and vanillin. Rogers detected vanillin in the radiocarbon samples but could not detect any vanillin from the samples from the *[other]* areas of the Shroud. From this he inferred that the original Shroud material is between 1,300 and 3,000 years old.
>
> Rogers also detected alizarin dye in the radiocarbon sample but no such dye in the original Shroud material. The dye was apparently used to make the color of the repair material match the color of the original Shroud (linen turns yellow over time). This particular dye was introduced in Italy in 1291, so the radiocarbon sample cannot be older than this date. Indeed, the central value of the radiocarbon date, 1325, is about three decades after the date of the first use of the dye in Italy. (Tipler 2007:177).
>
> *[Excerpt reprinted with permission of Random House.]*

So, many academics, even some from outside of the "Shroud crowd," began to notice Rogers' findings and report it in their writings. One advantage the reweaving theory had over some of the other explanations for why the C-14 dating was wrong was that there was some solid scientific and historical data that made the theory very plausible.

When the time for the conference came, D'Muhala had to withdraw at the last minute due to a family situation, but all of the other committed STURP members, as well as Pete Schumacher, were able to attend. We were fortunate to have Rex Morgan for our keynote speaker. Rex flew about 30 (!) hours to get to Columbus and delivered the best presentation on the Shroud that I think I've ever heard. He was given 90 minutes, and he finished in the nintieth minute. It seemed as if he never even came up for air. Readers should take the time to listen to this most amazing talk (Morgan 2008).

Archaeologist Paul Maloney presented an enlightening paper on the controversies surrounding the C-14 dating of 1988 and on the interpretation of data related to it. Several points in Maloney's presentation are worth noting. Maloney related that in November, 1987, he discussed with Luigi Gonella, the Cardinal of Turin's scientific advisor, the best location from which the sample should have been taken. At the time, Maloney was unaware of a photo of the C-14 sample area that had been taken by Barrie Schwortz in 1978. It is known as the "blue quad mosaic." The C-14 sample area shows a darker discoloration as compared with the Shroud image area. According to Maloney:

> [A] tool (never formally published by STURP) actually existed at the time of my meeting with Prof. Gonella, that, had I known about it, might have convinced Prof. Gonella to re-examine the question: the so-called "blue quad mosaic." Some years before his death, I talked with the late Don Lynn about the use of remote sensing and what specialized photography of the Shroud could reveal. By using black and white film but with different filters, red, green, blue, Lynn told me that it could reveal surface chemistry through its reflectance—a kind of spectrum indicating that the surface was different from elsewhere on the Shroud cloth. When one looks at the "blue quad mosaic" one sees something very different at the corner from the deep orangeish-red coloration of the image area. In the "Raes Corner" one sees a kind of "bluish-greenish cast. What causes this? Lynn told me that such special photography does not tell us what the chemical consistency is, it merely indicates that we must do chemical analysis to determine what that chemical signature is (Maloney 2008).
>
> *[Excerpt reprinted with permission of Paul Maloney.]*

Had the laboratories performed chemical analyses of the samples in 1988, they perhaps would have discovered that anomalies were present. Whether they would have informed the Turin authorities that those samples should not be dated and that different samples should be taken is an open question. (A picture of the "blue quad mosaic" can be found in Benford and Marino 2008.)

Maloney also noted:

> In March of 1981, the late Walter C. McCrone sent me several Kodak transparencies of shots he took looking at line fibers on the Shroud. On those slides, still preserved in my collection, McCrone had written the following note: "madder rose, linen fiber, medium (blue) sample 3 CB" and sample 3-AB. McCrone was referring to photomicrographs made on STURP sticky tape samples 3-CB and 3-

AB which came from the blood flow across the back nearest the side-strip, where someone would have been making repairs if the reweave theory is held to be correct. McCrone, of course, due to his belief that the Shroud was painted by an artist, was trying to prove that the Shroud had been in artist's studio. Hence, he sent me these photo-micrographs as a piece of that evidence. But he was faithfully preserving the fact of the presence of madder rose on the cloth. There is now a new way of looking at the presence of that madder rose. Although this is some distance from the "Raes Corner" such trace amounts can now be conjectured to explain the dye that was used, along with the aluminum mordant and the gum arabic as a binder to create the wash to color the rewoven area. Thus, it may now be seen not as a contaminant from an artist's studio, but rather a contaminant from the weaver's workshop (Maloney 2008).

[Excerpt reprinted with permission of Paul Maloney.]

In addition, Maloney presented some interesting findings about the cotton that the Derbyshire lab had found in 1988 (Maloney 2008). He stated:

It is now clear that the presence of cotton **spun inside** *[bolding in original]* linen yarns in the Raes' Corner [*i.e., the C-14 sample area*] is supported by the findings of five separate and independent investigators:

*Gilbert Raes, (1973-1974);
*STURP's own early analyses reported by STURP spokeswoman, Joan Janney, (1981);
*Investigators at Precision Processes (Textile lab) Ltd. in England, 1988;
*Ray Rogers' 2004 investigations;
*John Brown at Georgia Tech (2004).

[Excerpt reprinted with permission of Paul Maloney.]

Another highlight of the conference was a presentation by the aforementioned Robert Villarreal, which gives further support to Maloney's findings about the cotton. A press release summarized his paper:

August 20, 2008
PRESS RELEASE: Los Alamos National Laboratory team of scientists prove carbon 14 dating of the Shroud of Turin wrong

COLUMBUS, Ohio, August 15 — In his presentation today at The Ohio State University's Blackwell Center, Los Alamos National Laboratory (LANL) chemist, Robert Villarreal, disclosed startling new findings proving that the sample of material used in 1988 to Carbon-14 date the Shroud of Turin, which categorized the cloth as a medieval fake, could not have been from the original linen cloth because it was cotton. According to Villarreal, who lead the LANL team working on the project, thread samples they examined from an area directly adjacent to the C-14 sampling area were "definitely not linen" and, instead, matched cotton. Villarreal pointed out that "the [1988] age-dating process failed to recognize one of the first rules of analytical chemistry — that any sample taken for characterization of an area or population must necessarily be representative of the whole. The part must be representative of the whole. Our analyses of the three thread samples taken from the Raes and C-14 sampling corner showed that this was not the case." Villarreal also revealed that, during testing, one of the threads came apart in the middle, forming two separate pieces. A surface resin, that may have been holding the two pieces together, fell off and was analyzed. Surprisingly, the two ends of the thread had different chemical compositions, lending credence to the theory that the threads were spliced together during a repair.

LANL's work confirms the research published in *Thermochimica Acta* (Jan. 2005) by the late Raymond Rogers, a chemist who had studied actual C-14 samples and concluded the sample was not part of the original cloth possibly due to the area having been repaired. This hypothesis was presented by M. Sue Benford and Joseph G. Marino in Orvieto, Italy in 2000. Benford and Marino proposed that a sixteenth-century patch of cotton/linen material was skillfully spliced into the first-century original Shroud cloth in the region ultimately used for dating. The intermixed threads combined to give the dates found by the labs ranging between 1260 and 1390 AD. Benford and Marino contend that this expert repair was necessary to disguise an unauthorized relic taken from the corner of the cloth. A paper presented today at the conference by Benford and Marino, and to be published in the July/August issue of the international journal *Chemistry Today*, provided additional corroborating evidence for the repair theory (Press Release 2008).

[Note: Chemistry Today is a peer-reviewed journal.]

Chapter Fourteen: Moving Forward—Without a Key Player

Despite this and some other exciting papers, the media did not seem interested. Even though all the national and local media were notified, there was basically only one Internet story about it. The usual stories in the media about an image of Jesus that has supposedly appeared on a tortilla or myriad other strange objects appeared in the media, but a whole conference presenting strong scientific evidence that the 1988 C-14 dating was wrong was basically ignored. A further disappointment was that another Shroud story, which had previously been covered some months before, was published the same weekend (see *http://articles.latimes.com/2008/aug/17/nation/na-turin17*). It was essentially a rehash of material from an article from the previous spring. Even though it was a pro-Shroud story, given the importance of the Villarreal paper, it seemed that the latter should have been the subject matter instead of months-old material. So the lack of media coverage was a real disappointment. In attendance, however, was a representative from the Discovery Channel, which planned to produce a Shroud documentary in the upcoming months. On another positive note, many people said it was the best conference they ever attended. It also was the first Shroud conference in which all (with one or two exceptions) papers were later available online, although a written Proceedings was also produced.

There was one interesting development at the conference regarding the invisible reweave theory. Two individuals independently found an old 1962 book titled The Frenway System of French Reweaving, with the subtitle, "Detailed and complete instructions in the art of French Invisible Reweaving." Rogers hadn't been the only one who had thought we were part of the lunatic fringe. Many Internet bloggers had chastised our hypothesis as pure fantasy, not realizing that the technique really does exist. Although Flury-Lemberg had said that that invisible reweaving would be detectable on the back side of the Shroud, a book from the 1950s about French invisible weaving of which I became aware in 2011, stated:

> Occasionally you may be asked to reweave a damage invisibly on both sides....Invisibility is achieved on both sides by applying the face-weaving method to the back side of the fabric, *with a slight variation in the lock-in procedure.* After pick backs have been made,

the needle is inserted some distance to the right of the first one, and then glided thru the fabric *between the top and bottom surfaces. The needle must be kept hidden within the fabric until brought out at the pick-back.* On the left side of damage the procedure is reversed. *The needle enters at the point of lock-in,* and then glides thru the fabric and comes out some distance to the left. Thus when the protruding ends of replacement thread are clipped close to the surface the lock-ins will not show from either side (Hauser 1954: 61).

(Note: Italics are original to the quote. The term "face-weaving" indicates the technique is applied to the face of the fabric instead of the back. However, Hauser is saying that the even though there is normally a different technique for the back ["back-weaving"], face-weaving can actually be done on the back, which plays a role in the fact that a repair can be invisible on the back side of the cloth.)

Hauser has diagrams and photos (pp. 47-51) of the face and back of herringbone weaves, comparable to the herringbone weave of the Shroud. For those that say a repair would not have been done to the back side of the Shroud because of the Holland backing cloth sewn on by the Poor Clare nuns after the fire of 1532, Sue and I believed that the repairs were made after the owner of the Shroud, Margaret of Austria, died in early 1531, but before the fire of 1532 and thus before the backing cloth was added.

At the Columbus conference, an attendee, French physician Thibault Heimburger, was given the "Raes" thread that microscopist John Brown had analyzed. Heimburger did additional studies on the thread and soon concluded:

> The fact that the Raes/Radiocarbon area is strongly anomalous regarding cotton was already known. The present study of Raes #7 thread not only confirms this but also provides more information about the type, the amount and the layout of the cotton fibers in the thread.
>
> **Under the very probable assumption that Raes #7 is representative of the Raes/Radiocarbon area, the threads of this corner are blended linen/cotton threads. The two kinds of fibers were spun together and this has been performed likely deliberately as was typical in the Middle Ages. To the contrary, the main part of the Shroud is pure linen.**
> [Bolding in original.] [Excerpt reprinted with permission of Thibault Heimburger.]

Chapter Fourteen: Moving Forward—Without a Key Player

This alone would be sufficient to know that this area is not part of the original Shroud. If we add the other findings: the dye (Rogers, Brown), the splice (Rogers, LANL) with the resin binder (LANL)

and the amount of lignin/vanillin in the flax fibers of this area as compared with that found on the main Shroud fibers (Rogers), there is an extraordinary set of self-consistent data converging on the inevitable conclusion: the 1988 radiocarbon dating is invalid and nobody knows the true age of the Shroud (Heimburger 2005).
[Excerpt reprinted with permission of STERA, Inc.]

In September, the Discovery Channel called Sue and me and asked if producers could come to our home to interview us for their upcoming documentary. After a delay of about a week due to a power outage in our area caused by the winds of Hurricane Ike, the production crew came and spent the good part of a day with us and filmed. Around the time of the documentary filming, Sue discovered a relatively new treatment for breast cancer. It essentially was a miniature laser that was supposed to slowly zap the cancer. The laser had originally been designed as a weapon but then adapted for medical use. OSU had one of these miniature lasers, but they would only do one treatment, whereas a clinic in Arkansas that Sue found did multiple ones in a week's period. People were coming from all over the world to this clinic, which was having very successful cure rates. Even though Sue believed the cancer was in remission, she thought it would be a good idea to undergo the treatment. We registered to go for a week in October, and Sue completed the treatment. They informed us that her immune system would be affected due to the treatment.

In November, I co-authored with a retired NASA scientist, listing all the evidence that indicated that the area from which the C-14 sample had been taken from was not representative of the main cloth (Marino and Prior 2008). It also dealt with various problems with the C-14 dating process in general. Edwin Prior was agnostic, with no religious ax to grind. I had for some time been compiling data to write an article and discovered through a conversation with Barrie Schwortz that Prior was doing a similar thing. Barrie put us in contact with one another and we decided to combine our data and ideas. Our first article was 40 pages. After publication, Prior and I continued to find more data and we would later produce an appendix of 19 more pages. If one is convinced that the C-14 test was unquestionably valid and/or there is no reweave present in the sample area, 59 pages of data is quite a large amount of material to have to explain away.

The Discovery Channel completed the Shroud documentary fairly quickly, and it was broadcast three days before Christmas, 2008. Everything was going along nicely for Sue and me. The Shroud was getting its due renown, and Sue seemed to be feeling even better after the laser treatments at the Arkansas clinic. For some reason though, I found myself praying that I would die before Sue, because I felt she would be able to handle such a situation better than I would. I thought it was strange that I was praying that when things were going so well for us. I had no rational reason to be making such a prayer, but there it was. As I would soon find out, a reason would soon become manifest.

CHAPTER FIFTEEN

"SHE'S GONE"

One morning in January, 2009, Sue woke up with what she thought was an "infarcted omentum," which is a disorder of the immune system and something she had experienced when pregnant with her younger daughter. Since the clinic in Arkansas said that the immune system would be affected by the treatment, she thought the infarcted omentum was due to that. Sue was a nurse and an excellent researcher, so I was confident in her self-diagnosis. She knew of various people who had beaten cancer with a non-traditional approach such as she herself had taken, and I felt she would beat it that way also. She immediately made an appointment with her gastrointestinal doctor, but the soonest she could get in was March 22. The problem kept her from eating much, and she started to lose weight, which was not ideal for one who weighed just under a hundred pounds when healthy.

One Saturday in February, I drove her to an urgent-care facility, where she was given an intravenous drip, so she could receive more nourishment than she had been getting. But she obviously was not well. When the GI doctor saw her on March 22, he was very concerned and immediately admitted her to OSU hospital. After some scans, the doctors sadly determined she had Stage Four breast cancer. We were stunned—we had thought she had beaten the cancer, and she had even been feeling really good as recently as late December. If that wasn't bad enough, they also had to operate on her for ulcers and a blood clot. It was an unbelievable turn of events. Despite all this, Sue had a peaceful demeanor. Her younger daughter said to her, "You don't even seem that upset." Sue calmly replied, "Everything happens for a reason." Her calmness made an absolutely horrible and sickening situation more bearable for me. I did get upset at a remark that a doctor made to me. He had seen in her chart that she had decided not to undergo the normal cancer treatment regimen, and he asked me, "Did you have any input in her treatment?" This was hurtful to me because he was clearly implying that I should have insisted to her that she follow traditional treatment, and that I was stupid for not having done so. I told him that she was a knowledgeable cancer researcher and was even an oncology nurse, so I trusted her judgment.

The nurses would ask Sue questions to see how alert and cognizant she was. It was shocking and sad when the nurse asked her what year it was, and she got it wrong at first before correcting herself. But the cancer had spread to the brain. She had been so vibrant just a few short months ago, but she was now having trouble remembering basic facts. She was also having extreme trouble even swallowing. A respiratory therapist came and handed me a paper with about 19 exercises, of which Sue was supposed to do ten repetitions, and all of them were supposed to be done three times a day. She didn't have the strength or stamina to accomplish such a feat. Everything was starting to fail, including my hope. When it was certain she would not be able to overcome her progressing disease, she was moved to a hospice in early April. The thought of losing her was utterly overwhelming. It's cliché, but it just didn't seem possible that this was happening.

On April 5, Palm Sunday, as Sue lay near death in the hospice, the Discovery Channel rebroadcast the Shroud documentary, and the staff at the hospice wanted to see it. I was glad that the doctor and nurses there could see Sue as she was when she was healthy. It was hard to believe that it had been filmed less than seven months previously. The next morning, I had to make a trip to our lawyer's office for some urgent business. I whispered to Sue to wait until I got back. When I returned to the hospice, I fell asleep, exhausted from all the events of the past few weeks. Around 11:30 a.m., I felt a tug on my arm and Sue's cousin Sandy quietly said to me, "She's gone."

The person who had been the central focus of my life for the past ten years was no longer here. I would never again see that wonderful smile, never kiss her good morning, never feel her warm embrace, never send her emails from work telling her I loved her, never come home to her wonderful cooking, never experience the simple of joys of life with her, never do research with her and never kiss her good night. I broke down and sobbed.

Chapter Fifteen: "She's Gone"

Sue's work assistant Julie drove me home and one of Sue's cousins drove my car home. I just sat in Julie's car, looking blankly out of the window the entire ride back home. The horrible nightmare of life without Sue had begun. Sandy and Julie made the arrangements for the necessities that followed. I still find it so difficult to recall all of this, and Sandy's words—"She's gone"—continue to echo in my head.

Even though I knew it was coming, I found it difficult to accept the reality. Though many people came to the funeral service and I received many shows of support, when I returned home, I felt absolutely and utterly lonely. I had grown up in a family of seven and then lived many years with about 20 other monks. As my older stepdaughter Erika was already out of the house and my younger stepdaughter Alexis decided to live with her dad, I now faced the reality of living alone. It was a daunting prospect for me. I would lie on the couch many nights after work and literally wonder if I would be able to keep my sanity. One effect was that I lost quite a bit of weight. There was no sense of normality any longer. At times I would recall what she went through and become physically ill. Life was and has been difficult and challenging for me since Sue died. She was my wife, my best friend, and my soul mate. Here is the obituary that I wrote for the *British Society for the Turin Shroud Newsletter*:

> Sue Benford had an enormous impact on Sindonology from the time she first learned about the Shroud in 1997 until her untimely death on 6 April, 2009. She was formerly a registered nurse at Children's Hospital in Columbus, Ohio, in Oncology Pediatrics (the very place where she had survived a childhood cancer), was a World Champion Power Lifter in the 97-pound weight class and a prolific researcher on various scientific and medical topics. She was a co-author with American astronaut Dr. Edgar Mitchell on a paper presented at the Fifth International Conference on Computing Anticipatory Systems (CASYS'01) in Liège, Belgium, August 13-18, 2001.
>
> Benford's autobiography <u>Strong Woman: Unshrouding the Secrets of the Soul</u> (Nashville, Source Books, 2002), recounts how she got involved with the Shroud and eventually joined forces with another sindonologist, former monk Joseph Marino. Together, they wrote several papers theorizing that the 1988 C-14 dating was skewed by an invisible reweave. STURP chemist, the late Ray

Rogers, thought that this was nonsense and, having the necessary Shroud samples to work on, would prove them wrong in five minutes. Ultimately, he believed they were correct and went on to write, shortly before his death in March 2005, a significant peer-reviewed article in the prestigious journal *Thermochimica Acta* that asserted that the 1988 C-14 results were invalid because the samples that were dated were not representative of the whole cloth. Other researchers, including a group of nine scientists at Los Alamos National Laboratories in United States, corroborated Rogers' findings. Benford and Marino went on to have two articles published in the peer reviewed literature: "Role of calcium carbonate in fibre discoloration on the Shroud of Turin" *Chemistry Today.* March/April 2008, 26(2):57-62 and "Discrepancies in the radiocarbon dating area of the Turin shroud. *Chemistry Today.* July/August 2008, 26(4):44-50. The latter is accessible online at: http://chemistrytoday.teknoscienze.com/pdf/benford%20CO4-08.pdf.
Many other details about Benford and access to many of her writings can be found at: *www.homestead.com/newvistas*. She will be sorely missed by all who knew her.

I received several emails of condolences from individuals at the Turin Centro, including one from Monsignor Ghiberti himself, for which I was very appreciative.

Soon, I remembered that I had prayed the previous autumn that I would die before Sue. I firmly believe that the prayer had been put into my heart to help prepare me for what eventually happened. I believed wholeheartedly that she would make known her presence to me in various ways (I had, in fact, asked her to do so), and she didn't disappoint. I'll give just a few of the many situations where I feel she let me know that she was nearby. One night, I was awakened by seven clear, loud knocks. I saw nothing in the room. Sometimes one can wake up from a dream but then realize that it was only that. This definitely was *not* just a dream. I believe it was Sue announcing her presence. Another incident involved our dog, a Tibetan Spaniel we had owned since 2003 and whom my stepdaughter Erika named "Peanut." Peanut cannot be trusted to stay put outside, so she always has to be leashed. One sunny day I had to get something out of my car, which was parked in the driveway. I went through the garage, retrieved what I needed from the car, and came back into the house. I went back to close the garage door and noticed that the trunk of my car was open. That was strange—it hadn't been opened a few moments before when I had gotten what I needed from the car, and I couldn't have accidentally opened it via a control inside the car because there was none. The trunk had never come open on its own for any reason before that and never has since. I walked out to the car to close the trunk and, to my surprise, discovered Peanut on the sidewalk. She had slipped out without my noticing when I had first opened the garage. Amazingly, she hadn't run off to chase a squirrel or follow a playing child. I managed to coax her back inside before she wandered off. If the trunk hadn't been opened and I had just closed the garage door, I would have assumed she was in the house somewhere, but just out of sight. Had Peanut remained outside, she surely would have disappeared. She had a tag on her collar with my phone number, but the number was no longer in service, so if someone had found her and tried to call, they wouldn't have been able to reach me. I immediately went out and obtained a new tag. I'm totally convinced that Sue opened the trunk so I would walk out there and discover that Peanut was loose. Sue had managed to make a sunny day even brighter.

There were other strange events. Since 2002 we had a hot tub in an addition built onto the house. Sue hated the winter and loved soaking in the tub to cope with the cold. There are French doors leading from the family room to the addition, which I always make sure are locked before I go to work. One day in 2009, close to that time of year when we would start to use the tub a lot, I came home from work and found the French doors unlocked and several feet ajar. I have a neighbor, who arrives around midday on days that I work, to walk Peanut, so after making sure a robber hadn't been in the house, I called her and asked if she had seen the doors open. She said she did pass through the family room while checking on Peanut but hadn't seen any open doors. I told my neighbor that the only explanation I had was that Sue visited to say it was hot tub season! I know that sounds flippant, but I don't have any rational explanation for how those doors opened, and I'm very comfortable attributing it to Sue.

One last little anecdote: during Holy Week, 2010, I found the backyard gate, with a very hard-to-open latch, open on Monday and Wednesday. I never found it open before then or have at any time since. Later in the week, I realized that Sue had died on the Monday of Holy Week, 2009. I felt that she was making her presence known on the liturgical anniversary of her death and again two days later for good measure. I told a friend of mine about this and even let her try to open the latch—she was literally unable to do it. There are many more incidents I could mention, but let's return to the timeline of 2009.

In the summer of 2009, the History Channel was filming for what became the excellent Shroud documentary "The Real Face of Jesus." When producers contacted Barrie Schwortz about filming him, they mentioned that they were interested in interviewing me. Barrie kindly told them that because of Sue's death, it would not be a good time for me so they didn't contact me. As it turns out, the documentary only briefly mentioned the C-14 controversy, so I doubt they would have used any footage of my interview anyway. I'm always leery of appearing in these shows—with editing, they can twist your words and make them fit any agenda whatever. But this documentary, which was the first-ever two-hour Shroud program for television, was very well done.

When a spouse dies, one goes through a very difficult first year, especially at the various holidays and anniversaries that are full of happy memories. Christmas would be the most difficult one for me. My family suggested I fly back to St. Louis for Christmas week, which I decided to do. Not long before I was to leave, I got an email from a woman named Laura Clark, who happened to live in St. Louis. She said that she had seen the documentary that Sue and I were on. Laura was very taken by Sue's account of how she first learned of the Shroud, and intended to contact Sue to tell her of her own similar experience. However, she learned from my website that Sue had died. Laura said that she had written a just-published fiction Shroud screenplay titled <u>Sindone: The Divine Remedy</u> and asked if I would be interested in reading it. I told her I would, and she sent me a copy, which arrived just a few days before I was to leave for my trip. I decided it would be a good book to read on the plane.

When I got the book, I flipped through it and glanced at the back cover, which had a picture of Laura. The picture stopped me in my tracks. It struck me immediately that the picture of her was stunningly similar to a picture I had of Sue. I pulled out that particular picture of Sue and was startled to see that:

* they were both wearing dark glasses
* their hair color was about the same
* their hair length was similar
* their body angle matched
* the expressions on their faces were the same
* they both had something over the right shoulder

I immediately had the feeling that this couldn't all be coincidence. I brought the book and picture of Sue over to some neighbors, John and Joyce, to show them. Before I could get the whole story out, John said he thought the picture of Laura was a picture of Sue! John then asked me where Laura was from, and I told him that she was from St. Louis. John knew that I would be flying there in a few days and asked if I had planned to get together with Laura while I was there. I told him I hadn't planned on it. John, who loves to joke, said to me kiddingly, "If you don't look her up when you get there, I'm never going to speak to you again." "Alright, John," I replied, "I'll see if I can arrange to get together with her." I went home, emailed Laura and within a few hours, we had agreed to meet for lunch as soon as I landed.

I read the book on the plane. The theme of the book is the meaning of human suffering in the context of the Shroud. Given my long-time passion for the Shroud and the fact that I was going through tremendous suffering after having lost Sue (whom I met only because of the Shroud), I could not have had a more meaningful present for my first Christmas without her.

After I landed, I met Laura for lunch. In person, she didn't look all that much like Sue, but she did agree that the pictures were strikingly similar. While we were conversing, I had the feeling that this was the closest I would ever get to experiencing having lunch with Sue again. It didn't have anything to do with any romantic notion—it would have been way too early to even consider that, and Laura was in a committed relationship anyway. But since those two pictures were so similar, and they were both so passionate about the Shroud, I couldn't help knowing that this was a special experience, courtesy of Sue. I told Laura how appropriate the theme of the book was for me at that particular time.

Laura was like most passionate shroudies—she would love to work on the Shroud more, but she has to hold a normal job, working in anti-terrorism (perhaps a notch or two above "normal"). She had books published on that topic. Laura and I started to email each other quite often, which we still do. Along the way, I discovered some interesting connections between her and Sue, and between Laura and myself.

* Laura had first learned of the Shroud in 1997; Sue first learned of the Shroud in 1997.
* Laura had actually written the book in 2004, but firmly resolved on April 6, 2009, to get it published; Sue died on April 6, 2009.
* Laura had written a screenplay about the Shroud; Sue had first written her book as a screenplay.
* Laura's book and Sue's book both have blue and white on the covers and both have similar design patterns.
* Laura has a character in her novel named "Magdalena." Sue's real first name is "Magdalena," after her maternal grandmother.
* Laura and Sue were only about two-and-a-half years apart in age.
* Laura and Sue's birthdays are only five days apart.
* Laura and I are both native St. Louisans (although we didn't meet until after I moved to Columbus.)
* Laura had a sister who lived in Columbus. Her sister passed away in 2011. Her funeral was handled by the same home that handled Sue's.
* Laura has two brothers who attended the school that was run by the monastery I was in and both were there at the same time I was.
* Laura and I were very similar, psychologically and spiritually.

If there were any doubts that Sue had arranged for Laura and me to meet, there shouldn't be after looking at that list. Such events convinced me more and more that, just as Sue had said, everything happens for a reason. As hard as it was not having Sue, I felt that for whatever reason(s), she was destined to die at that particular time. I continued to show the similar pictures of Laura and Sue to various people and all were amazed. One person said, "They could be twins!" Another said, "They look like sisters." Another person's jaw literally dropped when he saw it. Laura added an interesting twist to her book by having the main character in it periodically blog on the Internet. Laura has wonderful insights about the Shroud, especially as it relates to suffering, which have been very helpful for me. (To read the blog, go to www.divineremedy.org.)

As the end of 2009 approached, I had already felt Sue's literal presence in my life in several ways and found (no doubt, with Sue's help) a new Shroud friend from my hometown, who would figure prominently in some important events that were to happen in 2010. In the midst of the terrible gloom after Sue's death, there had already been some positive experiences to lift my spirits and boost me forward.

CHAPTER SIXTEEN

NEW HORIZONS

After the Shroud had been exhibited in 2000, it was announced that the next public display would be in 2025. However, the Turin authorities requested and received permission from the Vatican to have an exhibition in April and May, 2010. Some Shroud experts thought that the date was moved up because Cardinal Poletto, who would be retiring later in the year and who had presided over the controversial restoration of the Shroud in 2002, wanted to end his time in Turin with a positive Shroud event.

In conjunction with the exposition, ENEA Senior Research Scientist Paolo Di Lazzaro, assisted by an international team of Shroud researchers, organized the "International Workshop on the Scientific Approach to the *Acheiropoietos* Images" in the Rome suburb of Frascati. "*Acheiropoietos*" is a Greek word meaning "not made by hand." Although papers on other relics were presented, the main focus was the Shroud. It would have been great to attend both the exhibition and the workshop, but I decided not to go. It certainly wouldn't have been as enjoyable without Sue, and I just couldn't justify the expense given my new situation. Besides, the exhibition announcement had generated a great deal of media stories on the Shroud and spurred the release of many new books, all of which were wonderful distractions for me.

One of the key papers at the Frascati conference dealt with a statistical analysis of the data from the 1988 Shroud C-14 dating. The authors wrote:

> The Shroud data relative to the 1988 radiocarbon dating show surprising heterogeneity. This leads us to conclude that the twelve measurements of the age of the TS cannot be considered as repeated measurements of a single unknown quantity (Fanti *et al.* 2010).
> *[Excerpt reprinted with permission of Giulio Fanti.]*

In other words, the data suggests that more than one cloth was dated, which is completely consistent with the theory of an invisible reweave.

Shroudies learned in the spring that Cardinal Poletto would be resigning in the fall of 2010; we also learned through the grapevine that the Vatican would exert more control over the Shroud than it had in the past. Given the overall lack of response sindonologists had received from Turin in recent years, I was as hopeful as other shroudies that there would be greater communication and collaboration with the authorities, but Shroud concerns closer to home were also on my mind.

When I was in the monastery, I kept my Shroud collection and an English-language bibliography well organized and current. When I moved to Columbus, other obligations prevented me from keeping everything up-to-date. Because Sue and I were doing so much research, many articles and books were pulled out, which added to the disarray. Since I arrived in Columbus, there had been two exhibitions, numerous conferences, and countless new books and articles in the popular press and on the Internet. I collected huge amounts of material during that time, but keeping it organized and adding it to the bibliography had been virtually impossible. In the autumn of 2010, I decided I would at least start to tackle and reorganize my collection.

One Friday night, as I began to go through materials, I ran across several emails from September, 2008, that made me freeze. They were from Fran Beauchamps, a member of a congregation headed by Ken Stevenson, who had been on the STURP team and now was a pastor. I had never met or heard of her before that email, in which she wrote: "a prayer burden came upon me for you. The LORD brought your name to me several times." She wanted to know if she could send a prayer cloth to me and Sue. The biblical basis for prayer cloths is Acts 19:11-12, which states, "Meanwhile God worked extraordinary miracles at the hand of Paul. When handkerchiefs or cloths which had touched his skin were applied to the sick, their diseases were cured and evil spirits departed from them" (*New American Bible*). I emailed her that she could, and wrote her back with some questions. Fran elaborated:

I don't know why the LORD brought your name so strongly to me this morning during worship. From my years of service unto him, I have learned NOT to ignore when I get a prompting in the Spirit like that. It doesn't matter whether I know any detail or not. (Sometimes the Spirit of GOD will reveal a thing or two, give an inkling of what's going, and sometimes He does not.) I don't really try to figure things out. God knows, that's what's more vital to us.

It could be that you are going through something right now that only you and your wife know about . . . or it could be that you're about to go through something . . .

I can tell you that a weeping came over me for you while Pastor Ken prayed, and there was a precious compassion for you that poured through me. When we're in prayer like that, we can literally feel the power of God pour through us, it's quite amazing and very blessed.
[Excerpts reprinted with permission of Fran Beauchamps.]

Those emails were dated September 7, 2008, just several months before Sue got sick. The phrase that really jumped out at me was *"or it could be that you're about to go through something."* I honestly feel there was something to this because, as noted previously, I distinctly remember praying in the fall of 2008, when Sue seemed fine, that I would be taken before her because I thought she would do much better without me, as opposed to the other way around. I believe that inkling was given to me to start preparing me for what was to soon happen. Fran's emails confirmed my ongoing feeling that Sue dying when she did was in God's plans. I'm not a big fan of the theology that when a young person dies from sickness or an accident "it was their time," or that "God wanted them," but in the case of Sue, I make an exception—and if there was ever a case of *"exception*al," it was my Sue.

I continued to communicate a lot with Laura, my newfound friend from St. Louis. During one phone conversation, she said she thought it would be interesting to hear various shroudies' stories of how they became interested in the Shroud. She suggested I bring the idea to Barrie Schwortz, for posting on his wonderful *www.shroud.com* website. When I talked to him, he liked the idea. Laura came up with a questionnaire, which I then sent via email to several hundred Shroud contacts. Laura and I edited the responses, which I then sent on to Barrie, who posted them on a "Reflections" page on his site. Normally I intensely dislike questionnaires, but since this one was about my favorite topic, I absolutely loved doing it. I called up one person who rarely, if ever, gets on the Internet, to ask her to fax me her responses. She was the artist and physicist Isabel Piczek, who had a fascinating story to tell about her involvement with the Shroud, including how she escaped from the Communists as a young girl before becoming a prominent artist, scientist, and sindonologist. Readers should read Isabel's story and many other interesting experiences that other shroudies have related. (Go to www.shroud.com, click on the Shroud image and then on the "Reflections" page.)

During the course of our conversation, Isabel suggested I write a book about my experiences with the Shroud. I had thought about it once or twice in the past, but each time, after about a nanosecond, I always decided against it because I knew how much work it would involve. However, since I also knew that Laura had published books, I decided I would at least talk with her to see what sort of financial investment it would take. I called her up one Saturday in November, 2010, and we chatted for almost two hours. Publishing a book would not break the bank, but I still wasn't convinced I wanted to do it. It was one thing to fill out a relatively short questionnaire, but quite another matter to write a whole book. Then Laura went for my Achilles heel—she said, "You know, it would be a great way to honor Sue."

Her words made me commit on the spot (how could I not when it was put that way?) and I immediately acquiesced, with no hesitation, to write this book. I started that very night and spent five hours putting together an outline and writing the introduction. The process quickly changed my sleep cycle. One Friday night I went to bed about 10 p.m., exhausted and woke up at 11:30 p.m. for no reason at all. I couldn't get back to sleep, so I worked on the book from midnight to 3:30 a.m. I even managed to work on the book several times before going off to work, which, considering I'm not a morning person, was close to a miracle. Writing it also has had a healing effect.

My decision to write a book fostered another positive event. One day I had a conversation on the phone with a work colleague about Sue's book and how the few copies still available on the Internet had become more and more expensive. I told her I would search some sites and see if I could find an inexpensive copy. To my amazement, one site that had two copies wanted

$205 for one copy and $378 for the other!! Sue was a good writer, but I didn't realize she was that good! Then the thought hit me: I could have Sue's book republished. Now Sue's book is back in print and available again at a reasonable price. *[See www.amazon.com*: *Strong Woman: Unshrouding the Secrets of the Soul.]*

As another Christmas approached, I prepared to return to St. Louis again for the holidays. This time, I didn't need any prodding from John, my neighbor, to arrange a meeting with Laura. We met over lunch again and discussed the book and other Shroud matters. We both expressed the thought that it was so nice we were from the same city and had a chance to get together when I was in town.

On Christmas Eve, I got a call from Rebecca Jackson, Dr. John Jackson's wife. She told me that the new issue of *Radiocarbon* had just published an article co-authored by a principal scientist from the Arizona laboratory involved when the Shroud had been dated in 1988. The abstract read:

> We present a photomicrographic investigation of a sample of the Shroud of Turin, split from one used in the radiocarbon dating study of 1988 at Arizona. In contrast to other reports on less-documented material, we find no evidence to contradict the idea that the sample studied was taken from the main part of the shroud, as reported by Damon et al. (1989).We also find no evidence for either coatings or dyes, and only minor contaminants (Freer-Waters and Jull 2010).
> *[Excerpt reprinted with permission of Radiocarbon.]*

It seemed strange that it had taken the laboratory almost six years to respond to Ray Rogers' findings. It was undoubtedly released on Christmas Eve to capitalize on the religious aspect, but only one paper in France carried a story about it. The rest of the world's media, which often trumpeted negative news about the Shroud's authenticity, was unusually quiet about the news.

One of the members of the Shroud Science Group, author Mark Oxley, wrote a superb critique that was published on Schwortz's *www.shroud.com*. The article concludes:

> Jull and Freer-Waters merely report that they found no evidence for any coatings or dyeing of the linen. As has been stated in the past, absence of evidence is not evidence of absence, and this must

surely apply to this paper. The work of Rogers, Brown and others has clearly shown coatings and other discrepancies in the area of the radiocarbon sampling. Prof. Jull cannot just dismiss it all in a few short sentences, without explanation. Their conclusion from their studies is that they find no reason to dispute the original carbon 14 measurements.

It is noteworthy that the results of the radiocarbon tests were diametrically opposed to a mass of other evidence indicating that the Shroud is much older than a mediaeval date, and that the results of Jull and Freer-Waters' study are diametrically opposed to the results of other studies on the same material. Even if the results of the radiocarbon tests could be seriously accepted as being scientific evidence of a mediaeval date for the Shroud, evidence is not proof and pieces of evidence must be weighed in the context of all the available evidence in order to be judged. The same applies to Jull and Freer-Waters' results.

It has to be concluded that the opaqueness of the procedures regarding the cutting and wrapping of the samples in Turin in 1988, the many unanswered questions surrounding the samples, not least the whereabouts of the smaller piece sent to Arizona, the questions about the tests themselves, notably the small sizes of the samples used and the failure to make use of detailed screening and testing procedures, and the subsequent studies that have called into question the dates given by the tests, all combine to deliver a fatal blow to the credibility and validity of the radiocarbon test results. They should be consigned to the scientific dustbin, where they belong. Science relies on precision, attention to detail, accurate record-keeping, proper reporting of results and impartiality on the part of scientists. All of these have been lacking in this sorry episode (Oxley 2011).

[Excerpt reprinted with permission of Mark Oxley.]

It was now increasingly clear to many people that the 1988 dating was extremely sloppy and questionable at best.

In early 2011, I bought a book called Praey to God, Vol. 1 by Annette Cloutier, as I heard that it contained much information about the Shroud. (The "a" and "e" joined Old-English style; it was originally titled Prey to God but some thought it was "Pray to God" so the author combined "Prey" and "Pray" into "Praey".) She mentions Sue often in her Shroud material. On page 173, Cloutier writes: "By April 6, 2009, I became convinced that the Shroud of Turin is the *Resurrection Fabric* of Jesus" *[italics in original].*

[Excerpt reprinted with permission of Annette Cloutier.]

I thought it rather odd that she would name a specific date that she became convinced. In any event, April 6, 2009, was a familiar date—it was the day Sue died. This was eerily similar to Laura having firmly resolved on that very day to get her Shroud book published. Annette, like Laura, has a Columbus connection. Annette had thought about becoming a Dominican nun and had attended school in Columbus in the late 1960s. I do believe Sue was from the other side inspiring people from the other side and sending them into my life. Just to make sure I got the point, both had various connections that indicated that more than just coincidence was at work. It truly felt that Sue was watching over me from above. What a blessing that has been!

In June 2011, I took some time off work to visit Barrie Schwortz at his home in Colorado. Barrie had for several years invited me to come, and the trip would be both business and pleasure, as I was on the Board of Directors for his non-profit corporation, "Shroud of Turin Education and Research Association, Inc." (STERA). A circumstance, somewhat negative, actually turned out to be the impetus for me to go. When I had booked my flight in October, 2010, for my trip to St. Louis for the Christmas holidays, I received a $259 credit that I would have to use before October, 2011. I decided to use it toward a flight to go visit Barrie. Colorado is a great place to vacation, with all its mountains and wonderful scenery. I was able to watch busy Barrie at work, doing various things like answering hundreds of emails from shroudies, constantly talking on the phone with others, and a slew of other Shroud-related activities. (Barrie devotes a minimum of twelve hours a day, seven days a week to STERA.) While I was there, Barrie videotaped me for STERA's archives for about two hours regarding my nearly 35-year involvement with the Shroud. I was able to see some rare items in STERA's collection and also found time to edit my book manuscript. I was really glad that I applied my airline credit to this fruitful trip.

Barrie and I also met with John and Rebecca Jackson, who live only about an hour away in Colorado Springs, and whose Shroud Center is in a different location since the last time I visited them. Between Barrie and the Jacksons, there is always a massive amount of significant Shroud work being done in Colorado. I was excited to hear Barrie and John discuss the possibility of collaborating on a book about their STURP experiences. That would be quite a fascinating book—Barrie and John, if you're reading this and haven't gotten started, get a move on!

In 2011, a peer-reviewed periodical, *Current Physical Chemistry Journal,* was planning to publish a special issue totally devoted to the Shroud. One of the papers was titled "Investigating the Radiocarbon Dating Sample Area of the Shroud of Turin Using Digital Image Processing Software" (Morgan *[in press]*). The author indicates that there are techniques available that can ensure that if another sample is ever taken for another C-14 test, it will be representative of the whole cloth and not anomalous like the 1988 sample.

In October, 2011, an Italian documentary, "The Night of the Shroud," exposed many of the suspicious, behind-the-scenes actions relating to the 1988 C-14 dating, based on many documents, including the matter of the one-million-pound donation to the Oxford lab. The documentary confirmed that politics predominated throughout the whole event. The documentary will eventually be shown in the United States.

Whether another C-14 testing of the Shroud will ever be allowed is uncertain, but it is good to know that technology is continuing to advance and that if another test is permitted, it might be able to definitively prove, in conjunction with the aforementioned paper by Morgan, that the original C-14 sample area was rewoven, just as Sue and I had always believed. How I wish she were here to continue with the research!

The title of this chapter is taken from one of my favorite Moody Blues' songs, written by Justin Hayward after his father had died. It in it he sings: "…I'm beginning to see / Out of mind far from view / Beyond the reach of a nightmare come true." This song has special meaning for me because I had also lost a special person to death. (To hear this wonderful song and also "Broken Dream," the one Sue and I considered "our song," mentioned in Chapter Six, go to *www.youtube.com* and search each title along with "Moody Blues." The beauty of both songs is absolutely breathtaking.) The human spirit is amazingly resilient. Even under the worst circumstances, we can overcome the nightmares of life and have dreams of a positive nature.

With the Catholic Church's problems retaining members and abuse scandals within its own clergy, I often think that it should allow more Shroud testing as a way to give itself a shot in the arm. I'm thoroughly convinced that although science can never definitively prove that the Shroud wrapped Jesus, it can come awfully close. If that's the case, it's hard to understand why the Catholic Church won't allow it. In one of his last interviews, Ray Rogers said "I believe that competent scientific efforts to understand the Shroud have a bleak future" (*British Society for the Turin Shroud Newsletter*, No. 60, December 2004, pg. 23). Certainly all of the shroudies, including myself will continue to wait—and dream—that our pleas for further scientific studies are answered. It could very well help answer the non-scientific question of Jesus, "Who do you say I am?"

EPILOGUE

There are two things that I think about every day—and will to the end of my life—the Shroud of Turin and Sue Benford. My life has been inextricably intertwined with one or both since 1977. I can't even imagine what my life would have been or would be now without either one. I certainly could have been occupied with the Shroud without Sue, but every fiber of my being tells me that she was part and parcel of the special call that I had always felt pertaining to the Shroud. I've never regretted my decision to leave the monastery. If I found myself in the same circumstances one hundred times, I would have made that decision each and every time. Whenever I think about it, there is a sense of peace and calmness, even though I've had to bear the pain of losing Sue to cancer. But Sue does continue to make known her presence to me in various strange ways similar to some of the experiences mentioned in Chapter Fifteen.

Although I wish that I could have had more time with her, I am grateful for the ten years we did have. I tell people, without exaggeration, that not only will I stand before God with a clear conscience about it, but I would have been afraid to stand before Him *not* having made that decision. I know that may be difficult for people to understand, but the Catholic Church teaches that one is obliged to follow one's (informed) conscience, and I believe mine was informed. Mother Teresa of Calcutta was in solemn vows in a community before she left to start the Missionaries of Charity. How many of the thousands of people she helped, especially the most destitute, would have said that it was wrong for her to have left her previous community? Sometimes God breaks through the boundaries of our theology. If you think about it, no matter what beliefs you hold, there will be literally millions of people who don't agree with them. Everyone needs to do what he/she believes God wants him/her to do. No matter what decisions we make, the only guarantee is that somewhere along the way we will suffer.

Pope Benedict XVI made the following remarks regarding the Shroud and suffering in a talk released by the Vatican Press office on December 19, 2010. He said the Shroud:

> ...invites us to meditate on him who took upon himself man's suffering of every age and place, even our sufferings, our difficulties, our sins.
>
> How many faithful over the course of history have passed before that sepulchral winding sheet, which covered the body of a crucified man, which in everything corresponds to what the Gospels transmit about the passion and death of Jesus!
>
> The Son of God has suffered, he has died, but he is risen, it is precisely because of this that those wounds become the sign of our redemption, of our forgiveness and reconciliation with the Father; they become, however, a test for the faith of the disciples and our faith: every time that the Lord speaks of his passion and death, they do not understand, they reject it, they oppose it. For them as for us, suffering is always charged with mystery, difficult to accept and bear.

Much of the suffering in life, such as natural disasters and disease, is beyond our control. But some suffering arises due to the conscious actions of ourselves and those around us. Despite almost two thousand years of Christian theology, the "Golden Rule," treating others as we would want to be treated, seems to be practiced less and less. The twentieth century was the bloodiest period in all of human history. Rampant greed, child sexual abuse, parents killing their young children, and other inappropriate actions by those in positions of power are just some of the situations that are all too common in our world.

Despite all our numerous gains in science and technology, we are nowhere near the utopia that many people believed would result (many of whom believed that there is no need for religion and/or spirituality). Many dream of a world with little or no suffering. Neither theology nor science nor technology has solved the mystery of the Shroud. It is an enduring cloth that somehow captured the image of one of the most brutal examples of mankind's inhumanity. It is still in our midst despite having been subject to fires, looting, an arson attempt and travels over long distances. It seems destined to be a constant reminder of the existence of suffering, but in that serene face that we see on the cloth, we are comforted and seem also to sense a feeling of hope.

Although we often feel that our personal sufferings, whether coming from outside forces or self-inflicted due to our own decisions, are burdensome, they will never approach being whipped, having thorns smashed into our heads, having nails put through our wrists and feet, and being left on a stake to die. The Shroud is a constant reminder of how Jesus gave his life for others—and how we should give our lives for others, as well. It is as if all of the suffering of the world is encapsulated in one image. There is no doubt in my mind that the Shroud, like the message of Christianity, will endure as long as humans exist on the earth.

REFERENCES

"1988 Test on Shroud is Disputed." 2005. http://www.zenit.org/article-12198?l=english. Retrieved 17 January 2011.

Adler, Alan. 1996. "Updating Recent Studies on the Shroud of Turin," [in] *Archaeological Chemistry: Organic, Inorganic, and Biochemical Analyses*, Mary Virginia Orna, ed. American Chemical Society: 223-228.

Adler, Alan. 1997. "Concerning the Side Strip on the Shroud of Turin." Actes Du III Symposium Scientifique International du CIELT-Nice, 12-13 May, pp. 103-105.

Antonacci, Mark. 2000. Resurrection of the Shroud: New Scientific, Medical, and Archeological Evidence. New York: M. Evans and Co.

Badde, Paul. 2010. The Face Of God: The Rediscovery Of The True Face Of Jesus. San Francisco: Ignatius Press.

Battaglia, Franco. 2005. "Certainly not medieval! The Shroud dates back to Jesus' time." Accessible at www.shroud.it/ILGIOR-4.HTM. Retrieved 17 January 2011.

Benford, M. Sue. 2002. Strong Woman: Unshrouding the Secrets of the Soul. Nashville: Source Books.

Benford, M. Sue. 2011. Strong Woman: Unshrouding the Secrets of the Soul. St. Louis: Cradle Press.

Benford M. Sue and Joseph G. Marino. 2008. "Discrepancies in the Radiocarbon Dating Area of the Turin Shroud." *Chemistry Today*, July-August, 26(4):4-12. Accessible at http://chemistry-today.teknoscienze.com/pdf/benford per cent20CO4-08.pdf). Retrieved 17 January 2011.

Benford, M. Sue and Joseph Marino. 2005. "New Historical Evidence Explaining the 'Invisible Patch' in the 1988 C-14 Sample Area of the Turin Shroud." Accessible at http://www.shroud.com/pdfs/benfordmarino.pdf. Retrieved 17 January 2011.

Boswell, Randy. 2002. A Fresh Attempt to Prove Shroud of Turin is No Fake. *Ottawa Citizen*, 21 August, pg. A1.

Brown, John L. 2005 "Microscopical Investigation of Selected Raes Threads From the Shroud of Turin." Accessible at http://shroud.com/pdfs/brown1.pdf. Retrieved 17 January 2011.

Cahill, T.A. et al. 1987. "The Vinland Map, Revisited: New Compositional Evidence on Its Inks and Parchment." Analytical Chemistry 59: 829–833.

Coghlan, Andy. 1989. "Unexpected errors affect dating techniques." *New Scientist*. 30 September, pg. 26.

Currie, Lloyd A. 2004. "The Remarkable Metrological History of Radiocarbon Dating [II]." *Journal of Research of the National Institute of Standards and Technology*, 109:185-217.

D'Emilio, Frances. 2005. "Shroud Could Be Older Than Initial Findings." http://spirit-bear.livejournal.com/46195.html. Retrieved 17 January 2011.

Damon, P.E. et al. 1989. "Radiocarbon Dating of the Shroud of Turin." *Nature*. 16 February, Vol. 337, No. 6208, pp. 611-615. Accessible at http://www.shroud.com/nature.htm. Retrieved 17 January 2011.

Evin, Jacques. 2002. Personal communication.

Fanti, Giulio *et al.* 2010. "A Robust Statistical Analysis of the 1988 Turin Shroud radiocarbon dating results." Presented at *International Workshop on the Scientific approach to the Acheiropoietos Images* 4-6 May at ENEA Research Centre of Frascati. Accessible at http://www.acheiropoietos.info/proceedings/RianiWeb.pdf. Retrieved 26 March 2011.

Freer-Waters, Rachel and A.J. Timothy Jull. 2010. "Investigating a Dated Piece of the Shroud of Turin." *Radiocarbon*, 52:4:1521-1527.

Frenway System of French Reweaving: Detailed and complete instructions in the art of French Invisible Reweaving. 1962. Privately printed and published by The Fabricon Company in a limited edition. The most significant part of the book can be accessed at http://shrouduniversity.com/frenchreweavinginstructionbook.pdf. Retrieved 28 June 2011.

Garza-Valdes, Leoncio. 1998. The DNA of God? London: Hodder & Stoughton.

Gove, Harry E. 1996. Relic, Icon or Hoax: Carbon Dating the Turin Shroud. Bristol and Philadelphia: Institute of Physics Publishing.

Hauser, Jeanette. 1954. Invisible French Reweaving, Vol. 1. La Mesa, California: Invisible Reweaving (Industries).

Heimburger, Thibault. 2005. "Cotton in Raes/Radiocarbon Threads: The Example of Raes #7." http://shroud.com/pdfs/thibaultr7part1.pdf. Retrieved 28 June 2011.

Kersten, Holger and Elmar R. Grubar. 1994. The Jesus Conspiracy: The Turin Shroud & The Truth About The Resurrection. Rockport, MA: Element, Inc.

"Local Scientist Dates Cloth to Christ's Time." 2005. http://www.redorbit.com/news/science/125172/local_scientist_dates_cloth_to_christs_time/index.html. Retrieved 17 January 2011.

Maloney, Paul. 2008. "What Went Wrong With the Shroud's Radiocarbon Date? Setting it all in Context." Presentation at The Shroud of Turin: Perspectives on a Multi-Faceted Enigma, Columbus, Ohio, 16 August. Audio/Video accessible at http://shrouduniversity.com/ohiocon2008.php. Retrieved 28 June 2011.

Marino, Joseph G. and Edwin J. Prior. 2008. "Chronological History of the Evidence for the Anomalous Nature of the C-14 Sample Area of the Shroud of Turin." Accessible at http://www.shroud.com/pdfs/chronology.pdf. Retrieved 28 June 2011.

Meacham, William. 1986a. "On Carbon Dating the Turin Shroud." *Shroud Spectrum International*, June, pp. 15-25.

Meacham, William. 1986b. "Radiocarbon Measurement and the Age of the Turin Shroud: Possibilities and Uncertainties." Accessible at http://www.shroud.com/meacham.htm. Retrieved 28 June 2011.

Meacham, William. 2005a. "Dallas Disgrace." Accessible at *http://freepages.religions.rootsweb.ancestry.com/~wmeacham/Dallas.htm.* Retrieved 28 June 2011.

Meacham, William. 2005b. The Rape of the Turin Shroud: How Christianity's most precious relic was wrongly condemned, and violated. *LULU.COM.*

Morgan, Jay. 2011. "Investigating the Radiocarbon Dating Sample Area of the Shroud of Turin Using Digital Image Processing Software" *Current Physical Chemistry Journal*, In press.

Morgan, Rex. 1988. "World Reaction to Carbon Dating a Farce." *Shroud News*, October, No. 49, pp. 3-18.

Morgan, Rex. 2008. "The Shroud: an Eternal Challenge." Presentation at The Shroud of Turin: Perspectives on a Multi-Faceted Enigma, Columbus, Ohio, 14 August. Audio/Video accessible at http://shrouduniversity.com/ohiocon2008.php. Retrieved 17 January 2011.

Murphy, Cullen. 1981. "Shreds of Evidence." *Harper's*, 265 (November):42-65.

Nelson, D.E. et al. 1986. "Radiocarbon Dating Blood Residues on Prehistoric Stone Tools. *Radiocarbon* 28:170-174.

Olin, Jacqueline S. 2003. "Evidence That the Vinland Map Is Medieval" (Reprint). Analytical Chemistry 75: 6745 – 6747.

Oxley, Mark. 2011. "Evidence Is Not Proof: A Response To Prof Timothy Jull." Accessible at http://www.shroud.com/pdfs/oxley.pdf. Retrieved 17 January 2011.

Petrosillo, Orazio and Emanuela Marinelli. 1996. The Enigma of the Shroud: a Challenge to Science. San Gwann, Malta: Publishers Enterprises Group.

PRESS RELEASE: "Los Alamos National Laboratory team of scientists prove carbon 14 dating of the Shroud of Turin wrong." 2008. Presentation at The Shroud of Turin: Perspectives on a Multi-Faceted Enigma, Columbus, Ohio, 16 August. Accessible at http://shroud.typepad.com/ohio_shroud_conference_me/. Retrieved 17 January 2011.

Rogers, Raymond N. 2001. "Comments On the Book 'The Resurrection of the Shroud' by Mark Antonacci." Accessible at http://www.shroud.com/pdfs/rogers.pdf.

Rogers, Raymond N. (and Anna Arnoldi). 2002a. "Scientific Method Applied to the Shroud of Turin: a Review." Accessible at http://www.shroud.com/pdfs/rogers2.pdf. Retrieved 17 January 2011.

Rogers, Raymond N. 2002b. "The Chemistry of Autocatalytic Processes in the Context of the Shroud of Turin." Accessible at http://www.shroud.com/pdfs/rogers3.pdf. Retrieved 17 January 2011.

Rogers, Raymond N. (and Anna Arnoldi). 2003. "The Shroud of Turin: an Amino-Carbonyl Reaction (Maillard Reaction) May Explain the Image Formation." Accessible at http://www.shroud.com/pdfs/rogers7.pdf. Retrieved 17 January 2011.

Rogers, Raymond N. 2004a. "Pyrolysis/Mass Spectrometry Applied to the Shroud of Turin." Accessible at http://www.shroud.com/pdfs/rogers4.pdf. Retrieved 17 January 2011.

Rogers, Raymond N. 2004b. "Testing the Jackson 'Theory' of Image Formation." Accessible at http://www.shroud.com/pdfs/rogers6.pdf. Retrieved 17 January 2011.

Rogers, Raymond N. 2004c. "Frequently Asked Questions (FAQs)." Accessible at http://www.shroud.com/pdfs/rogers5faqs.pdf. Retrieved 17 January 2011.

Rogers, Raymond N. 2004d. "The Sudarium of Oviedo: a Study of Fiber Structures." Accessible at http://www.shroud.com/pdfs/rogers9.pdf. Retrieved 17 January 2011.

Rogers, Raymond N. 2005a. "Studies on the radiocarbon sample from the shroud of turin." *Thermochimica Acta*, 425:189-194. Accessible at http://www.metalog.org/files/shroud/C14.pdf. Retrieved 17 January 2011.

Rogers, Raymond N. 2005b. "The Shroud of Turin: Radiation Effects, Aging and Image Formation." Accessible at http://www.shroud.com/pdfs/rogers8.pdf. Retrieved 17 January 2011.

Rogers, Raymond N. 2008. A Chemist's Perspective on the Shroud of Turin. Barrie M. Schwortz. STERA, Inc.

"Rogue fibres found in the Shroud." 1988. *Textile Horizons,* December, pg. 13.

Salamone, Gaetano. 2011. The Secret Gospel of Mark and the Burial Shroud of Jesus. *Xlibris.com*.

Savarino, P. and B. Barberis. 1998. Shroud, Carbon Dating and Calculus of Probabilities. London: St. Paul's.

Schwortz, Barrie. 2005. Personal communication.

Snodgrass, Roger. "Shroud may be older after all." 2005. http://www.lamonitor.com/articles/2005/01/27/headline_news/news04.prt. Retrieved 17 January 2011.

Sox, David. 1988. The Shroud Unmasked. Basingstoke, Hampshire: The Lamp Press.

Stevenson, Kenneth and Gary R. Habermas. 1990. The Shroud and the Controversy. Nashville: Thomas Nelson Publishers.

Thomas, Michael. 1978-1979. "The First Polaroid in Palestine: The Shroud of Turin." *Rolling Stone*, December 28/January 11:78-84.

Tipler, Frank J. 2007. The Physics of Christianity. New York: Doubleday.

Trivede, Bijal P. 2004. "Jesus' Shroud? Recent Findings Renew Authenticity Debate." http://news.nationalgeographic.com/news/2004/04/0409_040409_TVJesusshroud.html. Retrieved 17 January 2011.

"Vinland Map of America no forgery, expert says." 2009. *http://www.reuters.com/article/idUSTRE56G58320090717*. Retrieved 4 December 2010.

Wilson, Ian. 1998. The Blood and the Shroud. New York: Free Press.

Wilson, Ian and Barrie Schwortz. 2000. The Turin Shroud: The Illustrated Evidence. London: Michael O'Mara Books Limited.

APPENDIX A

TRANSCRIPTION OF HANDWRITTEN NOTES OF STURP'S DR. ROBERT DINEGAR DURING 1985 C-14 CONFERENCE IN TRONDHEIM, NORWAY

©1985 Robert H. Dinegar Collection, STERA, Inc.

[These notes provide some fascinating background material related to the politics of the 1988 C-14 dating of the Shroud. At least one major prediction regarding the dating came true. I have kept Dr. Dinegar's abbreviations and punctuation.]

One of the first persons I ran into at the opening reception of the C-14 conference on 6/23 was Harry Gove. He said he thought we ought to have a meeting and discuss what the group involved in the intercomparison tests were going to document, especially in relation to the Shroud. I agreed wholeheartedly and suggested that he "run with the ball" and arrange for a get-together. He said he would.

The paper on the laboratory intercomparison tests was presented 6/24/85 by Sheridan Bowman—neither Burleigh (scheduled to give papers) nor Mike Tite attended the conference. The presentation drew much attention and comment. One reason for this – in my opinion—was that she opened with V. Miller's picture of the Shroud and said the intercomparison impetus stemmed from the possibility of dating the Shroud. My only participation in the discussion was to comment publicly to Rainer Berger of Un. Of Cal. At Los Angeles that the real problem with dating the Shroud was not in doing the experiments but in the "politics" of getting the samples to date—and that I thought STURP could handle the getting of the samples and that the labs would do an excellent job in getting the date.

The question about which laboratory was associated with which date in the intercomparison arose. Bowman said Brit. Mus. Had agreed not to identify. At this point an unidentified attendee said he didn't see why the lab that got the "outlier" date was so insecure! Immediately, Hans Oeschger arose and said he didn't mind identifying his lab as the one who obtained this bad date. He also said they didn't know why this had happened as they had gotten good dates just before. He did indicate, though, that there had been a change in the sample preparation processing in between then and the intercomparison testing. I privately congratulated Oeschger on coming forth and removing any possibility of criticism of "protectionism," also saying that his laboratory was a member of the Shroud-dating project no matter what happens in the intercomparison. Nite of 6/26—at dinner: I learned they do know that it was a "goof-up"; a lot of internal embarrassment. I decided not to pursue it, convinced it was a "fluke."

At the reception 6/24 nite at the archbishop's Palace I conversed with several C-14 workers who brought up pros/cons about their findings about the dating the Shroud. Earle Nelson (Simon Fraser Un. Canada) explained his association with ASSIST very clearly, stressing he would give scientific comments-as-asked-on Shroud problems, but he would not be involved in "the work of dating a religious object."

Tuesday (6/25) Harry Gove announced that a meeting of those involved in the intercomparison testing/Shroud work would be meeting after the pm session. Just before the meeting (1500) he looked me up and dropped this "bomb": "several' (?-sic)* labs do not understand the place of STURP in Shroud dating; STURP has no function; the labs should 'go it alone'." I, of course, disagreed, pointing out that this was why Gar Harbottle was so important over the last couple of years. We went back and forth. Harry obviously feeling that the labs should be 'unencumbered' by any 'intermediary' like STURP.

At the meeting: Otlet (AERE, Harwell), Hedges (Oxford), Donahue (Arizona), Wolfli (not Oeschger, Zurich, Bowman (observers, British Museum), me (STURP) plus several various 'assistants' were present. Gove 'chaired' the meeting.

Topics: 1) Otlet emphasized we should act as a team; not individuals seeking 'the spotlight'. All others agreed but wanted to be able to do it "their way." Otlet was worried about premature leaking of a date; others felt bothered by the apparent 'distrust' of the integrity of the labs. Gove especially then proved this point Otlet was making by emphasizing how much his lab had 'profited' by work 'on this project.' The matter was dropped for obvious reasons.

2) Gove now brought up that there was no further place for STURP—(1) the labs had shown the ability to do the job; (2) the British Museum had the international reputation to distribute the Shroud samples and collate the data; (3) STURP had 'no standing as a reputable scientific body!' I now objected, agreeing with (1) and (2) but (3) taking offense at (3)! We now got into an argument as to whether Brit. Museum would do (2) or even should do it since Hall (Oxford) was a trustee. There was great discomfort with AERE, Zurich, etc. of the Brit. Mus. Functioning like this. The matter was dropped by everyone but Gove who obviously wanted Brit. Mus. To SUPPLANT STURP.

3) Zurich/Arizona now showed little knowledge about STURP and asked that I explain what we had done. Gove saw no reason to 'take up time' with me speaking! I got up and much to Gove's annoyance spoke for 10 minutes or so. Every minute or so, when I 'took a breath' Gove started to get up and take over. Finally, I asked him to 'wait a few minutes' until I had finished; grudgingly he sat in his seat.

Wolfli (Zurich) said he was unaware of all this. I pointed out my correspondence with Oeschger; he said he should have been told. I found out later there is tension and problems between the 2.

Donahue (Az) said he didn't know either!! At this point I said his name was on all correspondence (at Paul Damon's request) and he had been sent the proposal. He said nothing further!

Gove now resumed directing the meeting and we discussed 'getting the samples' and who would pass on the proposal and/or give permission! Gove then said he was tired of dealing with "clerics, Gonella, and STURP"—he would deal directly with his friends on the Pontifical Acad. Board. He now went into a diatribe on how he had been "ignored" by the Church and Gonella in 1978, his letters had never been delivered to responsible people etc. and that he had refused to work with STURP in 1979. I agreed, he had been treated badly in 1978, but that the non-membership in STURP was <u>his</u> decision—I had been right next to him in Santa Barbara when he said he wanted to go it alone. He then said that was going to act without any STURP involvement and get material for the C-14 community. He said he was going to write up 'a request' and circulate it for comment by others. It was now 7 PM. And we were tired (11 hr day!). Gove walked out; I saw no reason to try and deal with such an unreasonable person; the others <u>obviously</u> were in no mood to agree or disagree with Gove! The meeting ended! On the way home Otlet and Jill Watson of AERE gave me (and my daughter Janice) a ride. He said he didn't want to appear as taking sides in 'his various political problems' and so would say no more about the situation at this meeting, but invited me to stop by AERE where we could talk. I thanked him but said I saw no point in coming to England, to discuss the 'Gove attitude contra STURP,' the tensions in Zurich,' or any other confrontations! We then talked pleasantly about other things.

It was quite obvious: 1) Gove had come to Trondheim determined to get the group to follow his lead; 2) Gove's lead was to <u>exclude</u> STURP as not being qualified and; 3) for some reason the other labs saw no reason to <u>disagree</u> with Gove. I did not experience any hostility from others, but no one was pro-STURP enough to argue for us!

I returned to the hotel, determined that Harry Gove would never again (or further) be involved in any STURP effort; he would 'sink or swim' without us!

Wednesday 6/26. Janice and I went to breakfast in the Hotel (Brittania). Gove and (female – wife?) were there. We sat down behind them. He accosted me at the buffet table and asked that we join them. After 'small talk' he said: "I guess you're <u>peeved</u> at me." I assured him 'peeved' was <u>not</u> the word! He chuckled and said "worse than that, eh?" I made no comment. Gove then dropped another 'bomb', he said: "Bob, I think you <u>misunderstood</u> me yesterday; I certainly feel that there is a place for STURP in our team. After all, you people have done a great deal of work for years! Janice and I almost fell off our chairs! I remarked that I was glad that "he felt there was a place for STURP in the C-14 work." I did not agree (or disagree) that he had been <u>misunderstood</u> on Tues; in fact, I told the lady with him (who had been present on Tuesday)—when Gove went for more coffee—that I thought any reasonable person would have come to the conclusion on Tuesday that STURP was being excluded. She nodded, smiling weakly.

Gove now brought up this Brit. Mus. Doing the sample distribution and holding the sample keys, doing the collation of data, etc. I agreed they were <u>qualified</u> but not the only ones who could do these things. He now said <u>my</u> proposal had recommended that Brit. Museum do it! I pulled out a copy of the proposal sent to Gove et al 2/14/84 and said 'read it again.' Harry, it says the Brit. Mus. Will do this for the <u>intercomparison tests,</u> not the Shroud tests! He looked it and admitted he had received this copy and that it did say as I had indicated!

We now talked face-to-face. He said exactly what place he NOW thought STURP should play in the future; I assured him <u>STURP thought</u> its place was exactly as stated in this proposal. Further, I emphasized, that unless changed by Board of STURP, this would remain our position <u>when we got the threads</u>! I also admitted, if our proposal was turned down by the Church, of course, we had no part to play. Gove then asked us to walk to the meetings with them and continue the discussion. We did so, during which Gove: (1) said a lot of his actions on Tuesday had been an effort to 'take a stand' within the C-14 group of fellow workers! (I gathered he meant, he wanted to appear "hard-nosed and in charge" to the C-14 community); (2) "many" in C-14 community were worried about the religious statements on the Shroud by STURP members; and (3) since it would take money for C-14 labs involvement (mostly travel), how were STURP's finances?!!!

I assured him: (1) I understood and said STURP had a "positioning," but that our position was one of cooperation and helpfulness <u>with</u> "your experts." (2) this was unfortunate and we had done our best to disassociate science from religion; and that we believed we could raise sufficient funds <u>when</u> we had permission and a date to do the work. This ended our talk except for general topics and reminiscing. I said I'd wait for his letter and send him my comments. He did not say again he would write one! We'll see!!

Later on Wed (6/26) morning I ran into Otlet and Jill Watson. I asked if they had seen Gove the night before-Bob said 'no.' I mentioned Gove's conciliatory (?) ** approach and Otlet again said he wouldn't involve himself with any of the politics, wherever they were. He began to "talk" and we sat for about an hour. He brought up:

(1) belief some were not "team" players and wanted only "personal glory"

(2) Press hounds people for news about Shroud. Eventually they get it

(3) impossible to keep info from "leaking" if investigators know which sample is which

(4) <u>must</u> have at least 3: 1) Shroud; 2) unknown; 3) another unknown—some want only 2:

1) Shroud; 2) known; Otlet opposes.

(5) Otlet doesn't want Brit. Mus. 1) Teddy Hall on Board of Trustees just doesn't look right to the public view

(6) should have another "counter" lab—3 each [?] AMS and counter – 1) suggests Geyh of Hanover, Germany

(7) data collation <u>must</u> be C-14 institution with statistical background capability, not just one or the other. PLUS NOT INVOLVED in the determination. We both agreed Minzer Stuiver of Washington would be superb BUT that an <u>international</u> flavor would be better (non-English speaking)

He suggested 1) Reidar Nydal Nos. In Tech, Tron
 2) K.O. Munnich Un. Of Heidelberg

He said it would be difficult to pick one suitable to every investigator: e.g. he had originally suggested St. Fleming and Teddy Hall had violently opposed. We agreed it would be tough, but didn't have to finalize until this material was "in manu (in hand!). We then broke up, agreeing our meeting was very good and profitable! Otlet lived up to (and I told him so) Gar Harbottle's statement to me that "Bob's a great guy; you'll enjoy him"!

Nothing more transpired: C-14 dating of Shroud. STURP's JOB: Get the material. He who has the "threads" calls the shots!

The previous diary was written 6/26-27/85 in auditorium, Nory. Inst. Tech Trondheim Norway

[Signed]
Robert H. Dinegar

[This parenthetical "?-sic" is Dinegar's]
**[This parenthetical "(?)" is Dinegar's]*

APPENDIX B

SHROUD SYMPOSIA

Year	City/Country	
1939	Turin, Italy	
1950	Turin, Italy	
1950	Rome, Italy	
1977	Albuquerque, NM, USA	
1977	London, England	
1978	Turin, Italy	
1978	Rome, Italy	
1981	New London, CT, USA	
1981	Bologna, Italy	
1984	Trani, Italy	
1986	Elizabethtown, PA, USA	
1986	Hong Kong	
1987	Sao Paolo, Brazil	
1987	Siracusa, Italy	
1987	Turin, Italy	
1989	Paris, France	
1989	Bologna, Italy	
1990	Cagliari, Italy	
1991	New York, NY, USA	
1991	St. Louis, Missouri, USA	
1993	San Antonio, Texas, USA	
1993	Rome, Italy	
1994	Mt. Angel, Oregon, USA	
1994	Evansville, Indiana, USA	
1994	Milan, Italy	
1994	Los Angeles, CA USA	
1995	Paris, France	
1996	San Marino, Italy	
1996	Esopus, New York	
1996	Rovigo, Italy	
1997	San Marino, Italy	
1997	Nice, France	
1998	Turin, Italy	
1998	Dallas, Texas, USA	
1999	Richmond, Virginia	
1999	Rome, Italy	Included other topics besides Shroud
2000	Orvieto, Italy	
2000	Turin, Italy	
2001	Dallas, Texas, USA	
2002	Paris, France	
2004	Poza Rica, Mexico	

2005	Dallas, Texas, USA	
2006	Argenteuil, France	
2006	Santiago, Chile	
2006	Lima, Peru	
2006	Poza Rica, Mexico	
2006	Turin, Italy	
2008	Columbus, Ohio, USA	
2008	Poza Rica, Mexico	
2008	Ciudad Nezahualcóyotl, Mexico	
2009	Mexico City, Mexico	
2010	Poza Rica, Mexico	
2010	Frascati, Italy	Included other topics besides Shroud http://www.acheiropoietos.info/
2010	Lima, Peru	
2011	Toruń, Poland	Included other topics besides Shroud
2011	Argenteuil, France	Included other topics besides Shroud
2011	Detroit, Michigan, USA	
2012	Valencia, Spain	

APPENDIX C

AUTHOR'S CORRESPONDENCE WITH DR. WALTER MCCRONE

From Joseph G. Marino's Collection of Personal Correspondences

Letter from McCrone to Author on 5 June 1990:

Dear Br. Marino:

I was pleased to receive a copy of your newsletter in which you quoted some of the material from the paper I wrote for American Laboratory. I have no objection to your quoting anything of mine that appears in print. I'm taking the liberty of sending you a reprint of a more recent paper on the Shroud which may give you some more material.

I might point out that inclusion of any information from me or mentioning my name in other than a derogatory sense may lose you some subscribers. Your mention of the Shroud conferences in New York and St. Louis this year and next are the first words I've seen on the subject. I will certainly not wait for an invitation to appear at those meetings since I only heard of the conference in Spain as well as the one in Paris last year after the fact and by accident. You have run a great risk in associating with this "pagan who blasphemes the Shroud by calling it a painting." I thought it only fair to warn you.

Yours sincerely,
[signed]
Walter C. McCrone

WCM:dag
Enc.

P.S. I had misplaced your address, so couldn't let you know that you had my permission to reproduce the 1989 ACS Newsletter. I, in fact, spent quite a bit of time trying to track you down; knowing only that you were O.P.S. [sic] in the U.S.A. I tried with a number of Catholic institutions either trying to track down Br. Joseph Marino (which I did remember) or the fact that you published a newsletter. None of these efforts were successful. So, please accept my apologies for the delay.

Letter from McCrone to Author on 6 October 1990:

Dear Br. Joseph:

I appreciate receiving your newsletter "Sources for Informational Materials on the Shroud of Turin"; even though almost all of the material included is for the already fully convinced. I'm glad to have the opportunity to continue to read it.

I'm enclosing a reprint of my recent paper on the subject. I'm not by any means suggesting you reprint it or any of it but you might list it under "Recent Articles". Perhaps with the following parenthetical insertion: *the author will furnish copies of this reprint to anyone writing to him at* 2820 South Michigan Avenue, Chicago, IL 60616-3292. In consideration of the note accompanying your newsletter that the cost of production and mailing are becoming oppressive, I'm enclosing a small donation.

Yours sincerely,
[signed] Walter
Walter C. McCrone

WCM:dag
Enc.

Letter from McCrone to Author on 6 October 1990:

Dear Br. Joseph:

I am writing to say that I appreciate very much your sending me your Shroud Newsletter for the past several years. I hope that you will have an interesting and satisfying two years at the seminary.

You have done an excellent job of presenting a balanced picture of the various controversies surrounding the Shroud and in particular, you have done a nice job of presenting my side of the Shroud developments. I was particularly interested in your most recent newsletter with a copy of the paper presented by Rev. Dinegar in 1977 before the most recent scientific test in 1978. I was there at the time and remember a bit of what he said but it is very nice to have it all down in black and white to read over. I do think he went too far in suggesting that if the Shroud turned out to be too late to be associated with Calvary, that many people would lose their faith in the church itself. I see no reason why this should happen and I know for a fact that it hasn't happened with many scientists who have been convinced by my data and reinforced by the carbon-dating that the Shroud is medieval. It is still a beautiful representation of that important event. I have given a hundred or more talks on the Shroud since 1978—most of them presenting my data which proves the Shroud to be medieval. In all of those audiences, only two or three individuals have ever expressed doubt concerning my methods or my conclusion. Still, all of those that I have talked to assured me that finding the Shroud to be medieval had no effect on their faith in the church and all that represents. True, most of these audiences were scientific and I never expect non-scientists to understand the work that I did and the conclusions that I drew.

It does, still, surprise me that non-scientists, and particularly, those with long-standing and direct interests in the Shroud can ignore all of the scientific evidence which most scientists believe proves the Shroud to be medieval. I have, however, gotten used to the idea and am happy to sit back and read your newsletter and other sources that continue discussing the Shroud and future work on it as though it was beyond a doubt a first century relic. I am only disappointed that the absence of acceptance of my work and conclusions has prevented much of the scientific world from recognizing how powerful an analytical tool, the light microscope still is. If this had happened, my efforts to increase the use of the light microscope for the solution of important problems would have been much easier.

In any case, and although it is apparent that you are not convinced that I am right, you have been very kind to represent my views in your newsletter. I hope that Jim Fanning enjoys his new responsibility and that he is able to come close to your devotion to the subject. I am sending my subscription order in today. With best wishes.

Yours sincerely,
[signed]
Walter C. McCrone

WCM:dag

Enc.

Email from McCrone to Author on 4 April 1998:

Dear Father Joseph:

I appreciate your inclusion of my name on your e-mail list. I don't like everything I see there but it keeps me up-to-date and I do see signs of increasing acceptance of the Shroud as a medieval painting. As one example, the London Times of March 23 started one of their articles in the column titled "The Times Diary" with: "Despite overwhelming evidence of fakery, the Turin Shroud will not be allowed to rest in peace." It goes onto give a very negative review of Ian Wilson's new book "The Blood and the Shroud."

I would like to comment on your last message covering a news item covering the textile expert, Franco Testore's "New Research." He mentions Dimitry [sic] Konznetsov's [sic] criticism of the carbon-dating result to the effect that the heat of the 1532 Chambery fire changed the original first century date to the fourteenth century. I would like to point out that all of the samples for carbon-dating are, and always have been, burned to carbon-dioxide as one step in the purification step.

Dr. Testore also mentions that the medieval counterfeiter was clever enough to introduce Palestinian pollen on his medieval Shroud. I would note here that the set of 32 Shroud tapes I examined showed only a fraction of the number claimed by Max Frei on his set of equivalent Shroud tapes. Furthermore, Steve Shafersman showed conclusively that Max "forged" his data (see pp. 291-308 of "Judgement Day for the Turin Shroud" by that troublemaker McCrone).

    Sincerely,

    Walter C. McCrone
    McCrone Research Institute 2820 S. Michigan Ave.
    Chicago, IL 60616-3292

Appendix C 225

Email from Author to McCrone on 5 April 5 1998:

Dear Dr. McCrone,

I finally have a few minutes to respond to your remarks of April 1.

I'm not so sure that there is increasing acceptance of the Shroud as a medieval painting. Some people are still putting stock in the Picknett/Prince "Leonardo forged it" theory, some in Nicholas Allen's "medieval camera obscura," some in Kersten & Gruber's "myrrh and aloe paste" and some in Nickel's dauber method. All of those people are just as sure that they are right as you are about your theory.

I have not seen the *London Times* of March 23 article. I suspect Wilson's new book, which I have read and think is very balanced, got a negative review because he still thinks the Shroud is authentic and the reviewer, who obviously feels that it is clear that the Shroud is a fake, criticizes Wilson's work because of that view.

One thing seems clear to me: while critics of the Shroud may not agree on the method used to forge the Shroud, they all seem to have a non-appreciation of the complexity of the Shroud. It seems to me that if the Shroud really were a forgery, there would have been obvious indications in the 100 years of study of the cloth and in the over 250,000 hours that STURP put in to analyzing the data from 1978. Yet hundreds of scientists and researchers world-wide continue to believe that it is authentic. Not to mention thousands and thousands of Christians (and some Jews!). Just wishful thinking? I don't think so. The Shroud is not necessary for salvation—so why all the fuss. Perhaps it's the religious equivalent of Mt. Everest—because it is there—and yes, it will not be allowed to rest in peace because there are too many unanswered questions about it.

Regarding your comment about carbon dating samples having to be burned: I've always read that one of the cardinal rules about carbon dating is that the object should not be exposed to even smoke and soot, not to mention fire. Why would that always be said if it didn't matter because the sample is ultimately burned? I'm no scientist, so I don't know why there is the contradiction there.

Regarding Max Frei's work, he pressed harder into the cloth on his samples than STURP's pressure-sensitive applicator, so he picked up more material than STURP did. In regard to the "conclusive" evidence that Frei forged his data, Dr. Alan Whanger tells a different side of the story in an article that was published in *Shroud News* in 1996.

You seem to relish the role of being a "trouble-maker" as you referred to yourself. You'll always have proponents of your theory, just as the other critics will have their advocates. But if you think you're going to convince most people that the Shroud is a painting, you'll have plenty of self-inflicted trouble, because it just won't happen. I personally have had some religious experiences that also convince me that the Shroud is authentic. I accept that science doesn't accept those sorts of experiences as data, but there is still enough hard scientific data to warrant believing the Shroud is authentic.

Perhaps some day we will learn the truth about the Shroud. But to paraphrase a passage from the Acts of the Apostles: "If the Shroud is of human origin it will break up of its own accord; but if it does in fact come from God you will not only be unable to destroy it, but you might find yourselves fighting against God."

Sincerely,

Father Joseph Marino, O.S.B.

Email from McCrone to Author on 8 April 8 1998:

Dear Father Joseph:

Several years ago while you were doing your Newsletter, you mentioned you would be willing to consider "short articles that dispute the authenticity of the Shroud."

I have just done such an article and wonder if in lieu of your Newsletter you would be willing to send it to your e-mailing list. I've enclosed a copy to make your decision easier. Best wishes.

Sincerely,

Walter C. McCrone

Appendix C

The Painting Hypothesis
Walter C. McCrone
McCrone Research Institute
Chicago, IL

In 1980, I published the first of three papers covering work I had done on 32 sticky tape samples kindly taken for me by Ray Rogers of Los Alamos and STURP from the Shroud in October 1978. I reported: the image consists of yellow fibers and a pigment intentionally added. Later that same year, I reported our work now supports the two Bishops and it seems reasonable that the image now visible was painted on the cloth just before the first exhibition, about 1356. The third paper in 1981 confirmed the earlier results using scanning electron microscopy with its elemental analysis capability, an electron microprobe with its elemental analysis feature, the transmission electron microscope with its electron diffraction ability to identify crystalline compounds followed by X-ray diffraction, confirmation of the presence of hematite (a component of red ochre) and vermilion, another red pigment found only in the blood image areas. This paper totally confirmed the polarized light microscopy and my conclusion of the medieval painting hypothesis.

Since then, the 1988 carbon-dating by three top laboratories confirmed my, by then, 1355 date with their average 1325 date. My reasoning from the beginning had been the image is visible, it is therefore a chemical entity, perhaps biochemical. I should be able to identify that substance and draw a conclusion as to its source.

My approach was different from anyone else involved in Shroud research. I am a chemical microscopist trained at Cornell University over a 10-year period (B. Chem, Ph.D. in Chemical Microscopy and a 2-year post-Doc) applying those techniques to World War II problems. I then joined the Armour Research Foundation (now IITRI, the Illinois Institute of Technology Research Institute) where I built up a 25-scientist group doing microanalyses. After 12 years there, I decided to start my own company doing the same things. This company is still going strong solving chemical problems by microscopical techniques. I also started a school, the McCrone Research Institute, to teach chemical microscopy courses. Today, we teach about 1,000 students a year in nearly 100 intensive one-week courses. The subjects cover all areas of forensic problems, paintings authentication, asbestos identification, and other general small particle identification problems.

I have written 400 technical papers, chapters, articles for encyclopedias, and 15 books including <u>Judgement Day for the Turin Shroud</u>. I am an Honorary Fellow of the Royal Microscopical Society and the American Institute for the Conservation of Art Objects. I was Criminalist of the Year of the American Academy of Forensic Scientists in 1985, and have received 8-10 other awards. Were it not for the true believers working to discredit me, I could have expected to be elected to the American Academy of Sciences and received a few more awards and recognition. I have no trouble, however, understanding how almost anyone unfamiliar with my work would assume that at least a dozen authors of what reads (to non-scientists) like sound authenticity research would more likely be right than one lone microscopist in Chicago claiming the Shroud to be a painting. I have worked on more than 200 paintings during a 35-year period to identify the pigments and media, and to establish a date they were painted. I teach courses regularly at the Institute of Fine Arts of New York University, as well as Chemical Microscopy courses at Cornell University, University of Illinois, and Illinois Institute of Technology. In the past also, the Smithsonian Institution, Getty Institute, Courtauld Institute (London), etc. etc.

I justify this uncontrolled bragging to justify my position in Shroud research. The Shroud research fit perfectly my training and experience. I was chosen by Father Rinaldi in 1974 to study the Shroud. I proposed the sticky tape sampling of the Shroud, an established forensic technique I have used for nearly 60 years. The resulting samples were excellent. Each one of the 32 tapes held about 1,000 linen fibers from the Shroud. Eighteen of those tapes showed thousands of red pigment particles adhering to the fibers; all 18 were from image areas. Of these 18, at least 7 are definitely from blood-image areas and show vermilion. The remaining 14 tapes were all from non-image areas and showed no paint.

Elemental mapping proved conclusively that the Shroud blood-image areas were painted twice. The entire image was first painted with the red ochre paint and the appropriate spots were then enhanced with blood-red vermilion. All image areas showed the presence of gelatin, a popular paint medium in the Middle Ages. It was produced then from parchment scraps or directly from animal skins. No pigments or gelatin medium were found in the non-image areas.

I conclude with absolute confidence that:

1. The Shroud image is 100 per cent paint. There is no other colored matter in the image areas
2. There is no paint in non-image areas
3. There is NO blood on the Shroud, and
4. Any arguments to the contrary are totally wrong and specious.

Most of these specious arguments are ridiculous. Just a few of them:

1. Dozens of flowers (and all from Palestine!) on the Shroud
2. Biological materials (mold, bacteria, etc.) changed the carbon-date

Appendix C 229

from first to fourteenth century! That would require an amount of material that would have tripled the weight of the Shroud. The actual contamination of the Shroud is miniscule and especially after the heroic cleaning efforts before carbon-dating would have had no effect on the 1325 date.

3. Pollen on the Shroud from Palestine. I saw, on all 32 of my tapes, not more than 2-3 grains per tape. Max Frei, finding 54 different species of Near-East pollen, was guilty of wishful thinking and indulgence in fantasy. He and others felt justified in finding on the Shroud whatever should be there if it was authentic.

4. Others in 3 include those who profess to find blood on the Shroud. There is NO blood on the Shroud even though positive tests were obtained for known blood components and several scientists have typed the paint; its type AB.

5. The heat of the Chambery fire in 1532 changed the carbon-date 13 centuries to 1325 yet the carbon-dating procedure has always involved complete burning of the thoroughly cleaned sample to the gas, carbon dioxide.

I could continue with other similarly ridiculous authenticity arguments like the resurrection modified the date of the cloth or the image is due to the Kirlian effect. Frankly, I'm sick of reading books and hearing TV and radio programs ridiculing my work and extolling the conclusions of a group of non-scientific religious fanatics. I feel fortunate at times that they ignore my work (as unworthy of attention). A few such published comments follow:

1. McCrone's claims have been convincingly refuted in several STURP technical reports.
2. William Meacham in Usenet Newsgroup: alt. Turin-Shroud (1/14/98) says: Someone remarked to me that he didn't have time to argue about religion or debate with people who still think Joe Nickel [sic] or McCrone solved the mystery of the Shroud and he then added "Neither do I."
3. Its prominence, the painting source, as the main forgery theory is such that virtually all commentators expend great effort in disproving it. The notion has indeed been disproved so thoroughly and absolutely that it should be permanently buried.
4. Clearly, however, the cumulative effect is to place the painting hypothesis somewhat lower in credibility than notions of the Marlow authorship of Shakespeare's' plays or of Egyptian influence on the Mayas.
5. Attempts to interpret it as a painting (McCrone) are untenable . . . and need not be discussed further.

In one respect I should be in a very good position with respect to the authenticity argument. I do not have to argue against any of the preposterous arguments from the pro-authenticity crowd. If they say how could a medieval artist produce such an image, a negative, a perfect anatomical and scriptures-perfect rendition that is too faint to see in order to paint it? I can ignore all such pronouncements because I have proved that an artist did, in fact, produce the Shroud image—period. As much as I would liked have to find the Shroud to be authentic, it is not and the science supporting its medieval origin is too important for me not to defend it to the limit of my ability.

Email from Author to McCrone 8 April 1998:

Dear Dr. McCrone,

I'll be happy to send your paper out to my list. As it arrived to me with some computer language, I will have to do a little editing (I won't change any words!) to make it more readable. I should be able to get to it before Easter.

Sincerely,

Father Joseph Marino, O.S.B.

Email from McCrone to Author 9 April 1998 (Comments to Author's 5 April 1998 email):

Dear Father Joseph:

May I comment on your comments on my remarks? If yes, please read on. First off, I am not theorizing or hypothesizing with my views. I have studied very carefully thousands of actual linen fibers from the Shroud. I have observed directly the colored substances on thousands of the body and blood-image fibers. I used the instruments and techniques I have used for 60 years on a wide variety of samples from radioactive fallout particles and Leonardo's "Last Supper", to fibers that put Wayne Williams of the Atlanta murders of 28 young black males in prison for life as well as tissue from Martin Luther King Jr,'s neck wound to determine whether he was shot from behind or from the front. I have examined over 200 paintings attributed to old masters to determine their authenticity. This is done by identifying the pigments and media in those paintings to compare with the artist's known palette. I am well known in forensic circles, in air and water pollution areas, and in investigations of small particle contamination in all types of consumer products.

When I started microscopic study at 1000X magnification of the Shroud tapes, I saw immediately millions of red particles on the image tapes BUT they could not be blood—wrong color, wrong shape, wrong optical properties. They were a pigment I had seen in at least half of the paintings I've ever examined. After a few hours of patient study of many fibers from image and non-image areas I tried to warn STURP that we should be careful about what we said about the Shroud because I was finding paint and only in the image areas. Their immediate wholehearted rejection of my evidence made me spend a great deal of time over the next two years to test my conclusion which only resulted in proving beyond any doubt that the Shroud is an inspired medieval painting. I can now say there is no way anyone can prove the Shroud to be authentic. I tell you, Sir, the Shroud is a painting and eventually that conclusion will be accepted.

Everything I have read or heard from Ian Wilson, Max Frei, John Jackson, William Meacham, Alan Adler, Baima Bollone, Alan Whanger, Leoncio Garza-Valdez, et al., is contradicted by my findings. How can I explain how only I could be right and dozens of other "scientists" be wrong? Very simply, none of them are chemical microscopists, small particle microanalysts, nor have they studied the Shroud tapes against a background of familiarity with pigments, media and artist's paintings. If I am right, then all of their ideas are wrong and I am right.

I have no trouble convincing physical scientists that I am right. I lecture to at least 500 scientists a year and I have gotten only questions like: Why do we still hear about flowers on the Shroud, that the image is blood, that the carbon-dating is off because of biological contaminants on the cloth, that pollen from dozens of Near-East species of pollen on the Shroud, etc.? I have to answer that "they" want the Shroud to be real so badly they are blind to any evidence to the contrary and believe anything that could be true if the Shroud were authentic.

Your "cardinal rule" that objects for carbon-dating should not be exposed to smoke or soot is not correct. One popular object is charcoal from ancient hearths. I have carefully examined microscopically all 26 of Max Frei's tapes and I saw no more pollen on them than I did on my 32 STURP tapes. Max, himself, told me he saw only about one pollen grain per square centimeter of tape. There are additional reasons why Max was dealing in subterfuge. For example, many of his reported pollen sources were insect pollenated [sic] and would not be dispersed by the wind to reach the Shroud.

I do not relish the idea of being a "trouble-maker." I hate this situation. I have performed a straightforward application of time-tested scientific procedures, come to an obvious conclusion, and now find myself reviled, or often ignored. I do not like to see my favorite instrument and techniques maligned indirectly and I have to work many hours every week to try to hasten the day we can settle down and be grateful that my 1355 artist created such a fantastic image for us.

Interruption: I was just handed my morning e-mail including your message saying you would be happy to send my paper to your list. I thank you from the bottom of my heart and now feel I probably shouldn't send you what I've just written. Still, I probably will. I might add two other e-mail messages this morning along with yours help in my argument that the belief in the painting mechanism for the Shroud image is improving. One message from a Gerald Swica (unknown to me) says:

"Great Book!! <u>Judgement Day</u>."

"Dr. McCrone:

I must say I was quite impressed with your book. I have followed the shroud off and on for many years by reading whatever I could get my hands on in the local bookstores or from the popular press. Your book stands out as the best I've ever read on this subject.

For years I've been totally baffled by this object, but now I realize there are two shrouds. The first, the one you describe as a wonderful painting. And the second, a burial cloth created from belief. After watching Ian Wilson on CBS last night, I could see it in his eyes that the Shroud means the world to him."

The second message from Paul McDermott (also unknown to me) reads:

"Dr. McCrone,

I would like to thank you and your colleagues for your much-needed research. Religion needs to accept that science has a better toehold on the world, because it works! No wonder the pious (or is that the insecure?) are so disturbed by your work, even to the point of censoring it on the Web as you recount!"

Finally, I take to heart your reference to Acts of the Apostles 5:38-39 but I am fully at ease with my conclusion with no thought that I am "fighting against God" or that my work will "come to naught." I thank you for taking the time to comment on my remarks.

Sincerely,
Walter C. McCrone
McCrone Research Institute

WCM:dag

Appendix C

Email from Author to McCrone on 10 April 1998 (response to his email above):

Dear Dr. McCrone,

Some comments on your comments of my comments on your remarks:

Although you have studied sticky-tape samples of the Shroud, that carries considerably less weight than the fact that STURP examined the cloth directly. I think it is similar trying to make a diagnosis on a patient based only on the X-rays, without actually having seen the patient. In some cases, it might not be possible to examine anything more than sticky-tape-sample-type-evidence, but it in the case of the Shroud, that is not so. It is the most studied artifact in human history, and there has been ample opportunity for people to discover whether it is a painting or not.

You mentioned someone's comment that they could see in Wilson's eyes that the Shroud means the world to him. Does this mean that anyone who has a passionate opinion about something should be dismissed, simply because they have passion? Don't you have a certain amount of passion in your stance? Obviously, no one is totally objective. We all have pre-conceptions, biases, and world views that we operate under. We have to try to limit their influence. I think it's significant that a lot of people who do think the Shroud is authentic started out believing and/or tried to show that it was not authentic. I would think that there are many more of those than people who started out thinking it was authentic and then later came to believe it not authentic.

I find it hard to believe that chemical microscopy is so powerful that it can outweigh dozens of other disciplines put together. You said that none of the other scientists are chemical microscopists. CBS, on a program last year, interviewed a microscopist named Dr. John Brown, I believe, who disagreed with your findings. And not only have I seen scientists question your Shroud findings, but there have been questions about the Vinland Map research and your recent work on a Rembrandt. And no matter how much wishful thinking you think may be out there, I find it difficult to believe that so many intelligent people, including many non-religious people, over the course of so many years, can believe that the cloth is authentic unless there was a good basis for it. Your good friend, Ray Rogers, thought STURP would go in there and prove the Shroud a forgery in 30 minutes. Didn't happen. You referred to STURP in your painting article that I just sent out as a "group of non-scientific religious fanatics." There were very few devout believers in that group, which included Jews like Adler, who would have nothing to gain by saying the Shroud was authentic. And a lot of those scientists worked on our country's nuclear and space programs. So how can you call them "non-scientific?"

How many of the scientists that you have convinced that you are right know very much about the Shroud? I would guess that most of them know very little. Most scientists who think the Shroud is authentic have read a great deal and know a great deal about it; apart from you and a 1 or 2 other critics, most people who think the Shroud is a forgery know very little about it. If you were right, I would have to believe that a significant number of reputable and knowledgeable sindonologists would have accepted your findings by now.

As I have said, I'm no scientist. I take on faith a lot of what I hear from scientists. I had read on a number of occasions that C-14 samples should not be exposed to smoke or soot. Your contention that it doesn't matter is the 1st I've ever heard. I know Max Frei has his supporters, which included long-time researcher Jesuit Father Werner Bulst and others. Apart from critics of the Shroud authenticity, I have never heard anyone question Frei's integrity.

In your last email, you made no reference to my alluding to various religious experiences I've had, which is part of the reason I believe the Shroud is authentic. As I said, science cannot really make an airtight judgment on those types of experiences, even though sometimes it tries. I've had quite a number of these experiences. Naturally, from my point of view, they count for a lot. These experiences (and others have had them as well) could well play a crucial role in determining the authenticity of the Shroud. The fact that you did not say anything about that and the fact that you feel that STURP was a group of non-scientific religious fanatics suggests to me (and admittedly, I'm no psychologist, either) that you have some unresolved religious issues tied up with your stance.

When I cited the quote from Acts, I should have changed the word "destroy" to "debunk." Not doing so made it sound harsher. It was also a way for me to emphasize my own strong belief, based on my overall connections with the Shroud, especially my religious experiences, that God's wisdom can confound the best of human wisdom, which includes at times a certain amount of hubris in science. And hubris being what it is, it boggles the mind that if an artist produced the Shroud, he wouldn't have taken credit for it and his name has not come down to us.

John Jackson examined the cloth directly, and as I recall, he said that even under magnification, he could not tell the difference between the Shroud image and the scorched area from the fire. This correlates with their conclusion that the image is caused by the dehydration of the fibers. And since the image is so faint, it has been said that an artist would have needed a 6 ft. brush just to maintain his perspective. Isabel Piczek is an internationally renowned artist, and she cannot accept the idea that this was painted by an artist.

Sincerely,

Father Joseph Marino, O.S.B.

Email from McCrone to Author 13 April 1998 (response to Author's email above):

Dear Father Joseph:

I'm sorry to do this to you. It's not going to change your mind and you will be troubled that I continue to be a loose cannon rolling around. To me, however, I feel I have to try to right a great wrong. The Shroud is a beautiful image. Recognizing it as a painting doesn't affect my faith and I'm sure wouldn't affect yours either. It is very important to me to see that good science is not discredited.

I was delighted to read your 4/10 comments. You have brought up the questions about me and my work that I need to hear. I welcome the opportunity to have an intelligent discussion of the issues. I'll follow the order you followed.

First, I don't believe the question of the Shroud's authenticity could have been solved without the microscope. Our lab has essentially all of the scientific tools (valued at $2-$3 million dollars) for determining the composition of any substance. We have and use all of the analytical instruments and techniques used by the STURP scientists. But land the other 40 or more scientists in our laboratories always start with the polarized light microscope (PLM value $3,000) and we nearly always solve the problem with that simple instrument. We use the other instruments only to confirm specific parts of our conclusions and to impress our clients. The main function of PLM is, I think, easy to describe. It simply makes visible to us objects too small to see with the unaided eye. Neither you or I have any trouble recognizing thousands of objects at sight. Some may be big like Niagara Falls or the Eiffel Tower or small like a penny, a paper clip, the letter D, etc., etc. Our eyes are, by far, the most important analytical tool we have and we use it continuously during our awake time. PLM then simply extends this innate capability to objects too tiny to see otherwise.

Imagine, for a moment, trying to identify someone you are meeting at LaGuardia getting off a 747 and you have only a description — a middle-aged man 5 ft. 10 in., brown hair, blue eyes, Caucasian, etc. I think anyone would have a problem but if you have a photograph of the man you would be able to pick out the right person at once with confidence. If you are waiting there for someone you know well, you don't need a picture. It's already in your mind. A microscopist looking through the microscope is in exactly the same situation. He sees a tiny particle he recognizes as an old friend or he doesn't recognize it and he has to compare it with pictures of possible substances. Either way, he knows for sure that he knows what it is or he knows for sure that he doesn't know. Although this simple approach works better and better as one gains experience, it doesn't demonstrate the full power of PLM. We look at objects normally by reflected light and we see size, shape, and color but that's it. Microscopically, we see it is a uniform mixture of rounded particles closely similar in size and shape. We also see that part of most of the red ochre particles is crystalline with different refractive indices in different directions. Most of the particles are partly or wholly non-crystalline but with extremely high refractive indices. Only one substance in a million would have these properties but we are already sure it is red ochre, an artist's pigment. This took 120 seconds. There is no other instrument that would identify red ochre particles as such. Even the electron microscopes would not do so. No other instruments used by STURP or any other scientists working on the Shroud would be able to identify red ochre as such. This identification is much more difficult when you see only individual particles well dispersed on the surface of the linen fibers yet PLM does it in 120 seconds.

STURP was severely limited in their Turin examination in 1978 because the instruments were not as sensitive as those in a proper laboratory. They did not even detect any iron in the body-image. They thought they detected blood in blood-image areas because they found iron there; but if it was blood they should have found, along with iron, even more sodium, potassium chlorine, and sulfur but these they found were absent (Figures 65 and 66 in "Judgement Day for the Turin Shroud." They also used infrared-absorption spectra (Figure 67) but the result for the Shroud "blood" was very different from that for real blood.

PLM is a direct approach and it quickly solves problems like the Shroud. Those tapes were invaluable to me. I hope that Cardinal Saldarini is successful in his appeal for all Shroud samples be returned to him. Ray Rogers. Alan Adler, and other STURP members may still have some of the STURP tapes and Alan Whanger has all of the 1978 Frei tapes. If they can be recovered, it would make unnecessary any further tests on the Shroud itself. If they were re-examined by a good materials science microscopist, my work and conclusions would be readily confirmed. I can't help mentioning that the 1973 Italian Commission did a pretty good job. They found my pigment; they called them encrustations on the fibers and showed they were not blood. They did not go further to identify the encrustations but several of them did conclude the Shroud is a painting.

I must emphasize that I am the only microscopist to have studied the tapes and the only one trained to identify the Shroud paints, red ochre and gelatin, followed by vermilion and gelatin. Without microscopy, there is no way anyone could see that the Shroud body-image was painted first with red ochre and then a second vermilion paint was used to enhance the blood-images. I, on the other hand, am 100 per cent certain of this; make that 1000 per cent.

Email from Author to McCrone 19 April 1998 (Response to email above):

Dear Dr. McCrone,

Since this is the Easter season, I think it's appropriate to use an Easter analogy to say something about my stance on the Shroud. If Mary Magdalene and other disciples went to a psychiatrist and said that they had seen a dead man after he had risen from the dead, the psychiatrist would likely have explained that dead men do not rise from the dead and that they would have to attribute their experiences to some other explanation, e.g., someone stole the body. One would hardly blame the psychiatrist for telling them this. But their experiences are so strong, they maintain that they happened and continue, despite the unbelievable nature of the claims, to preach the story as fact. And the explanations that other people gave, e.g., someone stole the body, sounds plausible enough, but left some questions unanswered, like, why were the grave clothes left neatly behind if someone stole the body? Not only the experiences themselves, but all of their previous interaction with Jesus, enables them to believe that he really did rise from the dead.

When I first heard the claims about the Shroud, I was open to the idea of it being a forgery, because that's the most likely and plausible explanation. But as I read more and more about it, the evidence suggested to me that it was authentic. Along the way, I had some profound religious experiences that also indicated to me that the Shroud was authentic. Your saying that the Shroud is a painting is a seemingly plausible explanation, but it just doesn't fit with my own experiences. And it doesn't answer all the questions. For example, since the "blood" apparently went on 1st, since when the blood is abraded away, the cloth is white underneath, which means that the blood went on before the image. Now what artist would paint "blood" and then put the wounds on after the blood?

Speaking of questions and answers, I'm reminded of the question I asked you at the Elizabethtown Conference in 1986. I asked you how your supposed artist was able to incorporate details that were only able to be discerned several hundred years later after the invention of the microscope. Your answer to me was, "I'm not going to answer that—he just did it." Quite frankly, that was no answer at all, much less a substantive scientific answer. It's like when a child asks him parents why he can't do something and is told, "Just because."

In your comments of 4/13, you did not address most of the individual points I raised in my email of 4/10. You just continue to maintain that you are right and everyone else is wrong. Although you compliment the 1973 Italian Commission, you are probably the 1st one I've ever heard to do so. Everyone else I've heard critique them say that their science was not very good. Now, Adler is an expert on blood and he and Heller performed 13 different tests that indicated blood. And you just dismiss them (not specifically in yours of April 13 but in general). And you didn't comment about Isabel Piczek, who is an internationally renowned artist who says the Shroud could not have done by an artist. You didn't comment on Jackson's claim that the image is very similar to the scorch area of the fire. You didn't comment on the fact that CBS interviewed a microscopist who disagrees with your findings. And you didn't directly comment on the issue of religious experiences related to the Shroud. If I was the only one still advocating authenticity of the Shroud, it would be a whole different story. But there are still hundreds and hundreds of intelligent scientists and researchers and thousands and thousands of Christians who continue to believe it's authentic despite your supposedly airtight evidence. As they said in the ABC evening news broadcast on the Shroud on April 6, "science is a journey to truth, and we have not reached the truth." But you believe that good science can only be identified with your work. Obviously, a lot of people disagree with you.

Sincerely,

Father Joseph

Email from McCrone to Author on 19 April 1998 (Response to Author's email of 19 April):

Dear Father Joseph:

I will give you my last and final comments. I am not at all happy taking time on an exercise in futility. You say since the "blood" went on first; this is not so. The body-image was first so that the artist knew where to put the blood-image. There is NO doubt about that. The paint in the blood-image area shows separate applications of red ochre and vermilion. I can't say which was first by this observation but common sense says the body-image has to be first for an artist to put the "blood" in the right places.

If I had tried to answer your Elizabethtown question, I would have said:

"I do not know of any details known today that were unknown in 1355. The artist did a good job of reading the scriptures, looking at earlier artist's representations of Christ and the crucifixion, and thinking about how to portray Christ's body with all known details on a shroud. The idea of painting the locations where the cloth would touch the body (contact-points and not painting the non-contacting parts of the body; but shading artistically from the contact-points he registered the cloth-body distance effect that yielded a beautiful image).

I did not address many of the points you raised on behalf of Heller and Adler, Piczek, and Jackson because they are meaningless. They represent the will-of-the-wisps they have concocted to rationalize their belief in an authentic Shroud. All of them and Meacham, Frei, Whanger, Garza-Valdes, Wilson, etc., are "red herrings." They cannot be right because the Shroud is a straightforward artist's painting, no more, no less. It is 100 per cent red ochre, vermilion, and a gelatin base there is no blood on the Shroud. Most of the arguments of these people are based on no known facts but come from their imagination. The observations seemingly based on factual observations (Bollone's typing of my paint, Garza-Valdes biological contamination, Frei's pollen, Adler's positive tests for blood, etc., are either imagination or due to incompetence or deceit; Adler and Frei fall in that category. I could comment on each in detail but what good would it do? Jackson, for example, can't see any difference between scorched fibers and image. He sees what he wants to see. Any of the kids in my Saturday classes on microscopy for junior high school courses would have no trouble with that question.

There are millions of people who want the Shroud to be authentic. They have nothing to go on but dozens of apparent experts who support that view and who reassure them they don't have to worry about McCrone. I wouldn't hesitate to swear with my hand on the bible that the "Shroud" is a medieval painting and there is no blood on the Shroud. I'm not asking for any answer to this.

[no closing]

Letter from McCrone to Author on 20 October 1999 (with reference to copy of his Shroud book):

Dear Joseph:

I have made the corrections and changes in your copy of the Prometheus edition. I have enclosed a copy of a letter I recently received concerning one of the finest honors a chemists [sic] can receive. I will add that this scientific Society of 160,000 members (of which I've been a member for 58 years) would not have voted this honor for me if they thought I was wrong on the Shroud of Turin. This was emphasized in the letters they received from the nominators suggesting this presentation.

While I am bragging I may as well mention that I have also been awarded Honorary memberships in the Royal Microscopical Society (1990) and in the American Institute for Conservation of Artistic and Historic Works. (1993).

Best Wishes,
[signed]
Walter C. McCrone

WCM:aj
Encs.

Email from Author to McCrone on 7 December 1999:

Dear Dr. McCrone,

Just saw your new article on "A Protocol for Authentication of Paintings" in the new *Microscope*. Do you have any objections to me sending a copy of it to my email list?

I'm curious about the "37" at the end of the sentence on page 137: "A pretty complete coverage of what was then Harrington's 12-year authentification effort has been published." (You only list 3 references.)

Thanks,

Joe Marino

Email from McCrone to Author on 8 December 1999 (in response to Author's email of 7 December):

Joe Marino:

I am impressed by the breadth and depth of your peripheral Shroud interests. I am also flattered that you would wish to send a copy of the Protocol paper to your e-mail list. I'm sure they will be less interested than you are. I am sending by snail-mail other papers of possible interest as well as the reprints referenced in the Protocol paper including number 37—a typo—actually number 3.

You might be amused that, in the two dozen or so lectures on paintings that I give each year, I always remark near the end that my reputation is obviously overestimated because in one case (the Shroud) I haven't even been able to convince the world that it is a painting.

Best Wishes,

Walter

[This was the last correspondence I received from McCrone, who died in 2002.]

APPENDIX D

TURIN WORKSHOP ON RADIOCARBON DATING OF THE TURIN SHROUD—29 SEPTEMBER through 1 OCTOBER 1986 AND RELATED DOCUMENTS

Opening Address by Anastasio Cardinal Ballestrero, Archbishop of Turin

While warmly welcoming all of you in the city of the Shroud, I wish to begin by thanking you for your participation in this meeting. A very particular thanks I owe to Prof. Carlos Chagas, President of the Pontifical Academy of Sciences, for the care and competence he devoted to prepare the meeting.

I do not think it useless to point out a few data that are at the basis of this meeting.

Already at the time of the last Exhibition of the Shroud several investigating groups and scientists from all parts of the world had expressed the wish that a Carbon 14 test be made on the Shroud to date the Cloth. Authorization was then asked of, and obtained from, Umberto di Savoia, who died a short time later leaving the precious Shroud Cloth the property of the Holy Father John Paul II. Upon my repeated requests the Holy Father eventually approved that this Carbon 14 test be made, and also upon my person request, after having appointed me Pontifical Custodian for the conservation and the veneration of the Shroud, the Pope involved the Pontifical Academy of Sciences as scientific consultant.

Prof. Luigi Gonella, of the Turin Polytechnic, scientific and technical consultant of Turin Bishopric since the time of the last Exhibition of the Shroud, is here present not only for his specific scientific competence but also as my personal assistant for what concerns the responsibility bestowed upon me as Pontifical Custodian of the Shroud.

It seems to me worthwhile to state that this research, desired by the Church to be of a purely scientific character aimed at dating the Shroud cloth, does not mean, nor could it, address any issue of faith related to the death and resurrection of Jesus Christ.

It is my hope that the works of this meeting will proceed not only with the competence that may be expected by a gathering of such eminent specialists, but also with a capacity and willingness for comparison and integration as befitting to the method of Science in our times.

As my specific competence is not in the field appropriate to an active participation in the forthcoming discussions, I shall not take part in your talks, leaving to my assistant, Prof. Gonella, the task of liaison with me.

I hope that these days of study will bring out such conclusions to allow presenting a valid and acceptable project for at last carrying out the radiocarbon dating of the Shroud cloth, a test that, owing to the uniqueness and singular character of the object, certainly could not be easily repeated.

The project coming out of this meeting, including concrete operative proposals, will be submitted to the Higher Authority of the Holy See, as it is explicitly requested in the letter sent to me on Sept. 24 by the Secretary of State "... the proposals and observations that will emerge in the discussion will have to be submitted to the Higher Authority".

And as a final thought, at this point, it is only left to me to wish you all a serene and fruitful work.

LIST OF PARTICIPANTS

1. Prof. Carlos CHAGAS, President, PONTIFICAL ACADEMY OF SCIENCES, VATICAN CITY

2. Prof. Alan D. ADLER, CHEMISTRY DEPARTMENT, Western Connecticut State University

3. Mrs. Shirley L. BRIGNALL, DEPARTMENT OF PHYSICS AND ASTRONOMY, The University of Rochester

4. Prof. Vittorio CANUTO, N.A.S.A.

5. Prof. Paul E. DAMON, DEPARTMENT OF GEOSCIENCES, The University of Arizona

6. Msgr. Don Renato DARDOZZI, Co-Director, PONTIFICAL ACADEMY OF SCIENCES

7. Dr. Robert H. Dinegar, LOS ALAMOS NATIONAL LABORATORY

8. Prof. D.J. DONAHUE, DEPARTMENT OF PHYSICS, The University of Arizona

9. Prof. Jean-Claude DUPLESSY, Directeur, CENTRE DES FAIBLES RADIOACTIVITES Laboratoire mixte CNRS_CEA

10. Dr. Jacques EVIN, LABORATOIRE DE RADICARBONE, Universite Claude Bernard Lyon

11. Dr. Mechthild FLURY-LEMBERG, Head, TEXTILE WORKSHOP, ABEGG-STIFTUNG (Switzerland)

12. Prof. Luigi GONELLA, DIPARTIMENTO DI FISICA, Politecnico di Torino

13. Dr. Harry E. GOVE, DEPARTMENT OF PHYSICS AND ASTRONOMY, The University of Rochester

14. Prof. E. Teddy HALL, RESEARCH LABORATORY FOR ARCHAEOLOGY AND THE HISTORY OF ART, Oxford University

15. Prof. Garman HARBOTTLE, DEPARTMENT OF CHEMISTRY, Brookhaven National Laboratory

16. Dr. Robert E.M. HEDGES, Director, RADIOCARBON ACCELERATOR UNIT, Oxford University

17. Dr. Steve LUKASIK, J.P. GETTY CONSERVATION INST.

18. Prof. William MEACHAM, CENTRE OF ASIAN STUDIES, HONG KONG

19. Prof. Robert L. OTLET, ISOTOPE MEASUREMENTS LABORATORY, Harwell Laboratory (United Kingdom)

20. Rev. Enrico di ROVASENDA, Director PONTIFICAL ACADEMY OF SCIENCES, VATICAN CITY

21. Prof. M.S. TITE, RESEARCH LABORATORY, The British Museum

22. Prof. Dr. Willy WOLFLI, INSTITUT FUR MITTELENERGIEPHYSIK, (Zurich, Switzerland)

CONCLUSIONS AND PROCEDURAL STEPS

The Turin Workshop on "Radiocarbon Dating of the Turin Shroud" was held from 29 September to 1 October, 1986. Twenty-two persons, representing the Archbishop of Turin, the Pontifical Academy of Sciences, and laboratories in France, Hong-Kong, Italy Switzerland, the United Kingdom and the USA, participated in the workshop. After two and one-half days of technical discussions, carried out in a spirit of amity, the following conclusions and procedural steps were agreed upon.

1. This is the time for radiocarbon dating of the Shroud of Turin.

2. A minimum amount of cloth will be removed, which is sufficient (a) to ensure a result that is scientifically rigorous and (b) to maximize the credibility of the enterprise to the public. For these reasons, the decision was made that seven laboratories will carry out the experiment: five accelerator-mass spectrometer laboratories and two small-counter laboratories.

3. The samples should be taken from an unobtrusive part of the Shroud, and from a portion which is not likely to yield other useful information. The samples should not include charred material. They should be prepared in a form, not too small, so as to allow reasonable pretreatment processes. In addition to the Shroud samples, the British Museum will also prepare and provide two control samples for each laboratory.

4. For logistic reasons, samples for radiocarbon dating will be taken from Shroud immediately prior to a series of other experiments planned by other groups. Selection of the material to be removed and the actual removal will be the responsibility of Mrs. Flury-Lemberg (Abegg-Stiftung, Bern, Switzerland).

5. Seven samples containing a total of 50 milligrams of carbon will be taken from the Shroud. In addition, a single dummy sample will be

prepared by the British Museum. These Shroud samples and the dummy sample will be distributed to the seven laboratories in such a way as to ensure that the seven laboratories are not aware of the identification of their individual sample. This distribution will be the responsibility of the following three certifying institutions: the Pontifical Academy of Sciences (Professor C. Chagas), the British Museum (Dr. M. S. Tite) and the Archbishopric of Turin (Professor L. Gonella).

6. The taking of the samples will be done so that representatives from the seven laboratories will have complete knowledge of the process. Samples will be delivered by the three certifying institutions (See 5 above) directly and immediately to the representatives of the seven laboratories who will thereafter be responsible for the samples.

7. At this time, a date will be chosen for submission of experimental results from the seven laboratories to the following three analyzing institutions: the Pontifical Academy of Sciences, the British Museum, and the Metrological Institute of Turin, "G. Colonnetti". These institutions will keep the results in sealed envelopes until an agreed upon date, at which time they will be opened for statistical analysis.

8. After the analysis of the experimental results by the three analyzing institutions, a meeting will be held in Turin between the three analyzing institutions and representatives of the seven laboratories to discuss the results of the statistical analysis with the objective of deciding the final result of the measurement program.

9. The radiocarbon groups will, through correspondence, establish a common format for presenting the experimental results to the analyzing institutions.

10. The cost of the experiments and the analyses will be borne by the participating institutions. Travel and living expenses entailed will be provided by the Pontifical Academy of Sciences unless other arrangements are made .

11. Samples from the Shroud will be taken by May, 1987. It is hoped that the final result will be available by Easter of 1988. This final result will be published in an appropriate scientific journal as a collaborative paper.

(Note: After the Conclusions and Procedural Steps document was published, the representatives read a statement by Professor Luigi Gonella published in the Turin newspaper La Stampa on April 27, 1987 that only two or three labs would used instead of seven. In a letter of July 1, 1987 to Cardinal Ballestrero from the representatives of the seven labs initially considered for performing the C-14 test, the concern was expressed that doing so would jeopardize the reasonable certainty of the test results. Cardinal Ballestrero responded in the following letter.)

October 10, 1987

To all participants
in the Turin Workshop on the radiocarbon dating of the Shroud of Turin

Dear Sirs,

At the end of May I received positive instructions from the Holy See, personally signed by the Cardinal Secretary of State, on how to proceed to the radiocarbon dating of the Shroud of Turin.

The instructions agree to the main line of the proposal put forward at the Turin Workshop of last year, but do not accept a few items. In particular, they direct that no more than three samples be taken, to be used for measurement by different laboratories. As for the measurement, the instructions agree to the suggested procedure, i.e. to use the method of blind testing with control samples, to apply to the competence of the Shroud samples, and to entrust to the competence of the same British Museum and of the Institute of Metrology "G. Colonnetti" the statistical analysis of the measurement results.

As a consequence, in the first place I wish to express my thanks to all who participated in the Turin Workshop with generous availability, even though I find myself unable to take advantage of the competence of all participants, as it was in the wishes of the meeting.

The choice of the three Laboratories among the seven which offered their services was made, after long deliberation and careful consultations, on a criterion of internationality and consideration for the specific experience in the field of archaeological radiocarbon dating, taking also into account the required sample size. On this criterion the following Laboratories are selected:

    Radiocarbon Laboratory, University of Arizona
    Research Laboratory for Archaeology, Oxford University
    Radiocarbon Laboratory, ETH, Zurich

The operations for taking the samples have to be presided by myself, in my capacity as Pontifical Custodian of the Shroud. H.E. Professor Carlos Chagas, President of the Pontifical Academy of Sciences, will be invited to be present at the operation, as well as at the eventual final meeting, as my personal guest, in consideration of the collaboration he gave in working out the project. The instructions from the Holy See do not deem it necessary for representatives of the measurement Laboratories to attend the sample-taking operations.

The decisions took more time to be worked out than originally wished, owing to the situation without precedents created by a number of competing offers tied into a rather rigid proposal, and also by initiatives of some participants in the Workshop who stepped out of the radiocarbon field to oppose research proposals in other fields, with implications on the freedom of research of other scientists and on our own research programs for the Shroud conservation that asked for thorough deliberations.

Besides, when the competent Authorities advised me they deemed we ought to proceed with three samples, a concerted initiative was taken to counter the decision, with the outcome of a telegram sent to H.E. the Cardinal Secretary of State and myself by some participants in the Workshop, a telegram where the meaning of my introductory words at the Workshop was heavily misinterpreted.

After further deliberation and scrutiny of the situation with the Cardinal Secretary of State we are now proceeding on the already decided terms, that I was just going to write you when I received the above quoted telegram.

In consideration of the great attention from the public and the press that all of us know this measurement is attracting, it seems to me worthwhile to stress again what I said in my opening address at the Turin Workshop, about the purely scientific character of this enterprise, which does not mean to, nor could, address any issue of faith related to the death and resurrection of Jesus Christ. Nor do I mean with this analysis to charge the Laboratories that have been selected with the task of "authenticating" the Shroud of Turin: the analysis is strictly meant to ascertain the radiocarbon date of its cloth, as an objective datum to the scientific quest that has long been growing on the illustrious image entrusted to my stewardship.

[signed]
Anastasio Card. Ballestrero
Archbishop of Turin
Pontifical Custodian of the Shroud of Turin

APPENDIX E

LETTER FROM ARCHAEOLOGIST PAUL MALONEY TO FATHER PETER RINALDI

(Note: The following letter, addressed to Father Peter M. Rinaldi, SDB, is printed beneath a letterhead reading "The ASSIST Investigations Group: A Division of the Association of Scientists and Scholars International for the Shroud of Turin, Ltd.," whose president is Dr. Frederick T. Zugibe, Ph.D., M.D., Chief Medical Examiner of Rockland County, NY. This is published herewith by kind permission of Paul C. Maloney, General Projects Director, ASSIST.)

The setting for the contents appearing in this letter was in preparation for a special meeting by Prof. Maloney with the Science Advisor to His Eminence, Anastasio Cardinal Ballestrero, Archbishop of Turin, Prof. Luigi Gonella, held at the Ryetown Hilton Hotel, Ryetown, New York on November 21, 1987 some 5 months prior to the actual taking of the sample that would be used to radiocarbon date the Shroud of Turin. Prof. Maloney was providing Father Rinaldi a summary of his research in advance of the meeting. Father Rinaldi, Rector of Corpus Christi Church, Port Chester, NY, was official emissary for ASSIST to the Turin Archdiocese where Cardinal Ballestrero was, at that time, custodian of the Turin Shroud.)

Nov. 16, 1987

Rev. Peter M. Rinaldi, S.D.B.　　Office of General Projects Director
Corpus Christi Church　　　　　　Box 334
136 South Regent Street　　　　　Quakertown, PA 18951
Port Chester
New York 10573

Dear Father Peter,
　　During our conversation last week I mentioned to you some of the

possible objections the scientific community might raise if the planning for the carbon dating moves in the direction of only one or two samples as now appears to be the case. I had reflected a conversation I had had several years ago with Dr .Stewart Fleming, Director of MASCA (Museum Applied Science Center for Archaeology) at the University Museum of the University of Pennsylvania. You will recall that you requested me to set these comments in a letter.

I drafted a preliminary copy of this letter after discussing it at length with Dr. Fleming last week and sent it to him. I have just discussed this draft with him by phone this morning and now want to get this to you immediately so that you'll have it before Prof. Gonella arrives from Turin this week.

Given the current state of development of AMS (Accelerator Mass Spectrometry) Dr. Fleming would agree that the original protocol for carbon dating the Shroud is the best one—i.e. that two small proportional counters and five accelerators be involved in the testing; that all these labs each receive one or more samples from the Shroud; and that blind samples be included for each of these labs. When completed we would have at least 7 dates of material from the Shroud. The average from these results would be a sounder base than those resulting from any other alternative proposed to date, which, as you know, would comprise fewer labs, drop the use of the small proportional counter, or reduce the number of samples removed from the Shroud to one or two.

There are good reasons why the original protocol is best. First, Dr. Fleming points out that all labs have worked with "Rogue samples". These are samples which deviate wildly from the expected date. Dr. Fleming referred to a case where the date produced from the shell of a hazel nut was drastically different from material from the same tree! He suspected that perhaps one in ten samples handled by laboratories were "Rogue samples"! In fact this could easily be checked out if one were to go to the published data on carbon dates (in *RADIOCARBON*, for example) and check on the actual material dated by the very labs which will be a part of the protocol—Brookhaven, Harwell, Lyon, Oxford, Rochester, Tucson, and Zurich—to discover how prevalent this is. Who is to say that the Shroud will not have such rogue samples? So many factors may be at work here: methods of handling the cloth in ancient times, extraneous sources of contamination throughout its history, and the lack of complete knowledge about whether or not or how these various factors will affect the date which is finally derived. The greater the number of labs, the greater the variation in technique (i.e. both small proportional counter and AMS), and the greater the number of samples, all contribute to a sounder base for drawing conclusions. In this light Harwell's request for eight samples is not at all out of line. In fact, Dr. Fleming says that any program should use 20 or more samples of all types of linen. He believes that if each lab received at least one sample from the

Shroud this should be acceptable if all labs—small proportional counter and AMS—are involved as planned in the original protocol.

A second line of reasoning is this: Dr. Fleming is not certain that linen has been adequately tested using AMS—it may require a special chemistry. By this I interpret that the existing data base for linen in general is not enough to provide a proper evaluation of the results from testing the Shroud. Therefore, it would be important to do—as was originally suggested—tests on many different samples from many different types of areas on the Shroud. This would include material from beneath the patches where the Shroud has been burned. And in order to get enough of the non-burned material for the small proportional counter one could recommend removing linen from tile same area from which the "Raes Sample" was taken in 1973.

Dr. Erle Nelson, Director of the Simon Frazer University AMS laboratory, referred to a study done some years ago where the ratio of carbon 12 and 13 to carbon 14 was different than, say, that found in cotton. He suggested that if, as Bill Meacham claims, fractionation had drastically affected the linen in the burn areas, tests done by the same lab on samples taken from both burn and non-burn areas could identify this change. This would then provide a scientific accounting for any resulting deviation. In other words, the peculiar signature of the "normal" linen ratio would act as a check on the final results. This alone argues strongly for labs to be able to have more than only one sample from the Shroud to test. Science likes to account for whatever problems it encounters. This would put it in a better position to do so.

A third factor makes Dr. Fleming reluctant to see only AMS labs the sole testing agent for the Shroud. He pointed out that with the accelerator technique there is a lot of pre-testing chemistry. With each step in the process there is the possibility that extraneous contamination could be introduced. For example, as you will recall, the Zurich lab—so well known for being one of the best accelerator labs in the world—produced an outlier of 1000 years on one of the linen samples in the pilot test supervised by the British Museum. They later admitted that the sample was improperly prepared—another way of saying the outlier was a lab induced result.

Dr. Fleming pointed out that if only a few AMS labs are used and, say, only one of those labs dates a sample from the Shroud, how can the results be evaluated if a radical outlier is produced from the testing? Dr. Fleming's analogy was, "It's like playing Russian Roulette!" The fact that one of the best AMS labs in the world has already produced such an outlier ought to make us very cautious about the protocol currently being promoted. He noted that labs can always rationalize ways to account for their outliers but if it is after the fact it has already muddied the picture. Those who are scientifically oriented, those who are avowed skeptics, or even those who are committed to the view that the Shroud is probably 2000 years old, would be able to point out to such unclear results in support of their own case. In essence, nothing would have been accomplished by the carbon dating and, technically speaking, it would have to be done over again—<u>correctly</u>—in order to obtain results which could be properly evaluated. In the long run this would require <u>more</u> samples than would be the case if done properly now. But it might have a devastating psychological impact on any future carbon dating plans. It would therefore be better not to do any carbon dating at all than to do the job halfway.

Dr. Fleming notes a fourth factor. When dealing with cultural items one likes to have as tight a data as possible. If a lab could take their testing to one standard deviation—say +/- 35 years, this would provide a relatively tight "window"; but characteristically, labs may regard 2 standard deviations—+/- 70 years—to be a proper measure of precision. Unfortunately no AMS facility is currently achieving that precision; +/- 150 years is more common. And to this one must add a certain amount for calibration. If <u>only</u> AMS is involved, if only a few of such labs are testing, or worse, if only <u>one</u> of those labs gets an actual sample from the Shroud—if those final results turn out to be plus or minus 300 years, or 450 years or more, the window is so wide as to be capable of many different interpretations. True, one may be able to produce a date in, say, the third or fourth century AD and successfully remove the date from the fourteenth century or the first century—but with so wide a window one has only transplanted that debate from one time frame to a different one. IF the goal is to test the case for authenticity it is most desirable to produce as small a window as possible.

As you already aware there are scholars who have promulgated views which would place the Shroud within a few centuries of the time of Christ. Dr. Robert Drews of Vanderbilt University would find a carbon date based on such a wide window as supportive of the case he has built. James R. Foye, of San Diego, has taken Dr. Drew's position a step further by suggesting that the Carpocratians made the Shroud. He too would find a "wide window" as supportive.

Dr. Fleming states, "The whole purpose for testing is to cut out ambiguity." He believes that anything less than what has already been proposed in the original protocol could well spell disaster for the entire effort.

One issue which has been raised by Turin is, "What precedent will we set if we allow a larger number of samples to be taken?" My answer is: "No precedent at all!" The reason for removing these samples is to obtain the best scientific results achievable under the current state of scientific ability. If 7 labs are required for checks and balances, and multiple samples are needed to create an average date from each lab and to minimize the possibility of "Rogue samples", then this is a one time procedure that should have nothing whatsoever to do with samples needed for testing unrelated to carbon dating either now or in the future.

Finally, it is important to point out here that when the testing is finished and the results are published, it will be the radiocarbon scientific community—those uninvolved directly in the testing—that will take the hardest look at the manner in which the testing was conducted. If it does not approve, you can be quite sure that it will become one of the most publicized critiques of a carbon test ever to become available to the general public. If the current plans proceed as now projected—<u>any</u> resulting date will raise a storm of protest.

Dr. Fleming would be happy to discuss this matter with you . . . .

Please feel free to use this letter or its contents in whatever manner you see fit. The issues at stake are so terribly important that we must apprise the authorities of the ramifications of the current planning . . . .

                        With warmest regards

                        Paul C. Maloney
                        General Projects Director, ASSIST

cc:
Dr. Stewart Fleming, Dir. MASCA, Philadelphia, PA
Rev. Albert R. Dreisbach, Dir., Atlanta International Center, Atlanta, GA
Father Adam J. Otterbein, C.SS.R., Pres., Holy Shroud Guild, Esopus, NY

APPENDIX F

Article by Bill McClellan of the *St. Louis Post-Dispatch* (McClellan is the son-in-law of Dr. Douglas Donahue of the University of Arizona laboratory that was one of the three that carbon dated the Shroud in 1988.)
[Reprinted with permission from St. Louis Post-Dispatch.]

Secrets Of The Shroud
By Bill McClellan
St. Louis Post-Dispatch
May 15, 1988, Everyday Section, pp. 1 and 13

FAITH AND SCIENCE COLLIDE IN ARIZONA AS A SPACE-AGE MACHINE BEGINS EXAMINING A SACRED CHRISTIAN RELIC

TUCSON, Ariz

PAUL DAMON looked up from his microscope. "The problem is in the cleaning," he said.

Damon is a geoscientist and the co-director, with Douglas J. Donahue, of the National Science Foundation-Arizona Accelerator Facility for Radioisotope Analysis. That facility, at the University of Arizona, is in the carbon-dating business.

It uses a nuclear accelerator to date objects that previously were undateable. Since the facility began operating in 1982, it has dated more than 3,500 objects. The results have not always been pleasing to the scientists who have delivered the objects for dating.

Take, for instance, the skeletal remains of the "Yuha Man" and the "Sunnyvale Girl."

On the basis of amino acid testing, the scientists who discovered the bones had estimated the "Yuha Man" to have lived 20,000 years ago. The "Sunnyvale Girl" was estimated to have lived 70,000 years ago.

If these estimates were accurate, the discoveries were historic. The common consensus among anthropologists is that humans arrived in the New World no earlier than about 12,000 years ago.

The bones were carbon-dated, and the results showed that the 'Yuha Man' lived 4,000 years ago, the 'Sunnyvale Girl' 5,000 years ago.

Those results, like the results of all the other tests produced by Damon and his colleagues, were of interest almost exclusively to the scientific community.

However, the object under Damon's microscope was of much wider interest. He was looking at a quarter-inch-square piece of the Shroud of Turin, the linen cloth that many people believe to be the burial shroud of Jesus Christ.

As viewed under the microscope, the sample, already cleaned and ready for testing, looked like a gauze bandage, the kind you might buy at a corner drugstore.

By immersing the sample in a series of chemical solutions, and then washing it in distilled water, Damon and his colleagues had removed the pollen, hair and other stray particles that had gathered on the cloth over the centuries. Of major concern had been the removal of the incidental carbon left from the grease and oil of the countless fingers that had touched the material.

Now there was only the cloth, the linen thread. The linen came from flax. Damon looked up from the microscope and nodded to a technician. The scientists were ready to determine when that flax had been harvested.

Of all the mysteries of the Christian faith, none has been more tantalizing than the Shroud of Turin.

The cloth itself is a strip of linen 14 feet 3 inches long and 3 feet 7 inches wide. Faintly visible on one side of the cloth are images of the front and back of a human body, in a head-to-head fashion. The images appear as if the body had been laid on the shroud and then the shroud had been pulled up over the body. The images are reversed like a photo negative, so that pale tones, such as flesh, appear dark. The image is that of a 5-foot-11 bearded male.

There are what appear to be wounds and bruises on the body, corresponding to those suffered by Christ in the New Testament account of the Crucifixion.

Ten years ago, a forensic pathologist examined a photograph of the shroud and concluded that the images were of a man who had been beaten, whipped and crucified. The man had died of cardiopulmonary failure, which is the cause of death one would expect in a crucifixion.

After examining blood-flow patterns, the pathologist concluded, "The pathology and physiology are unquestionable and represent medical knowledge unknown 150 years ago"

Appendix F

The history of the shroud is hazy. In about 1357, it was publicly displayed in France after its purchase by a noble family. Supposedly it had been seized by Crusaders during the sacking of Constantinople in 1204.

In 1453, the shroud was purchased by the Duke of Savoy, the ancestor of the family that later was to rule and unify Italy. When ex-King Umberto II died in 1983, the shroud was willed to the Roman Catholic Church.

The church has never officially claimed the shroud to be the burial cloth of Christ. Yet in 1973, Pope Paul VI declared the shroud to be "the most sacred relic in all of Christianity." In 1978, during an exposition to mark the 400th anniversary of the shroud's arrival in Turin, more than 3 million people viewed it.

Those who believe the shroud to be the burial cloth of Christ contend that the image on the cloth was miraculously imposed during the resurrection.

That contention was bolstered in 1978 when a team of 40 American scientists examined the shroud. This team was called the Shroud of Turin Research Project. Its conclusion, almost a unanimous one (more about that later), was that the image on the shroud was not the product of an artist.

"There are no chemical or physical methods known which can account for the totality of the image, nor can any combination of physical, chemical, biological or medical circumstances explain the image adequately. . . . Thus, the answer to the question of how the image was produced or what produced the image remains now, as it has in the past, a mystery," the report concluded.

The one scientific test that could solve the mystery - or at least determine if the shroud is a hoax from the Middle Ages - was not permitted. The shroud was not carbon-dated.

That's because conventional carbon-dating would require the burning of a handkerchief-sized piece of the shroud. The church was not prepared to allow such a large sample to be destroyed.

But even in 1978, the science of carbon-dating was undergoing a revolution. A new method was being perfected, a method that would require a sample 1,000 times smaller than that required by the conventional method.

In 1986, the church agreed to allow the shroud to be carbon-dated by the new method. Three labs in the world ultimately were selected - one in England, one in Switzerland and the one in Tucson.

Earlier this year, scientists from the three labs went to Turin to receive their samples. Each lab was given a sample the size of a postage stamp.

The mystery of faith and the precision of science were finally to collide. The collision occurred this month in Arizona, as atoms of carbon screamed through an accelerator at a speed of 2,000 miles per second.

To a layman who sometimes deals with nuclear physicists (or, as in my case, marries the daughter of one), the scientists sometimes seem to operate on a different plane than do the rest of us, with all their talk of 10 to the umpteenth power, big bangs and curves in space. The curves, incidentally, are what cause galactic protons to come roaring into our atmosphere, creating the collisions that lead to the formation of carbon 14.

Perhaps the best example of this different plane in which the physicists seem to operate is provided by a story about one of the scientists who is involved in dating the shroud at the laboratory in England. He recently bought a new car. He drove it until it ran out of gas.

"You're out of gas," his passenger said.

"I can't be," said the nuclear physicist. "The gauge says I've got half a tank left."

"That's the temperature gauge, the passenger said.

"I thought I was getting awfully good mileage, said the scientist, who makes his living running a complicated nuclear accelerator.

Nevertheless, laymen can relate, perhaps, to the fact that the big breakthrough in carbon-dating occurred over a few drinks. It was at the American Physical Society's annual meeting in April 1977. Harry Gove, a professor at the University of Rochester, and A.E. Litherland, a professor at the University of Toronto, were enjoying the hospitality suite of K.H. Purser, the head of General Ionex Corp., a company that manufactures nuclear accelerators.

The three physicists were discussing the possibility of directly counting carbon 14 atoms in a material. Conventional carbon-dating measures the amount and rate of decay of such atoms, and requires a large sample. If the atoms themselves could be counted, the procedure would require only a fraction of the material necessary for conventional carbon-dating.

Mass can be measured. Mass is weight, and in atomic and molecular terms, mass equals the number of protons and neutrons in the nucleus of an atom. Thus, carbon 14, with its six protons and eight neutrons, has a mass of 14. So does nitrogen, with its seven protons and seven neutrons. So do any number of molecules. Carbon 12, for instance, with six protons and six neutrons, will often combine with two hydrogen atoms, each with a single proton, to form a molecule with a mass of 14.

So any attempt to count carbon 14 atoms by counting particles with a mass of 14 seemed doomed. There would be no way to differentiate among carbon 14, nitrogen or molecules with a mass of 14. All weigh the same.

"Over a couple of glasses of wine, we got an idea," Gove recalled. "You can't add an electron to nitrogen."

That realization was the breakthrough.

You see, to fire a particle through a nuclear accelerator - be that particle an atom or a molecule - the particle must be charged. In their normal state, atoms and molecules are neutral. They have as many negatively charged electrons as they have positively charged protons.

One way to charge a particle is to add an electron, giving the particle a negative charge.

The three physicists decided to conduct an experiment. They would take a sample material, add an electron to all the particles that would accept an electron, shoot those negatively charged particles through an accelerator and count the particles with a mass of 14 that came out the other side.

Because nitrogen would not accept an additional electron, the nitrogen would not be accelerated.

The only particles that could be confused with carbon 14 - the only other particles with a mass of 14 - would be molecules. The physicists decided they could attack that problem by generating a collision inside the accelerator that would break all the molecules into atoms. Theoretically, only the carbon 14 atoms would arrive at the other end of the accelerator with the appropriate mass.

"It seemed simple once we thought of it," Gove said.

The experiment was conducted at the University of Rochester. First, the scientists tested graphite that had come from petroleum. That material was millions of years old, old enough so that all carbon 14 would have long since decayed. No particles with a mass of 14 were detected. The nitrogen had not been accelerated, and the molecules with a mass of 14 had been broken down.

Delighted with this result, the physicists went to a grocery store and bought some charcoal briquets, which of course would have a high content of carbon 14. Sure enough, the reading was positive. The carbon 14 atoms raced through the accelerator and were counted at the other end.

The results of this experiment, and the fact that this new method of carbon-dating would require only a tiny fraction of the material required by the conventional method, were reported in Time magazine.

Shortly after the article appeared, Gove received a letter from a priest connected with the Holy Shroud Guild, an organization dedicated to furthering scientific study of the Shroud of Turin. The letter invited Gove to attend a conference in Italy with the scientists of the Shroud of Turin Research Project.

"I'd never heard of the Turin shroud before," said Gove, who describes himself as "a lapsed Episcopalian."

He arrived in Turin in 1978, shortly before the Shroud of Turin Research Project conducted its experiments. Despite the fact that these scientists came from prestigious facilities - the Air Force Academy, Los Alamos Laboratory, Sandia Laboratory - Gove was decidedly unimpressed.

"Almost without exception, they were people who honestly believe it is Christ's shroud," he said. "It's a well-known fact that scientists can produce whatever result they want. If you believe that passionately in something, you can steer the results. My God, we've all been guilty of that."

Science, not diplomacy, is Gove's long suit. He made no friends during his visit to Turin.

But still, the church was interested in carbon-dating the shroud. In fact, if there was a debate inside the church about the wisdom of getting a final determination on the age of the cloth, that debate was kept inside the church.

At a news conference after the Turin meeting of 1978, a church spokesman said: "The decision not to include at this time the carbon 14 test was not arbitrary. A prerequisite is that only minimal parts of the cloth be used. The moment we will have this assurance, and not just from one source, we will certainly move on this test."

For the next several years, Gove corresponded with the church.

"We had a language problem, and I don't mean Italian," he said. "I'm a scientist."

Still, the church officials Gove talked to seemed sincerely interested in dating the shroud.

"My impression is the church is doing its best to move out of the relic business," Gove said. "Besides, one bishop I talked to put it pretty well. He said: 'If the shroud turns out to be 700 years old, it won't affect my faith. If it turns out to be 2,000 years old, it might do something to yours.'"

That view is echoed by the Rev. Robert Wild, a New Testament historian who has written about the shroud. Reached in Chicago, where he heads the Jesuit Province, Wild said: "I don't think the church has a lot of emotion tied into the shroud. Certainly, there are those who would be delighted if it turns out to be a first-century artifact, but I really believe the people with the largest emotional investment are the (Protestant) fundamentalists. They're the ones who are hoping for an artifact to prove the literal truth of the Scriptures."

Wild, incidentally, has written that he believes the shroud to be an artistic work of the Middle Ages.

One group of people with an emotional investment in the shroud are the scientists who participated in the Shroud of Turin Research Project. John Heller, for instance, wrote a book about the project, in which he concluded that it is easier to believe in the authenticity of the shroud than to disbelieve.

Reached at his home in Connecticut, Heller pointed out that even if the shroud turns out to be 2,000 years old, the debate about its authenticity will continue.

"I've often thought that if in the left-hand corner of the shroud, it said in Hebrew, 'This is my burial shroud, ' and was signed by Jesus Christ, it still wouldn't change anybody's mind."

But the debate would certainly end, would it not, if the shroud turns out to not be from the first century?

"The data are the data," Heller said.

The lone dissenter in the 1978 project, Walter McCrone, a particle expert from Chicago who believes the image on the shroud was painted, gave himself credit, after a fashion, for the church's decision to carbon-date the shroud.

"I'm rather surprised" the church is letting the test be done, McCrone said in a telephone interview last month. "I think one of the big reasons is the way my results were so vigorously attacked. I think the church believes this test will prove the shroud to be 2,000 years old. I'd bet all the money I have that it dates to the fourteenth century."

For whatever reason, in October 1986 the church, under the auspices of the Pontifical Academy of Sciences, convened a meeting in Turin to discuss the procedures under which the testing would be conducted. A decision was reached that seven laboratories, including Gove's in Rochester, would participate.

One year later, the archbishop of Turin, Cardinal Anastasio Ballestrero, notified the seven laboratories that only three would participate. Among the four excluded labs was Gove's.

Gove and Garman Harbottle, the head of a lab at Brookhaven Institute, which also had been excluded, responded in a news conference and in interviews with several newspapers. Gove said the archbishop was getting bad advice from his scientific advisor, Luigi Gonella, whom Gove referred to as a "second-rate scientist."

"He's a professor of metrology, whatever that is. He's a man nobody ever heard of," Gove said.

Gonella shrugged off the criticism. "I do not have to account for my credentials to Gove and Harbottle," he said. Despite initial protests from the three labs approved for the testing - a petition asking that all seven labs be allowed to participate was sent to the archbishop - the project moved ahead.

Gove's lack of tact had knocked him out of the project, insiders suggested. Gonella had been extremely supportive of the Shroud of Turin Research Project's work, and Gove's criticism of that work had not gone unnoticed.

Gove seems to have mellowed, but only a bit.

"Seven labs would have been better than three. If one lab makes a mistake and comes up with a result that's way off, you'd know it was a mistake if you had six other results that were the same. My real problem is this: The Pontifical Academy is a first-rate scientific body. I can't understand why the scientists from the academy weren't given complete charge of the project, instead of Gonella.

"I shouldn't have said those things (about Gonella), although they're true. I wish I knew how he got to be scientific adviser. Maybe all the top-notch physicists in Turin are communists or something."

The Saguaro cactus was in bloom in the Sonoran desert, but the scientists who work at the National Science Foundation-Arizona Accelerator Facility for Radioisotope Analysis were too preoccupied to enjoy the weather.

Damon has been involved in carbon-dating for more than 25 years and has dated thousands of objects. Some have had great scientific significance, but no project has been more intriguing than the dating of the shroud.

"It's all confusing," he said. "I remember when we went to get our sample in Turin. In the chapel where they keep the shroud, there's a large crucifix. Like all the crucifixes you see, the nails are through the palms of the hands. That's not how the Romans did it. The nails went through the wrists, because the palms would not have supported a man's weight. The image on the shroud has the nails through the wrists, so if the shroud is a fake, I would think that the person who did it would have to know something about real crucifixions. How would someone in the Middle Ages know that? The Romans ceased the practice in the third century, but I believe the Turks continued into the ninth century.

"So, you see, I don't know what to expect."

Asked about his religious affiliation, Damon smiled. He said his parents were Catholic and Baptist, but he became a Quaker during the Vietnam era.

"I was involved in the protests against the war, and I found that a lot of the people in the early days of the movement were Quakers."

He continues with his activism. Two years ago, he went to Nicaragua to help with the cocoa harvest.

It was this kind of mind-set that sent Damon into science. He went into the Navy during World War II and had planned on making a career of the military.

"Then the atomic bomb came along, and war seemed absurd, obscene. I decided to get out," he said.

The co-director of the lab, Douglas Donahue, also came to science through the Navy, but in a different manner. He started college at the University of Oregon with the intention of becoming a sportswriter.

World War II intervened, and the Navy sent Donahue to Park College in Parkville, Mo. He was fed an intensive curriculum of math and science. He discovered an aptitude for physics.

After his stint in the Navy was completed - he was in the Pacific, but saw no action - he returned to college and studied physics.

So instead of becoming a sportswriter and concerning himself with the speed at which a lefthanded hitter can run from home to first base (approximately 4.5 seconds), he became interested in things like the lifetime of a nucleus in an excited state (approximately a millionth of a millionth of a second).

Like Damon, Donahue noticed the crucifix in the chapel at Turin. He said that in many ways, the whole experience with the shroud has been, well, other-worldly.

"I remember coming back through customs with the sample. The customs agent in New York asked me what I had brought back from Europe.

'A bottle of gin, some chocolates and a piece of the Shroud of Turin, 'I said. She smiled and waved me through."

Donahue is a devout Catholic and has been all his life, although he's quick to add that his faith is not dependent on relics.

"Strangely enough, I had never even heard of the Shroud of Turin until a few years ago," he said. "It's funny. Right now, it seems like everybody has heard of it."

Including the parish priest of Donahue's childhood in California. He recently wrote Donahue a letter from Ireland, where he now lives. The priest had seen a news story about the decision to date the shroud, and Donahue had been mentioned in the story. The priest wrote that he had been studying the history of the shroud for 30 years. The priest also remarked that he remembered Donahue for the troublesome questions he asked as a child.

Was there anything in physics - the orderliness of the universe and so forth - that heightened Donahue's faith?

"Some people make that argument, but I don't," he said. "I keep my faith and my science relatively separate."

On a recent Friday morning, faith and science were together, but perhaps separate, in the lab.

A piece of the Shroud of Turin, one quarter the size of a postage stamp, burned to create approximately three cubic centimeters of carbon dioxide and then converted to graphite and compressed into a target pellet one millimeter in diameter, was loaded into the tandem accelerator mass spectrometer.

The machine, incidentally, was built by General Ioenx Corp., the company that hosted the hospitality suite in which the wine was consumed 11 years ago.

Atoms of Cesium, propelled by 10,000 volts, were fired at the target. Cesium is used because a cesium atom has a loose electron - that is, an electron in a loose orbit that readily disassociates itself from the nucleus of its host atom.

The cesium struck the target pellet, and particles in the target picked up the loose electrons, thereby gaining a negative charge. These negatively charged particles - carbon atoms and molecules, mostly carbon 12 atoms with two hydrogen atoms, but also carbon 13 atoms with a single hydrogen atom - sputtered out of the target and began their trip through the 50-foot accelerator.

In the beginning of their trip, the particles traveled at approximately 200 miles per second.

"They're just poking along at that point," was the way Donahue explained it.

An injection magnet steered all particles with a mass of 14 to the left, into the main body of the accelerator. As the particles with the proper mass veered into the main body of the accelerator, drawn toward a power source of 2 million volts, their speed increased to 2,000 miles per second.

Then those particles ran into a cloud of argon gas. This provided the collision that Gove and his colleagues had envisioned, the collision that would smash the molecules into their atomic components.

In addition to breaking up the molecules, the collision knocked four electrons off of each carbon atom. So instead of having an extra electron, and a negative charge of one, each atom now had a positive charge of three.

With their journey almost complete, the atoms spun toward another magnet, which directed particles with a mass of 14 into a detector. Only the carbon 14 atoms were detected.

This process went on for one minute.

Then the injection magnet was slightly altered to steer particles with a mass of 13 through the accelerator. In this way, the carbon 13 atoms were counted.

Then the magnet was readjusted for a mass of 14. Then readjusted for a mass of 13. Then back to 14. The cycle was repeated 10 times.

The procedure was repeated with a modern sample, a sample of known age. This is done for calibration purposes.

Then two samples of ancient material provided by the British Museum, which is coordinating the tests, were carbon-dated. Museum officials, but not the scientists doing the testing, know the dates of the material. This step is done to determine accuracy.

The entire test was repeated five times.

The results printed out on a computer. The modern sample always comes out as a reading of 20, so a reading of 10 would indicate that the object being tested was 5,700 years old.

In this instance, for the Shroud of Turin, a reading of 16 would indicate that the flax, from which the linen shroud was woven, had been harvested 2,000 years ago. If the flax had been harvested in the fourteenth century, the reading would be closer to 18.

Donahue was the first person to read the results. The second was Harry Gove, who had been invited to Tucson by Damon and Donahue to observe the test.

The evening of the day the Shroud of Turin was dated, Gove visited Donahue's home. The two men sat outside on the porch, enjoying the cool spring night. They talked about physics and mutual friends and the desert.

Everything but the results of the testing of the Shroud of Turin.

In the coming days, the Tucson lab will be testing the other three pieces of its original sample of the shroud. The results then will be sent to the British Museum, which is coordinating the tests. The other two labs will do the same.

Appendix F

All data will be forwarded to the archbishop of Turin, who will announce the results.

"If the results don't leak out first, it will be a miracle," said a nonphysicist.

The scientists barely smiled.

The official announcement is expected later this year.

APPENDIX G

Column by *St. Louis Post-Dispatch* columnist Bill McClellan, 10 October 1988, Everyday Magazine.
[Reprinted with permission from St. Louis Post-Dispatch.]

BROTHER Joseph Marino lives in a small room at St. Louis Priory. The decor is simple, as befits a Benedictine monk. No rugs cover the cement floor. A desk, a sink, a small bed, a bookcase and a file cabinet comprise the furniture. Yet the room is not without a distinct personality.

Just as a child's room will often reflect a passionate interest in sports, Marino's room reflects his passion with the Shroud of Turin. Photographs of the Shroud are on the walls. The file cabinet is filled with the results of years of correspondence with other Shroud aficionados, "Shroudies," they irreverently call themselves. The bookcase is full of books and video tapes dealing with the Shroud.

Marino gives formal lectures on the Shroud, complete with a slide presentation. He was instrumental in getting an exhibit on the Shroud to come to the Priory. More than 5,000 people viewed it, which consisted of photographs, drawings and representations of the Shroud. Needless to say, the Shroud itself was not there. It is in Turin, where it has been since the fourteenth century. That's when Crusaders brought it back from Constantinople.

At least that's what the believers have always said.

The Shroud, purported to be the burial cloth of Jesus Christ with the image of Jesus miraculously imbedded on the fabric during the moment of resurrection, has a solid history dating only to the fourteenth century. But believers can paint a plausible portrait of its earlier history, how it was secreted away from the Holy Land by early Christians, how it eventually ended up in Constantinople, how it was liberated there and taken to Europe.

Ten years ago, a team of scientists investigated the Shroud in an effort to determine how the image, that of a crucified man, was imbedded on the Shroud. The scientists determined that that was undeterminable.

In other words, it looked like a miracle.

All of this was incorporated in Marino's lectures. Medical evidence (the pathology of a crucifixion was accurately depicted), scientific evidence (the image was inexplicable) and, of course, spiritual evidence.

"The Shroud has been a source of inspiration to many, many people," Marino told me.

Now I should add that Marino has a charming habit, evident even to those who know him only slightly, of seeing spiritual inspiration.

"What you call coincidence, I call providence," he says, with a disarming shrug.

So maybe it's easy for him to tell stories of people who have read about the Shroud, or seen photographs of the Shroud, and have then been spiritually inspired. He even knows a lawyer who dropped out of the dog-eat-dog world of law to become a scholar of the Shroud.

Earlier this year, the Vatican allowed the Shroud to be carbon-dated. The results have not been officially released - that could come any day - but there have been a number of unofficial reports. All contend that the carbon-dating show the Shroud to be a product of the fourteenth century.

In the wake of these unofficial reports, I visited Marino. He readily conceded that the "Shroudies" were going to take a public relations beating.

"We're going to look very bad in the public eye for a while," he said. "The public has this idea that carbon-dating is infallible. It isn't, and the technique that was used is less than 10 years old."

He also talked about the scientific tests of 10 years ago.

"They spent thousands of hours, did hundreds of sophisticated tests, and they couldn't prove it was a fake. It's just unfathomable that some fourteenth century artist could do something that 20th century scientists couldn't figure out," he said.

Needless to say, Marino's religious faith does not depend on the authenticity of the Shroud. His faith is much deeper. The Shroud is, in some ways, almost a hobby.

It's not quite a hobby to me, but I have read an awful lot about it. Earlier this year, I wrote a long story about the carbon-dating of the Shroud. While I was working on that story, I thought a lot about the collision between science and faith. I wondered how the "Shroudies" would react to a "bad date."

And I felt rather pleased to hear that Marino, the No. 1 "Shroudie" in the St. Louis area, was not willing to concede anything.

"I'd really like a chance to do one of those 'At Your Service' programs on KMOX," he said. "This recent testing will not be the final word."

APPENDIX H

ARTICLE BY JOSEPH G. MARINO IN *SHROUD NEWS*, DECEMBER 1988, PP. 48-51. IT WAS WRITTEN UNDER THE PSEUDONYM "JUSTIN LODGE."

An article entitled "On the Physical Death of Jesus Christ" was published in the March 1986 issue of the *Journal of the American Medical Association* and suggested that, based on analyses of the Shroud of Turin as well as both Christian and non-Christian historical documents, Jesus was dead before he was taken down from the cross. The article produced the greatest correspondence the journal ever received on any topic. Most of it was negative and criticized the journal for delving into a "religious" subject. Australia's Rex Morgan, editor of *Shroud News* commented, "It is interesting to speculate again on why science seems to run scared when Christ is mentioned in the hallowed columns of scientific literature." [1]

It is not surprising that the Shroud enters into this question. The unmistakable link between the death of Jesus and the Shroud has often led to controversy. Since the beginning of its recorded history in 1357, it has caused much debate among religious, scientists, historians, and scholars. When the Shroud was exhibited publicly in 1389, it was alleged to be a painting by the bishop of the diocese, Pierre d'Arcis. Ironically, the Shroud was pronounced authentic by an agnostic scientist, Yves Delage, in a report to the famed French Academy of Science more than 500 years later, in 1902. The Academy, populated by many "free thinkers," derided Delage for having belied his position as an agnostic and accused him of having betrayed the spirit of science. Delage replied that he recognized Jesus as an historical person and saw no reason why anyone should be upset by the fact that material traces of his life still existed. He also added that problems were caused because a religious question had needlessly been injected into a scientific question.

While one must admire Delage for taking the stand that he did, one must question whether he was being realistic in trying to eliminate the religious question from the scientific question of the Shroud, which is similar to trying to separate the Jesus of history from the Christ of faith. This writer believes that neither can be done. Is there not an obvious correlation between the image of the man in the Shroud and the unique person of Jesus? Delage believed that the image was caused by a natural formation process (the "vapograph" theory), which has proven to be untenable. Shroud of Turin Research Project (STURP) scientists and European scientists who have studied the cloth have not been able to find a natural explanation that fits all the data. Even if they eventually discover a natural-formation process, it would not destroy the unmistakable correlation between the Shroud and Jesus. Perhaps Delage, like some scientists of today, have done, would reconsider the religious question if he saw the current advanced stage of Shroud research, which still has not been able to totally solve the mystery.

It is usually stated, and with good reason, that the Shroud is not necessary in Christian faith. Then why has it been so important to so many people for so long? What is it about the Shroud that makes so many people passionately involved, either in support of it or opposition to it? Advocates who are believers seem to find an added dimension to their faith because of the Shroud. Even more powerfully, a look at the face on the Shroud has been for many people the decisive moment when they decided to commit their lives to Jesus. I say "advocates who are believers" because there are some advocates who are not believers, just as there are Christians who are not advocates. Delage is a good example of the fact that one can be an advocate of the Shroud but not be a Christian. D'Arcis is a good example of the fact that one can be a Christian and not be an advocate of the Shroud. Skeptics who deny the authenticity of the Shroud are often atheists, and many of these atheists are in the forefront of Shroud opposition. They are not willing to acknowledge the possibility of the supernatural and find it safer to dismiss the Shroud as a forgery, even when it flies in the face of all the evidence. Quite simply, the reality of the Shroud and its possible ramifications scares them. They know that an authentic Shroud of Turin puts their atheism on shaky ground.

A comment by a bishop to one such skeptic really puts the whole significance of the Shroud in perspective. The bishop told him, "If the Shroud turned out to be 2,000 years old, it wouldn't really affect my faith, but it might affect yours". Thus in a real sense, the Shroud is more important for skeptics than it is for Christians. It penetrates to their deepest philosophical levels.

Christians and atheists both claim to be searching for the truth. Christians believe that the ultimate truth is a person, Jesus. The closest an atheist comes to having an ultimate truth is his almost unwavering belief that science can or will eventually be able to explain everything. Most reputable scientists realize that science is only a tool that can help us to explain some truths. The atheists would have everyone believe that a truly objective scientist must be an atheist or at least agnostic. They do not seem to realize that their atheism

Appendix H

requires as much faith as the religious believer. It is foolish to restrict reality to the knowledge, especially that gained through experience, that we physically perceive. Every person, whether atheistic or religious, works under certain pre-conceptions and assumptions. However, this does not mean that we cannot arrive at certain truths. Persons must acknowledge their own prejudices, be willing to change their opinions if the evidence warrants it, and let the search for truth be the main concern.

Shroud skeptics usually have at least two things in common: they accuse STURP scientists of being religious zealots out to prove that the Shroud wrapped Jesus, and they often are arrogantly confident in their conclusions, despite the fact that they haven't examined the cloth first-hand (as the STURP scientists did) and despite the fact that they usually disagree among themselves on how the image was allegedly forged. Even though their charge that the STURP scientists are religious zealots is patently untrue, and the skeptics' conflicting solutions, like the 19th century Rationalists' attempts to explain the Resurrection, help to point out the weaknesses of their own positions, they may be helping to stimulate the thinking of STURP scientists and all Shroud advocates.

The skeptics' usual procedure is to push seemingly negative facts (all of which can be readily explained) while ignoring all other evidence that contradicts their positions. An example is their treatment of the famous d'Arcis memorandum, which they use to back their contention that the Shroud is a forgery. D'Arcis wrote a memo to the Anti-Pope Clement VII in Avignon, denouncing the exhibition in 1389, stating that an artist had admitted producing the Shroud image in the time of his predecessor. However, no name of the artist or any other information was given. It simply was an unsubstantiated allegation (and we only have a draft of the letter, not the actual letter itself). The skeptics never point out the fact that Clement imposed perpetual silence on d' Arcis about the matter, which suggests that his case was not strong, or that d'Arcis successor, Bishop Louis Raguier, maintained the Shroud's authenticity in three official documents. [2] Raguier is not to be believed at face value any more quickly than d'Arcis is, but if one is aiming for the truth, **all** important facts should be divulged, not just the ones favorable to one's position.

Skeptics continue to claim that the Shroud is a painting because of traces of artists' pigments found on the cloth. The maxim from mathematics, "necessary but not sufficient"[3], applies here. For the Shroud to be a painting, it is necessary to find paint on the Shroud, but it is not sufficient to prove that it is a painting. One must look for other reasons why paint may be on the Shroud. It is well known that many artists who made copies of the Shroud touched their copy to the Shroud to "sanctify" it. This is a more plausible explanation why there is paint on the Shroud than saying a medieval artist painted a negative, 3-dimensional, superficial image showing knowledge hundreds of years ahead of his time.

One must also consider the possibility that some skeptics crusade against the Shroud as a way of getting publicity for themselves; some have made quite a name for themselves by maintaining that the Shroud is a forgery. Indifference and hostility regarding the Shroud even from some Christians is not uncommon. One Christian evangelical magazine went so far as to solicit one of the foremost skeptics of the Shroud to write a negative article for them. Despite all this, one is almost surprised that there is not more opposition to the Shroud than there is. But perhaps there is more sinister opposition occurring; the Archbishop of Turin recently named eight new exorcists for the city.

Advocates and skeptics alike often focus on the often-stated implication that the Shroud image points to the Resurrection of Jesus, which is admittedly an article of faith and beyond scientific proof. All Christians know that they must take some aspects of their beliefs on faith, which co-exists with their reason. Atheists rely on reason, and their faith is in their own conviction of their stance. Christianity could not stand without belief in the Resurrection. The Shroud possibly brings us face to face with the Resurrection and/or divinity of Jesus. When one realizes that on the Shroud, one may be looking at the man who said that our eternal destiny depends on our response to him, one can understand the emotionalism of the Shroud issue. Science can and should co-exist with religious faith. However, if science attempts to set itself up as the ultimate truth, it will continue to "run scared when Christ is mentioned".

NOTES

[1] Rex Morgan. "Editorial", *Shroud News,* Issue 35 (June 1986): p.2.
[2] Clement J. McNaspy, 'The Shroud of Turin", *Catholic Biblical Quarterly* 7 (1945): 149.
[3] John Heller, <u>Report on the Shroud of Turin</u>, (Boston: Houghton Mifflin, 1983): p. 193.

APPENDIX I

SHROUD ARTICLES/PRESENTATIONS BY MARINO (AND BENFORD)

Publications with Marino as principal author:

1984: "The Shroud of Turin: a Love Letter from God?" *St. Louis Priory Journal,* Spring 1984, 20:8.

1988: "The Shroud, Science and Faith." *Shroud News*, October 1988, pp. 48-51. (Written under pseudonym "Justin Lodge".)

1989: "The Shroud of Turin and the Carbon-14 Controversy." *Fidelity,* February 1989, 8(3):36-45.

1996: "The Disciples On the Road To Turin." Presented at Holy Shroud Guild Retreat/Conference—August 23-25. Accessible at: http://www.shroud.com/marino.htm.

1999: Jewish Burial Customs, The Burial of Jesus of Nazareth and the Shroud of Turin. Monograph. (Out of print.)

1999: "The Shroud of Turin: Bridge Between Heaven and Earth?" *Journal of Religion and Psychical Research.* April 1999, 22(2):95-105, co-authored with M. Sue Benford.

2000: "Rebirth, Resurrection, and the Millennium." *Journal of Religion and Psychical Research.* January 2000, 23(1):17-26, co-authored with M. Sue Benford.

2000: "Evidence for the Skewing of the C-14 Dating of the Shroud of Turin Due to Repairs." Presented at "Sindone 2000 Congress in Orvieto, Italy, 26-28 August.
Accessible at

http://www.shroud.com/pdfs/marben.pdf, co-authored with M. Sue Benford.

2008: "Chronological History of the Evidence for the Anomalous Nature of the C-14 Sample Area of the Shroud of Turin." Internet paper: *http://www.shroud.com/pdfs/chronology.pdf*, co-authored with Edwin J. Prior.

2009: "Addendum to Chronological History of the Evidence for the Anomalous Nature of the C-14 Sample Area of the Shroud of Turin." Internet paper: *http://www.shroud.com/pdfs/addendum.pdf*, co-authored with Edwin J. Prior.

Publications with Marino as secondary author:

2001: Benford M. S., Marino J. "Finding the Shroud — in the 21st Century." Internet paper: http://www.shroud.it/MARINO.PDF.

2002: Benford, M. S., Marino J. "Historical Support of a sixteenth Century Restoration in the Shroud C-14 Sample Area." Internet paper: http://shroud.com/pdfs/histsupt.pdf.

2002: Benford, M. S., Marino J. "Textile Evidence Supports Skewed Radiocarbon Date of Shroud of Turin." Internet paper: http://shroud.com/pdfs/textevid.pdf.

2004: Benford M. S., Marino. J. "Did C-14 Dating Bury the Shroud of Turin?" *Phenomena*, Issue 2, Jan/Feb 2004, pp. 52-55.

2008: Benford, M. S., Marino, J. "Role of calcium carbonate in fibre discoloration on the Shroud of Turin." *Chemistry Today.* March/April 2008, 26(2):57-62.

2008: Benford M. S., Marino J. "Discrepancies in the Radiocarbon Dating Area of the Turin Shroud." *Chemistry Today*, July-August 2008, 26(4):4-12. (Accessible at http://chemistry-today.teknoscienze.com/pdf/benford *percent20CO4*-08.pdf). Also presented at The Shroud of Turin: Perspectives on a Multi-Faceted Enigma, Columbus, Ohio, 16 August. Audio/Video accessible at http://shrouduniversity.com/ohiocon2008.php.

APPENDIX J

CORRESPONDENCE BETWEEN THE AUTHOR AND M. SUE BENFORD

Email from Benford to Author on 14 August 1997:

There's an interesting "coded" message in the Bible that I want to share with you. In Genesis 48, "Israel," e.g. Jacob, blesses Joseph's sons born of foreign heritage and raises them above all the others. Joseph, a great visionary/prophet, propagated the "nations" or groups of people that would carry on this visionary heritage through these non-Jewish offspring.

God is making a statement here about "outsiders" being accepted by insiders and even bringing the world vision-induced information. Christ tried, unceasingly, to reiterate this point of accepting those who may not, on the surface, appear "strong" but who, in actuality, were the ones closest to God. Maybe that's why He made me the strongest woman in the world—to make a point that appearances can be very deceiving.

Given all of this, I still have no visions of grandeur about how my thoughts will be accepted. That's why I will rely on people like you and the Jacksons to research and report to the various groups anything relevant that may come from my insights. I hope that all my theories are pursued in coordination with the appropriate resources who can verify and validate them. Maybe you can eventually take them to the Pope!!

In terms of my lack of being "Catholic," in one very important respect, I think that I am. The term Catholic is Greek for "universal" which, to me, is pretty darn inclusive. Christ is the Big Brother, first born, and Savior to all of us regardless of surface affiliations or beliefs. It's like a person trying to deny he has older siblings, he can do it of course but that doesn't make it a valid observation.

I belong to the Universal Church the same as you or the Pope or the Hindu guy down the street. We may each be on our own path, if you will, but our goals and endpoint are the same. And for each one of us, Christ is the guy at the side of the river holding the life preserver out to his little siblings who are treading water: whether we recognize, acknowledge, or accept him is the difference between us.

Someday, if you're interested, I'll share more of my early Christian beliefs with you that are truly very Catholic or inclusive of all of Christ's teachings. I was led to these just as I was led to the Shroud and I have been able to document many mysteries that would be impossible for me to have simply "guessed" at....

Email from Author to Benford 16 August 1997:

I wanted to ask you a few more questions related to your visions.

* When Jesus 1st appeared to you, did you know it was him right away, and if so, how?
* Do you actually see him like a flesh and blood person?
* What color is his skin?
* Does he look noticeably different than the Shroud image? (I assume he does not have the wounds shown on the Shroud)?
* When he leaves, what manner does the departing take?
* Do you have any inkling when he's going to appear or does he just come out of the blue?
* Is there anything else significant about the Shroud that he said that you haven't mentioned yet?

Some of these questions are mere human curiosity, but hopefully you can give some info on all of them . . . .

Email from Benford to Author, 16 August 1997, in response to email of 16 August:

I thought you might be interested in my original recorded journal entry related to the Shroud. I have never shared my actual entries with anyone before but I've been guided to do so now.
March 24, 1997
"I was told that Jesus' death shroud called the Shroud of Turin is authentic. It represents the radiated markings left by the release of the Spirit

from the soul's receptacle after Jesus' death. The subatomic particles acted like radiation waves and marked the exact outline of the body. We have been left this remnant to have a guide leading to our discovery of the spirit. We will be able to replicate this effect by the discovery of the subatomic particle release of the newly discovered photons and other particles in physics. When we have exactly replicated the Shroud's markings we will have mastered the formula and composition of the spirit. Thus, we will be able to measure waves and particles emanating from humans still alive to ascertain spiritual DNA and levels of spirit in the soul. We can then put people on 'spirit-gaining' exercises to increase spiritual mass!"

NOTE: This is free-flowing thought and is fraught with errors, i.e. "outline" instead of "image." This is because I usually am more concerned about getting things down on paper and then later refining them with additional guidance. Also, my physics stuff was very primitive at this point and was later refined with more insights and understandings leading to the composition of my paper you read. This is how they do it with me—they introduce a concept and some elementary truths then augment as I begin to understand (like teaching young kids in school).

Please read the paper I sent you very carefully and with an open mind for that is the only way truth can enter. Ask for guidance on its message and your role.

I've saved the best for last—the answers to your questions about my meetings with Jesus. When Jesus first appeared to me I was dwarfed, dumbfounded, diminished before him like a flea at his feet. His energy, radiated first as a brilliantly glowing light around his body, overwhelmed me with its intensity—like I was a 1 watt bulb and he a 1,000,000 watt bulb. I couldn't speak at first. I wasn't afraid just in a state of awe like you can't even imagine.

The brilliant light began to dissipate and it left only him standing before me (I was still flat on the ground). He looked exactly like the image in the Shroud except he didn't have any facial hair. His hair was to his shoulders, dark brown, parted in the middle. His skin was olive toned but radiant. His face was serene and his expression one of calm and collection. His confidence and love were palpable. John, who had first introduced me to him, had moved back to one side. He was smiling (John always is cheerful and in a good mood).

Jesus extended his hand to me and said, "Arise, my child, don't be afraid." I reached up, took his hand and stood up. He was wearing the same thing they all wear, a long white robe tied at the middle by a robe cord. I still couldn't form the words in my mouth to speak. He said, "Come. Walk with me."

We walked over to a nearby pond of still water. He sat on a large rock on the side of the water. I sat at his feet. I looked over at his sandals. They were leather and had straps. I reached out and touched one of them like a baby inquires about its surroundings.

My book goes into exact detail on our conversations so I won't rewrite it here. But to answer your other questions:

Yes, I knew it was him right away. First of all, I had specifically asked John to talk to Jesus plus there was just no way, once I met him, that it could be anyone else. The more we have talked and gotten to know each other the more sure I am that he is who he says he is. A skeptical friend of mine once asked me, "Are you sure it is Jesus and not the devil who is a deceiver?" I took that question to Jesus and he said, "You are right to be skeptical. Believe no image, including mine, that steers you away from my one true message." I asked him, being ignorant, "what is that?" He said, "The answer is always love. Any other answer is not of God no matter who says it." That one statement has guided me in numerous situations since.

Yes, I actually see him like flesh and blood and I actually talk to him like we talk now. Of course, it's all with "the third eye" and through the mind. He is a big brother to me in the truest sense. He's extremely patient with me, my moods, my skepticism, and everything else I constantly put him through. In fact, I think I told you about the one night, after we had debated for several hours, he finally called his mother in! It was the first time I met Mary and I gained a new appreciation for her. Jesus really respects her a lot, too.

You asked about when he leaves. That's funny you mentioned that because until you brought it up I didn't realize that he's never left our sessions before me! I usually become so exhausted that I fall asleep or must break off the meditation. I notice when I'm receiving the insights, I usually am excessively tired as a result. It's physically draining and requires a lot of my energy. That's one of the reasons we have to put the efforts of this world aside to focus our energy on the spiritual world.

When I ask for him he appears. At other times, like during the day, the origin of my insights are much more nebulous and indistinct. In fact, I don't know if they are coming from John, Paul, Thomas, Jesus or whoever. It might be from angelic messengers I'm completely unaware of (the real angels stay pretty well hidden and unidentifiable which is much different than many new agers would have you believe).

In terms of the Shroud, I finally asked him to show me everything the other night. He obliged. I've written it in some detail in the paper I just sent you. It was an awesome experience. It took a lot of energy for me to stay with it through the end. I've been exhausted for days as a result. Now I see why he disciplined me to be a world class athlete!!

There's so much more I need and want to share with you. I'm happy we finally met (I have to laugh—I asked them to send me a soul mate who could comprehend my spiritual journey. It's John's sense of humor that I was sent a monk!) But, as they told me, it is from our differences that we learn from each other. New life, both physical and spiritual, springs only from the joining of opposites (think about it). We have much to learn from each other.

Email from Benford to Author 21 August 1997:

I received *four* faxes from my young physicist friend at Fermi yesterday. I think I'm really blowing his mind with my theories. He's calculated that a typical antimatter-matter annihilation involving a human body would basically have blown up Jerusalem!

What I have him looking at now, however, is not the standard model for annihilations but annihilations that occur at the very tiniest level between the quarks (normally quarks and antiquarks don't annihilate because they are protected by the electromagnetic field within the neutrons).

But, according to my theory, this electromagnetic buffer field is disrupted by the burst that occurs at death causing a catalytic chain reaction deep within the atom structure leading to an implosion that annihilates the atom from quark up. This annihilation produces gamma rays which act as the image forming substance. Gamma rays are far more energetic than regular x-rays meaning that only a miniscule amount would have been needed to leave a trace like the one on the Shroud.

I had a very restless night last night because of all the incoming information I was receiving on this subject. I haven't been able to piece it all together but the snippets include: the reaction occurred from inside out and from top down, the reaction occurred over the course of time (between death and resurrection) and in a systematic manner, the reaction involved a series of catalytic events that I already described, the experiment to prove this will be at the most minute level our science can possibly explore today (e.g. quarks).

My mind was swimming and now I'm pretty exhausted. They really want me to understand this but, unfortunately, they're not talking to the smartest caveperson among us!! I'm convinced it's going to take someone like Dr. Jackson to help piece all of this together—I can only provide the big picture and some sense of direction to pursue. Hopefully, he'll find time to examine some of these concepts . . . .

Email from Benford to Author 22 August 1997:

I'm convinced, by every fiber of my being, that I truly know the Christ in the way he wants us to know him. Part of his instruction to me, early on, was that, "All my words must be heard. It's time." I initially didn't know what he meant until he led me to the early Christian Gnostic texts that had been condemned for political reasons.

When I questioned him about the "heretical" texts, he said, "Who among you, living or dead, is worthy of judging which of my words has meaning or not?" I didn't know how to respond besides saying "no one."

Point being, humans determined the canon of the New Testament, not Jesus. His message, as I told you, has been twisted and perverted by man to serve a worldly purpose. I have made it part of my mission to tell what I know of the true Jesus and his message. He is so much more than anyone can imagine. It is only this true realization of him that will save the world. This will be his second coming!

Email from Benford to Author 26 August 1997:

WOW! I just finished reading the articles you sent me. I can't believe some of the overlaps with my theories, especially the article on the "Electromagnetic Biophoton Emission." Has Dr. Jackson seen this yet?? If not, he REALLY needs to.

I'm more convinced now than ever that my theories are on target. Put all of what we know together about the Shroud and the resurrection and what have you got? Basically, a body that disappears /annihilates (e.g. resurrection), gives off a burst of light (most likely supported by an outside source coming in through the crown region), and leaves a radiation-induced image on a cloth.

I have a feeling gamma rays are the key. They are highly energetic little buggers that, I believe, could cause all of this at very minimal levels (e.g. between quark and antiquark annihilations). At death, when the electromagnetic field collapses, the quarks and antiquarks (e.g., body and spirit) annihilate to create a catalytic reaction on a subatomic level imploding the cells of the body from inside out (this is why Jerusalem didn't blow up) and producing gamma rays (radiation) as a by-product. The gamma rays act like X-rays and could easily have caused the image to be created.

Of course this death-related reaction is directly proportional to the resting energy level of the aura/minisoul such that the implosion is 1000x the resting level. Thus, Jesus alone had enough antiquarks, or spirit, in his minisoul (or influxing into his aura) to create such a thorough annihilation response. This is due to his spiritual-self equaling his physical-self proportionally (e.g. he achieved perfection).

I believe this is what he wants us to learn, this is what we are to strive for—equilibrium between the "two faces of Adam . . . ."

P.S. He said to tell you: "You'll see it when you believe it. The truth is all around like raindrops. Take your umbrella down." What were you asking him???

Email from Benford to Author on 29 August 1997:

I'm so excited I can hardly see straight!! Guess what?? Okay, I'll tell you. ..I have a meeting scheduled for next Friday with a researcher in Nuclear Medicine regarding testing the gamma-rays in the surrounding aura around the body. Ohio State University has a full body gamma ray detector that can do the job. I don't know if I told you before but I'm the President of a biotechnology company that funds several research projects at OSU so when I call, generally, they listen. When I described my theory the researcher said, "I've never heard anything like this before." I told him, "that's why they call it 'new' research." HA HA.

I've been in touch with my young physicist at Fermi who's helping me posit some experimental parameters. I'm proposing that he come up with an estimate of how much antimatter would have been necessary to annihilate Jesus' body without blowing up Jerusalem. We can then use that for the high end estimate of "spirit" (reflected in gamma rays produced) and use a cadaver to get the low end.

I have to tell you another funny story about my conversation with the Nuclear Medicine researcher. I explained to him that one of things we wanted to test was the "light shout" that radiated from the body at time of death. He asked where we would get human subjects for this and I explained that we could work with patients dying at Hospice. He grew silent for a moment then responded, trying to be diplomatic, "I think you might have some trouble with human subjects regulations if you proposed euthanizing patients to test the light radiated at time of death." He actually thought I was talking about killing people in order to test my theory! . . . .

Email from Benford to Author on 12 September 1997:

Just a couple thoughts that I've been told to relay to you as extensions of our conversation last night regarding people working "from the light" versus the darkness or "the world." They said you are now at the point where you can begin to discern between these two perspectives.

Here is a simple way to understand what I'm talking about. Start really becoming aware every time you think about someone, talk with someone, or interact with someone how it makes you feel—body and soul. Some people make us want to move away from them because of a negative or distasteful "vibe."

Others use such tactics as to cause shame, guilt, or fear within us (perhaps parents or bosses) causing both a physical and emotional set of reactions, e.g. how does your body and soul respond to stress and put-downs? The opportunities for spiritual gain within our souls when we are around people like this are slim to none.

On the other hand, there are people and situations which bring light into our soul. These experiences we can also easily discern. Like moths drawn to a bright light, we swarm to be near them. In their presence we find warmth, growth, and most of all, unconditional love. In relationships with them we find the freedom to make our own choices and decisions which is necessary for our continued spiritual growth. Most times our bodies respond along with our spirit (as both are a part of our soul). How do you feel when you are around people of the light? Begin to record, on paper, what you are thinking and feeling in different situations and interactions.

It is to your advantage, both now and in the future, to get in touch with this type of discernment and to act in the direction that grows your spirit. Remember, the spirit is like a fetus constantly needing the light for its nourishment. Unfortunately, many become "anorexic" by refusing to discern what is truly of the spirit/light and what is of the world/darkness. They, ultimately, kill their spirit.

On another note, I wanted to share with you the response I got from an email I sent to the Polish physicist, Dr. Slawinski, who did the studies on the "light shout."

Dear Dr. Benford,

Professor Slawinski has forwarded me your letter.
I see you are interested in the detection of the optical radiation. We are also interested in the detection of the optical radiation, mainly in UV radiation. We have used a TL detectors for UV-C radiation detection for the dose range 25-6500mJ/cm2. Now we are going to start with the CR-59.

We should be very grateful if you could send me more information concerning your research program.

>Best regards,
>Marta WASILEWSKA-RADWANSKA, Ph.D.
>Head of Medical Physics Department
>Faculty of Physics and Nuclear Techniques
>University of Mining and Metallurgy AI.Mickiewicza 30
>PL-30-059 KRAKOW, POLAND

Isn't it wonderful how all of this is coming together? I know our mission is being blessed.

Email from Benford to Author 20 September 1997:

...when I was leaving the gym today after my workout, one of my first soul mate's employees came up to me and said, "I was watching you today and you weren't into your workout. There's something going on with you, what is it?" This guy is a trucker—not a mystic—and has never before inquired into my personal condition in any way. Naturally, I was afraid of what might come next so I made a quick beeline for the door! It's like I'm giving off some invisible radar signal broadcasting all of this.

Another thing that I didn't tell you last night but ties into all of this, when I was watching you being interviewed on the Shroud tape I received an insight very similar to the one I got that told me my name wasn't Margaret. Only this time it told me that you were my mate. I watched it a dozen times and got the same insight each time. This occurred after my lunch meeting so I'm trying to pass it off as related to my thought processes from that episode.

In addition, even if you are one of my soul mates, that doesn't mean that we must physically link or marry legally for a lifetime. That's important to understand. Perhaps the lessons we are to learn from each other are transient and temporary. All I know is that this is a very dramatic episode in my life that has no previous counterparts.

Email from Benford to Author 29 September 1997:

How "ironic" the first thing you asked me in your email was if anything happened at Church or Bible Study. Until now, I had wondered whether or not to tell you about our Scripture lesson from yesterday which made me sit up and take notice.

I had been thinking that we have free will to do as we please in this situation and that we really don't have to go where Jesus is leading us if it would make us too uncomfortable. Then my minister started reading this passage from James 1:22-25 "Do not merely listen to the word, and so deceive yourselves. Do what it says. Anyone who listens to the word but does not do what it says is like a man who looks at this face in a mirror and, after looking at himself, goes away and immediately forgets what he looks like. But the man who looks intently into the perfect law that gives freedom, and continues to do this, not forgetting what he has heard, but doing it—he will be blessed in what he does." Another coincidence?

Also, after the service, Carol (the one predicting our marriage) came up to me and asked for an update on our situation. I told her we were going to meet with your spiritual director. She nodded her head and said, "I'll tell you what's going to happen, you're going to end up teaching *them* about the Spirit." I thought that was an interesting comment considering she doesn't know anything about my Gnostic understandings or the stuff we've been talking about.

I had a real "soul to soul" talk with Jesus about this last night. I asked him why he wouldn't just give us some really big sign like appearing before us or sending an angel. He said that the signs he was sending were "right for the time." As things progress, the signs will also escalate. Almost immediately after he said this, the wind (or something) whipped open the front door of my house. I thought there was a burglar or something. It scared me to death. He then reminded me that we had once talked about how I would be really frightened at a "big sign." The little signs suit me much better!

Email from Benford to Author 30 September 1997:

I have bounced my revelations off just about anybody who will listen. Unfortunately, I learned early in the game that there is a great deal of fear among the Orthodox for anything mystical in nature. This has made most of their input less than useful since it is fear-based, e.g., they think everything out of the ordinary comes from the devil.

Since most of my revelations of Biblical importance came last year (and I'm really mostly following that guidance now) I haven't been back to see my friend *[name intentionally omitted]*. Although he was very supportive he, too, didn't know much about Gnosticism or mystical relationships with Christ. I finally have come to the conclusion that I need to have confidence in my own beliefs and callings and that I need to proceed accordingly, e.g. with my book, screenplays, research, you, etc.

I trust others of the "light" which includes you and my close friend Carol who also hears about my revelations quite often. In addition, I share things selectively with the Stephen Ministers who are still pretty basic in their understandings but they are a good Christian group to be a part of. I also have shared much of this with my mother who is supportive but not really in tune with the mystical. I have no problem sharing my insights with others but I have turned over my spiritual guidance exclusively to Christ. He, above all, I trust.

I hope that doesn't sound pretentious but I have learned (mostly the hard way) over the past year that we are all at different levels of understanding on our spiritual journeys. To keep myself "in line" I have in the past asked my close friends to let me know if I ever act toward them in any way other than "loving" as a result of my revelations and then I will suspect my guidance has gone "astray." I would ask you the same thing. That's the best way I know to continually discern the messages I am receiving.

As Jesus once told me, "The answer is always love." He also said that any image, including one that even looked like him, that didn't have that as the answer wasn't of the light. I have used that guidance *many* times over the past year. Where unconditional love is present, God is present.

Email from Benford to Author 5 October 1997:

I forgot to put this in my last email. I saw on a TV documentary recently where some scientists have conclusively identified the dating of "the great flood" in the Mesopotamia region as having occurred 7,640 years ago. As you may recall, in my Two Faces of Adam article I stated that the flood occurred as a result of the melting from the last Ice Age which began 10,000 years ago and ended approx. 8,000 years ago.

My prophecy, of course, flew in the face of conventional orthodox wisdom on the dates for creation, the flood, etc. It was from this insight that I also was able to calculate the rest of the timeline of creation and "the fall" of Homo spiritual is. This gives me a very real affirmation that the revelations and insights I've been receiving are on target. It should be comforting to you, as well, to see that some of the things I've disclosed are now being scientifically documented (or maybe not!)

Just wait until we prove the existence of the spirit within the soul! :)

Email from Benford to author 16 October 1997:

Boy, this is strange one. Have you heard of the newly released book entitled, "The Messengers: A True Story of Angelic Presence and the Return to the Age of Miracles?" It's about a businessman that has a series of strange spiritual experiences, along with several of his close friends, and who ends up going through hypnotic regression only to learn is he used to be the Apostle Paul.

Well, as you know, I don't believe the apostles are back as whole spirits but only that they may have reproduced some of their spiritual "splendors" into other human souls. In my book, and in my revelations, Jesus refers to it as "spiritual DNA." Anyhow, because of that, I have avoided the book—that is until I was told to read it today.

I really didn't want to because I am knee deep in other projects so I called the library to see if I could borrow it. Unfortunately I was 19th on the waiting list for it but I thought, "oh well, see guys at least I tried." They said, "nope, go buy it today." To avoid a big debate over the subject I agreed and bought it at the bookstore.

One of the things that this guy "Nick" does when all the signs start coming to him is contact a woman who claims to be able to "talk to his angels." This is identical to the woman who I first talked to that got me started to look at this as a spiritual venture. His contact person, Sara, said that some major events were about to take place in the world and he should publish his manuscript before they occur. Then she said, "There is information in the manuscript that is coded, and people who have the correct spiritual DNA will be moved by the book and understand it . . . " She went on to explain "[J]ust as people have different DNA in their cells, people also have different spiritual DNA."

Needless to say I am speechless to see this terminology and description published elsewhere. Plus, I was also told that part of my job was to "awaken those who had ears to hear, the offspring of the apostles now here on earth." An identical message, perhaps, being given to a variety of people?

Listen to what I wrote nearly a year ago about spiritual DNA in my book:

"If a person reproduces, then it is easy to see how part of that person can technically live forever through its progeny. But that is only in the flesh and blood world. I wondered if it was a coincidence that my work in the physical world to develop a treatment for the prevention of premature delivery or miscarriage of human babies had any correlation to these new understandings and preventing the miscarriage of souls? Was there such a thing as "spiritual

DNA" and, if so, what scientific and spiritual documentation could I find to support this wild idea?"

"We are the tree we will become at the time of our births. We choose it with God as co-creators of our own destiny: our families, our unique life experiences, challenges, talents, opportunities, everything that we will do or become. We draw up the plans and bring them with us when we are born—in the form of spiritual DNA."

"One night in meditation Jesus told me that the seven psychical substances mentioned in The Secret Book of John used to create our bodies and souls would soon be discovered by scientists. These substances combine to form the spiritual DNA we inherit from our spiritual parents—like that transferred from Elijah to Elisha. Encoded in these substances are matching codes to our soul mates, angelic and planetary splendors. He said that science will prove the existence of the Spirit and, ultimately, the existence of God!"

Well, you get the point. How can all of this be a coincidence? I know what the events are that Sara is referring to. I'll keep you in suspense . . . .

Email from Benford to Author 16 November 1997:

I had Stephen's tonight and Carol (the one with the "intuition" about us marrying) came up and asked me how things were going. After I briefly updated her on the past month's visit, etc. she reiterated her belief that we would be married. In fact, she asked if you had already decided to leave the monastery!

She went on to say that there was something very different about me since I first talked to you. She said it was a special kind of "peace" that I never had before. She added, "truly divine intervention played a part in this relationship." I told her that there were so many miraculous signs that we could write a book and she just nodded her head. She said she looks forward to meeting you someday....

What did you think about the stuff on Thomas that I emailed last night? Perhaps you should also share my article called "The Two Faces of Adam" with Tom [Father Santen], also. He probably should know that I'm publishing many of my revelations in Christian magazines with large circulations (The *Church Herald* circ. is 110,000) and on the Internet. I figure that's as good a way as any to share my insights and put my theories to the test . . . .

Email from Benford to Author 18 January 1998:

This morning in Bible Study was really extraordinary. We are working our way through the bible and were discussing various chapters in Genesis and Matthew. I shared several of my "insights" and understandings which seemed to have a real impact on several of the group who saw things in anew and clearer light.

A couple people approached me afterwards asking more questions and inquiring about my writings. I really think this is a sign that my words need to be heard and that I should pursue getting my book published. What do you think? Any suggestions on how I might do this or who I could contact? . . . .

This was a strong affirmation for me that the things Jesus, et al have been revealing and teaching me will have a definite and positive effect on "those with ears to hear." Like you, many are now starting to look at religion and spirituality in a renewed light—just as Jesus predicted would happen. Although, so far my understandings have only been heard by a few, the reactions give me hope that I am on the right track. It should make you feel better, too.

Email from Benford to Author and an acquaintance, "Jeffrey" 26 March 1998:

Well, it finally happened—physical contact with "someone" from the group last night, or more precisely, 3:11 a.m. this morning!! A couple nights ago, while in one of my more skeptical moods, I requested, or somewhat demanded, that Jesus provide an overt sign of his involvement in all that is happening. He said that he would and that the sign would come in the middle of the night.

I woke the following morning and realized nothing had happened of any significance. Well, I should have remembered that time viewed from their perspective doesn't coordinate with time as we perceive it. They had taught me that a long time ago. Last night, I awoke to the sound of a gentle shuffling of footsteps coming down our carpeted hallway. Naturally, I figured it was one of the kids coming into my bedroom.

A minute or two passed and no child materialized. As soon as I realized that the sound wasn't caused by one of the girls, I felt a very distinct pushing against my back (I was laying on my left side not facing the door). It felt like someone had pushed against me with the fleshy part of their upper thigh— in other words, it wasn't like a kick in the back. I immediately panicked and knew it wasn't a person doing this. I looked over at the clock and documented the time as 3:11 a.m. just to prove to myself that I wasn't sleeping.

I was still frightened so didn't turn around to see what or who it was. Amazingly, I was able to fall right back to sleep (which is not typical when I've had a bad dream or fright of some kind).

In the morning, "the guys" told me that they orchestrated this sign via an angel—it wasn't them directly but was their doing. I had totally forgotten, until they reminded me, that I had asked for an overt sign the other night. They also told me that my fright was to demonstrate why they don't go around giving these kind of signs to everybody—we'd all be having heart attacks right and left!! They felt, at this point, I could handle a small physical sign. Now I realize that if Jesus pops out of the Shroud, I'll be there with you guys on the floor passed out!!!!

APPENDIX K

IAN WILSON'S COMMENTS IN THE *BRITISH SOCIETY FOR THE TURIN SHROUD NEWSLETTER*, No. 54, NOVEMBER 2001

[Reprinted with permission of Ian Wilson.]

Throughout the twenty-odd years that I have edited this Newsletter, I have felt the task to be a very privileged one and have greatly valued your support. However this is to let you know that this will be my last issue . . . .

I have always believed it to be better to bow out of any venture before reaching your 'sell by' date twenty years being quite long enough for anyone. However in this instance my departure is in direct protest at the current state of US-led Shroud politics.

For one of this Newsletter's prime functions is to report, comment on, and reflect the activities of leading Shroudies and Shroudie groups around the world. And while constitutionally the Society has no 'party line' on the issue of the Shroud's authenticity, it is no secret that the great majority of members favour authenticity, myself likewise. My bias as an Editor has therefore naturally favoured this, yet always mindful—and this is the crucial factor—of respecting those with sincerely differing, even conflicting views, and maintaining fairness and cordiality towards them. As but one expression of this, this present Newsletter carries two obituaries, both for individuals whom I personally knew, one, Dr. Robert Bucklin, definitely from the pro-authenticity camp, the other, Professor Edward Hall, equally definitely of the other persuasion. Despite many Shroudies regarding Professor Hall as an adversary, I certainly did not feel this. To me it is axiomatic that both he and Dr. Bucklin should be treated with equal sympathy and objectivity, and this I have tried to do. Likewise this issue includes a contributed article suggesting an interesting alternative hypothesis to my identification of the Edessa Mandylion with the Shroud. Although I do not agree with this hypothesis, I respect the writer very highly and believe it only right for members to be aware of his views in order to come to their own properly reasoned evaluation. It may be recalled from when I was living in England that I invited Dr. Walter McCrone, Professor Averil Cameron and other sceptics to address the BSTS, in much the same spirit.

Of late, amongst the current oligarchy of leading Shroudies, those (mostly American) whose activities and contributions to international conferences I am obliged to report, such a sense of fairness and openness has been in serious decline, accompanied by a preference for issues of often the most marginal credibility, let alone public interest. In 1999, while attending the Shroud conference at Richmond, Virginia, I was outraged at the organisers' denial of any platform to Shroud sceptic Dr. Emily Craig, likewise so excruciatingly bored by some of the speakers who had been allowed speaking time that I wondered whether they could be talking on the same subject as that to which I had devoted so much of life.

This set in train the erosion of a vital sense of my belonging to the world 'Shroudie' community, ultimately to snap altogether this July over the AMSTAR (American Shroud of Turin Association for Research) conference being held in Dallas, at which I had been invited to give the keynote address. After my having accepted this invitation, and agreed also to give a historical paper, I learned that the conference organisers had refused an important scientific paper from the University of Texas microbiologist Professor Stephen Mattingly. This even though Professor Mattingly is pro-authenticity, was speaking from the standpoint of his own professional expertise, and the conference was being held in his own home state of Texas. Since Professor Mattingly had lodged his application as early as April, AMSTAR's excuse that the speaking slots were full carried no credibility. All the indications were that the organisers were unprepared even to listen to an argument differing from their own 'party-line'. And only last year in Turin I had struggled far too hard persuading the late Dr. Alan Adler to take Professor Mattingly seriously (see Newsletter 51, pp. 9 & 10), to let this latest rebuff go unchallenged.

Rashly, therefore, I decided to take a stand. First I offered up my own history paper timeslot so that Professor Mattingly could give his microbiological paper in its place. Then I surrendered my keynote speech. Finally, when both offerings proved to no avail, I withdrew from the entire conference with a formal 'on record' declaration that should the Shroud be found to have suffered irreversible microbiological damage when next opened up, I would consider AMSTAR directly culpable, particularly given that the Dallas conference provided a unique opportunity for Professor Mattingly's microbiological insights to be heard by Cardinal Poletto's leading scientific advisor, Professor Bruno Barberis.

What happened next was positively Macchiavellian. Without the slightest reference to my self-sacrificial lobbying, AMSTAR suddenly flurried to find a slot for Mattingly, as if this had always been intended. At the same time it put about that my stand had been directed, not at giving Mattingly a speaking platform at the conference, but at securing him a place on the AMSTAR board of directors. My first reaction was to suppose there had been a genuine misunderstanding, since a year earlier I had conversationally suggested Mattingly as a replacement for the AMSTAR board's then recent losses of Dr. Alan Adler and Don Lynn. However not only did AMSTAR insist—untruthfully and, to me, utterly ludicrously—that my intention was a full-blooded board 'coup', as events further unfolded, including the refusal of a paper from Joe Marino and Sue Benford, it became clear that AMSTAR and I shared absolutely no philosophical common ground. Instead of any scientific openness and fair play in the selection of speakers their so-called 'peer review' committee's deliberations are conducted in secret, and by scientists whose identities apparently can under no circumstances be revealed.

The idea, therefore, of my giving a keynote speech to such a 'closed shop, closed mind' organisation, even should any reconciliation have been possible, violated every principle of the fairness and openness that I hold most dear. One remark in particular, by the AMSTAR peer review committee's chairperson, said it all: 'We [i.e. AMSTAR] will neither invite nor accept papers from controversial people. No Walter McCrone, Emily Craig, no C 14 maniacs, has-been STURP members who lost their faith, or anyone else who wants to bring outdated contact image ideas.' Put simply, this means 'we will not listen to strangers'.

Having become more and more weary of the bulk of material that *is* selected for Shroud conferences, and gaining absolutely no satisfaction from my sounding forth ever-more strident criticisms, I therefore decided that it would be altogether for the best, not least in the cause of general harmony, for me to quit not only the Dallas conference, but the entire scene of 'Shroudie' politics. Underscoring the rightness of this was the response to an explanatory round robin which I sent to a number of those whom I knew to be attending the Dallas conference. While this produced some kind notes of sympathy, which were greatly appreciated, no-one except Joe Marino was prepared openly to support my stand against AMSTAR on the fundamental principles of fairness, openness and honesty. So if not talking to outsiders, and positively debarring any dissident opinion is to be the colour of Shroud politics for the future, then I can no longer feel any sense of belonging, and must take my place outside, with the subject's outcasts and even its skeptics.

This said, please be assured that my departure is neither from the Shroud as such, nor from my continuing publicly to uphold its authenticity. In fact, I am hopeful of being able quietly to research and serve the subject rather better than has been possible for the last two decades. But at least until the emergence of a very different political mood in the subject, my days as a general commentator on Shroudies via the medium of this Newsletter, are very firmly over. I know that most of the present Shroudie oligarchy positively welcome this . . . .

APPENDIX L

DOCUMENTS FROM THE TURIN AUTHORITIES PERTAINING TO THE 2002 RESTORATION

Information for the Press

An important series of interventions has been completed on the Shroud in the period between last June and July, in the area of the Turin Cathedral:

1. **the Shroud has been completely unstitched from the Holland cloth, on which it had been fixed since 1534; all the 'patches", sewn by the Clare nuns of Chambery, have been removed and a new support has been joined to the Shroud Cloth;**

2. **the complete digital scansion, both on the image side and on the posterior one, has been carried out;**

3. **a new complete photographic documentation of the Shroud has been realized.**

All the operations have been carried out under the surveillance of the Papal Custodian, the Archbishop of Turin Card. Severino Poletto. The works have been followed, in all their steps, by the Assistants of the Custodian, Mgr. Giuseppe Ghiberti and Prof. Piero Savarino, with the collaboration of the diocesan Commission for the Shroud and of the Commission for the conservation. The interventions have been executed starting from the indications worked out by the Commission for the Conservation since 1992; the program has been approved by the Custodian and the owner (the Holy See).

1. *Unstitching and substitution of patches*

Dr. Mechthild Flury-Lemberg, emeritus director of the school of restoration of the ancient cloths near the Abegg Museum of Bern, executed, in collaboration with the restorer Irene Tomedi, the wide and complex intervention of unstitching of the Shroud Cloth from the patches and the underlying "Holland cloth", the lining to which it had been joined since

1534, when the Clare nuns of Chambery intervened in order to repair the damages of the 1532 fire.

The separation of the Shroud from the Holland cloth was necessary in order to reduce the problem of the folds on the Cloth and to limit the damages caused by the carbon residues: after the decision to conserve the extended Shroud, not rolled up anymore, there is a further improvement of the conservation conditions, just because the seam points (along the edges, in correspondence of the patches and other zones) stretched the Cloth in an irregular and uncontrolled way, with the risk to deepen the existing folds or to create some new ones. Moreover, the conditions of cleanness of the lining had become remarkably worrisome.

The intervention of the patches removal has been equally important: the interstices between the patches cloth and the Shroud Linen had accumulated dusts and debris for centuries, and a remarkable amount of microscopic fragments of carbonated cloth.

All the material removed from the Shroud has been collected and catalogued, with the relative photographic documentation, and is guarded by the Archiepiscopal Chancery of Turin.

Dr. Flury-Lemberg has substituted the old Holland cloth with a new support, sewing along the perimeter and in a "wide" way in correspondence of the burns edges, so that it is possible to verify in every point the "non-invasiveness" of the intervention carried out.

The substitution of the Holland cloth will allow the future conservation of the Linen in a condition of greater safety as to the cloth tensions. The "cleaning" of the burn residues and debris from the edges guarantees, moreover, a better conservation.

The opportunity of this intervention had been emphasized with force by the lamented Prof. Alan Adler, member of the Commission for the Conservation.

2. *Digital scansion*

For the first time the complete digital scansion of the two "faces" of the Shroud (the first partial scansion had been carried out in November 2000) has been realized. The intervention has been executed by Prof. Paul Soardo, of the "Istituto Elettrotecnico Nazionale Galileo Fenoaris" of Turin, in collaboration with Doctors Jacomussi and Rossi.

The complete digital mapping will allow to carry out a wide series of non-invasive studies on the Shroud.

3. The new photographs

The interventions carried out, and, above all, the removal of the patches, has given back a "image" of the Shroud that, at the first impact, is a bit different from the one everybody remembers. For this reason, the Giandurante studio has carried out a new complete series of photographs, of which some samples are given. The most representative images are published in the issue published for the press conference, and are available on the official website of the Shroud (*www.Shroud.org*). The scientific and photographic documentation of the interventions of sewing again and digital scansion will be published in the volume, which is being prepared and completing the documentation of the "season of the exhibitions", concluding what had been started with the publication of "The two faces of the Shroud". The new volume will also contain the scientific documentation of the interventions of sewing again and digital scansion.

Turin, September 21, 2002

Press conference
Intervention of [Professor] Piero Savarino

The jobs for the conservation began in 1992 when His Eminence the Cardinal Saldarini reunited a narrow number of experts in conservation and restoration of ancient cloths in order to obtain indications on the jobs to carry out.

The group supplied the suggestion unanimously to conserve the Shroud extended, deprived of the edges and drapes that accompanied it, in an inert atmosphere. Moreover, it suggested, then, to continue the works with the removal of the patches and the Holland cloth. On this last point, the opinions were not unanimous. Some, in fact, suggested, with the politics of the step after step, to act, while others preferred to carry out preventive surveys of data in order to act later.

Starting from these indications, at first it has been seen to eliminate the drapes and the edges, and subsequently to conserve the Shroud in extended position overcoming a long series of technological difficulties (construction of the case and the related pressure compensation systems, inert gas and its conditioning, control system of all the system, etc). In the course of these works, the Shroud has been the object of a series of careful observations. As an example, it had been found that under the patch situated near the foot a considerable amount of foreign substances was present. Therefore, the possible presence of polluting systems also under the central patches had been feared. The decision of intervening, guaranteed by the Holy See, has been taken with the will to proceed by degrees and intervene with means proportioned to the situation that, moreover, had to be verified moment by moment.

In fact, the imagination had not succeeded in previewing the real situation. Look at figure 2, [not shown here] in which it is noticeable, on the edge of the patch, a worrisome presence of the most fine dust of carbonic material.

A microscopic observation, carried out with the equipment placed at disposal by Dr. Tomedi, has evidenced that the carbonic material is present on the Holland cloth and also on Shroud sites far from the burns. On the Shroud sites not closely adjacent to the burns it has not been intervened, in order to avoid to alter and to make successive searches impossible.

The intervention has followed the following criteria:

a) Improvement of the conservation conditions removing the polluting parts on the edges of the burns, avoiding obviously of damaging the Shroud.

b) Collection, cataloguing (on the basis of the position) and delivery to the Papal Custodian of the parts removed on the edges of the burns and without carrying out cuts.

c) Replacement of a cloth of support in order to supply an adequate mechanical support to the Shroud.

d) Carrying out of observations and measures (on the posterior part) difficultly feasible in successive times. The surveys have been executed using a purposely constructed instrument and in a position to directly carrying the various sensors of the instruments on the sites of measure. The system has been studied by the Eng. Ardoino and realized by the company ADL. In this context photographic surveys (work group directed by the Giandurante studio) and scanning (work group directed by Prof. Soardo) have been carried out. Photographic surveys in fluorescence (executed by the work group of the scientific police of Turin directed by Dr. Cella). Moreover, recordings of reflectance spectra UV-VIS, spectra of fluorescence and Raman spectra have been carried out. The fluorescence and reflectance spectra have been carried out by the company Laser Point, cured by Dr .Pellegrini and Dr. Caldironi. The Raman spectra have been executed by the Renishow company, cured by Dr. Tagliapietra and Eng. Orsi. The results of the measures have been delivered to His Eminence Cardinal Poletto, Papal Custodian of the Shroud, to be put at disposal for successive researches.

e) On sites object of spectrophotometric measures on the back of the Shroud, they carried out sampling, with the methods of the suction and the adhesive tape. The sampling, carried out in the presence of the Chancellor of the Curia, have been sealed and taken by the same Chancellor. The choice of the sites has been carried out by Prof. Baima Bollone with the approval of the entire commission. Prof. Baima Bollone has moreover seen to carry out the sampling in the presence of the same commission.

f) Carrying out of a series of microscopic surveys with the use of the equipment supplied by Dr. Tomedi.

The particulars and techniques connected more specifically to the operation of conservation will be later described by Dr. Fleury-Lemberg on single demand of the present ones. Here we only describe the most important operations that Dr. Fleury-Lemberg has executed with the aid of Dr. Tomedi. The Shroud has been at first supported on neutral paper of rice with the image turned down. Then, the Holland cloth has been unstitched and after the patches. All the carbonated material has been removed from the sites under the patches. Such material was made up by a very fine dust. Without cuts, the material still weakly connected to the cloth has been removed. Subsequently the over cited surveys have taken place. At the end of such surveys, the operation of sewing again the Shroud on the new cloth of support has begun. The operation has been led turning the Shroud (without ever raising it extended) by a careful series of position variations, that have guaranteed its absolute safety. We are not giving technical details, even if interesting, but we want to emphasize here the absolute very high level of professionalism shown by Dr. Lemberg and Tomedi who carried out their engagement with dedication, ability and respect for the Shroud. The results obtained are noticeable in the following figure, in which the photographs of the Shroud before and after the intervention are compared.

Therefore, the comparison does not leave doubts on the positive quality of the work carried out.

Turin, September 21, 2002

THE SHROUD OF TURIN IN 2002:
THE NEW IMAGE*

1- Tuesday, 23 July 2002. The Shroud lay on the 'Microtecnica couch' in the decorous humility of its nakedness regained. It had left its chapel and the 'Alenia casket' five weeks earlier and was about to return. On the arrival of Mons. Lanzetti, all those who had been waiting in the glass-lined corridor entered the 'new sacristy'. A few moments of contemplative silence were followed by a brief comment on the present event in the history of the Shroud. Then the Auxiliary Bishop, acting on behalf of the Archbishop, who had gone to Toronto to join the Pope on the occasion of World Youth Day, led a prayer. Next the procession that was to accompany the Shroud back to its chapel was formed. It was with an aching heart that Mechthild Flury-Lemberg and Irene Tomedi stood to one side and watched the procession move away: "it seemed like a funeral cortege". Then when all was over their inner feelings came out: "During our work we took care not to think too much about the mysterious object that was passing under our hands and determined to keep our minds on what we had to do. Yet each time we finished a day's work a shiver of wonderment returned. Towards the end there was an ever-growing desire to remain with the Shroud, to be able to speak to that Sufferer. But now there is no time left." An impression shared by all who had been intensely involved in the events of the previous five weeks.

From the evening of Thursday 20 June to the evening of Tuesday 23 July, 2002, the Shroud remained outside its casket and its chapel. It now returned, in a way rejuvenated. But how many things had happened since it was first laid in the 'Alenia casket' in November 2000 at the end of the two Expositions!

2- The idea of undertaking conservation work on the Shroud, based on the repairs made by the Poor Clares of Chambery in 1534, had been considered long before by the members of the Shroud Conservation Committee.

Cardinal Saldarini had been entrusted with the Shroud at the time of the most heated polemics following the carbon dating analyses. His instructions were to refrain from considering further scientific research and embark upon a systematic approach to the question of conservation[1]. So in 1991 he formed a small group whose task was to prepare a meeting of persons competent to work on the question. We were all new to this approach and greatly influenced by a past that hung like a millstone. Strict secrecy in all our doings had to be maintained from the beginning. Following a day spent in preparation at Pianezza, a small and still somewhat informal committee spent several hours on 7 September 1992 in what is now called the 'old sacristy' of the Cathedral (though historians will tell you it is not the earliest) examining the Shroud to work out some ideas and opinions on how it should be conserved. A host of proposals were put forward for improving its condition which, being obviously the outcome of its long history, was not in keeping with the results that could be achieved by applying modern techniques for the conservation of ancient fabrics.

The main concern was expressed with regard to the increasingly numerous and harmful wrinkles on the sindonic figure, especially the face. Everyone agreed that the Shroud should no longer be kept rolled up and that it should also be freed from the numerous restraints that were binding it: the upper 'lining' and the blue-green silk surround with silver stiffeners in its short sides. Removal of the patches—seemingly a utopian idea—was also brought up, resuming a discussion already broached in 1969 during the work of the scientific committee formed by Cardinal Pellegrino.

3- But nothing was done. The Shroud had to be taken back to its niche in the 'glory' on Bertola's altar and no one knew when it would ever be taken out again. Providence, however, moved events in a mysterious way and only later did we begin to glimpse them as a part of a plan. On 4 May 1990, the Feast Day of the Shroud, just as Mass was drawing to a close, some chunks of marble fell from the ribbing of Guarini's cupola. No one was hit, but the authorities decided to close the chapel and undertake a thorough restoration of the cupola.

What was to become of the Shroud? The cardinal discussed the matter with the competent Superintendences and decided to transfer it to the choir of the Cathedral in a glass monument designed by architect Bruno. On 24 February 1993, Ash Wednesday, the Shroud left the chapel that had been erected for it and inaugurated three hundred years earlier, in 1694. For four years it remained in the choir, until, ten days after Easter of 1997, when in the night of Friday-Saturday, April 11-12, a furious fire broke out throwing panic in the Cathedral. The flames spread to a wing of the Royal Palace and wreaked havoc in Guarini's chapel. No harm came to the Shroud, but it was taken away for a year.

4- The events of these intervening years encouraged the Conservation Committee during its meetings to take another look at the ideas it had been working on since 1992. Cardinal Saldarini had become increasingly convinced that it was no longer possible to put off the decision to provide for the permanent safekeeping of the Shroud, laid out full length and at rest on a couch. This, however, raised a problem. Guarini's chapel had been designed on a circular ground plan to accommodate a casket measuring a little more than a meter. Now one had to place there a casket four times larger without modifying the original architecture. Suggestions, trials and proposals were advanced in endless discussions between architects, representatives of the Superintendences, and members of the Committee. But before a satisfactory solution had been found, the fire intervened and damage to the Chapel was so extensive that the problem would have to be shelved for many years. It was readily agreed that the new 'Chapel of the Holy Shroud' should be in the Cathedral below the royal tribune at the left end of the transep[2].

The time was now ripe for a review of the whole question of the conservation of the Shroud. Alan Adler, an American scientist who combined a rare degree of competence and authority with a unique love of the Shroud, was invited to join the Committee in 1994. He had been closely associated with Father Rinaldi, a Piedmontese Salesian transplanted to America, where he spread a deep interest in the Shroud[3]. Adler now became the providential link with American researchers and the important results of their investigations. He came to Turin on several occasions, including the symposium held at Villa Gualino in March 2000, but died suddenly on June 12 before the second Exposition. We owe him many suggestions for conservation, for example, that of preserving the Shroud in an inert gas atmosphere.

5- Adler worried about the possibility of the damaging effects of material from the 1532 fire that was trapped under the patches applied by the nuns of Chambery. When he spoke during the Committee meetings, he did not retreat from the most advanced hypotheses. One of these (certainly not new, as mentioned above, but backed now by the weight of his authority) was to remove the patches and the Holland cloth. This idea remained as a dead letter until the official photos taken in 2000 revealed how much pulverous material had accumulated between the patches and the backing cloth.

In preceding years, some steps had been taken to free the Shroud as, for instance, the removal of the silk surround with its silver stiffeners. They had all shown the benefit to a fabric that was now allowed to breathe. Would it not be advisable to carry the project to a definite conclusion? After long reflection, the issue was clarified in the words expressed by Dr. Carla Enrica Spantigati, a member of the Conservation Committee and Superintendent of the Artistic and Historical Heritage of Piedmont. The nearly five hundred years spent by the Shroud in the company of its Holland cloth and its patches had established a characteristic of a stable tradition in the life of the Shroud familiar to generations of worshippers and visitors. In respect of this history and to all who have known the Shroud with these characteristics, it would be wise to continue the present situation. Were it to be shown, however, that there were well founded reasons for thinking that a substantial advantage for conservation would be conferred upon the Shroud by the removal of its patches and Holland cloth, then the sentiments of a traditional past must give way to the needs urgently arising from the object itself.

All the members of the Committee agreed with this line of reasoning. A document was composed and signed by all, and presented to Cardinal Poletto, the Papal Custodian of the Shroud[4]. Cardinal Poletto examined the document and decided to send it to the Pope. The Secretary of State, Cardinal Sodano, carried it to the Pope, who personally took it under consideration and gave his permission to go ahead with the measures proposed. Cardinal Sodano's reply is dated 3 November 2001.

6- Having obtained permission, it was advisable to proceed without delay. But there were still many problems to resolve. First of all, where to take the Shroud for conducting the work. The destruction of the Twin Towers in New York, on 11 September 2001, had brought home to the opulent West a full awareness of its vulnerability. Italy's major cities are full of predictable targets and the Shroud topped Turin's list. A meeting attended by the city's civic and religious authorities had discussed the need to find a refuge for the Shroud concluding, however, in favor of the status quo. But now, would not moving the Shroud increase the danger? If the news were to leak out, a chain of perverse reactions could bring harm to an object so precious.

Several locations were considered. In the end, however, Cardinal Poletto, the Papal Custodian, opted for the 'new sacristy', which had already been the scene of all the operations preceding and following the last two Expositions. The Shroud would thus remain within the bounds of the Cathedral; every necessary precaution would be taken. The first of these was silence[5]; for major security reasons it was decided to tell all those who might seek information that nothing at all was going on. The police were alerted, together with the private surveillance organization "Cittadini dell'ordine" (one of whose guards had been on duty at every Exposition since 1978). A fence was erected, aimed to serve as a kind of rampart between the 'new sacristy' and the piazza, while seeming merely to be an extension of the one surrounding the work going on below the Cathedral.

7- The preparations were slowed by careful thought and discussions on the details of the operation. Everyone agreed that the old Holland cloth was due for a museum, given its fragile and sullied condition. What would happen to the patches? They would have to share the same fate as the Holland cloth. Did that mean new patches should be substituted? Although there was a precise leaning toward "no" in the November 2000 proposal, and this orientation had been accepted by the papal custodian and by the Pope himself, the door was left open for further reflection: the final decisions could be made during the course of the work.

It soon became apparent, however, that there was no need to return to the discussion. Mechthild Flury-Lemberg came to the last preparatory meeting with a specimen of the work she proposed to do. On a piece of Shroud-like cloth (prepared and dyed by Piero Vercelli) a burn mark had been produced similar to those on the Shroud, and underneath the hole a piece of the lining that would be used to substitute the original Holland cloth was applied. This Shroud-like cloth and its lining were perfectly joined by almost invisible stitches. The committee unanimously agreed that the result was totally convincing and readily confirmed its original decision to simply remove the patches without substituting them.

I do not want to bore the reader with a description of all the preparatory work that led to the final result. To say that an excellent job was done is somewhat meaningless, but in human terms it is possible to affirm that every effort was made to leave nothing to chance and to avoid every possible kind of risk.

8- One great concern remained: to document as much as possible what would happen and to gather as many data as possible to place at the disposition of the scientific community. When the work was finished, the aspect of the Shroud would be partly new, but an Exposition that would permit the viewing of a large number of persons was out of the question. Therefore it was necessary to provide for an immediate gathering of images to distribute as soon as possible. Moreover, during the course of the work, the underside of the Shroud, the side customarily hidden, would be visible when the Holland cloth and patches were removed. But this would be only a temporary exposure because it was absolutely necessary to attach a new lining. The Shroud linen has certainly remained exceptionally strong considering the many vicissitudes that have studded its history. Even so, it needs a backing cloth both to allow it to be safely handled when an Exposition takes place and. above all, to hold firmly the parts damaged by the fire of 1532. Once the new lining was in place, the back of the Shroud would again be invisible for who knows how long.

It was thought that the solution was to provide images in several forms. Studio Giandurante, that had produced the official photos of 1997 and 2000, was commissioned to provide new traditional photos of the front of the Shroud (with ordinary and digital cameras) and the first (and for a long time to come, the only) traditional photos of the backside of the cloth in its entirety as well as details in reduced size. Provision was made for total scanning of front and back by Paolo Soardo's team at the Istituto Elettrotecnico Nazionale Galileo Ferraris, that in 2000 had already conducted a partial scan of the Shroud. Giuliano Marchisciano and his assistants would take care that the main moments of the work would be documented by instant photographs to illustrate the reports. Television coverage of the more significant moments was entrusted to Daniele Dr Aria and Vittorio Billera from Telesubalpina.

9- The possibility of gathering other data was also discussed and one had to face, as usual, limitations of time and the nature of the Shroud itself, because it was necessary to avoid any risk. For example, X-ray fluorescence spectroscopy was excluded since it is a delicate technique and some of the results obtained in 1978 still exist, while the Committee decided to carry out reflectance (UV VIS), fluorescence and Raman spectra measurements. The eventual removal of tiny specimens from the back of the Shroud was the subject of considerable discussion. The general opinion was that this should not be done as the "visual findings only" criterion had been adopted. It was pointed out, however, that a long time would probably elapse before any other operations could be conducted on the back. A compromise was reached when Cardinal Poletto gave permission for the removal of some specimens with scotch tape (completed by vacuum in the same places) reserving them for his sole use and filing in his Shroud archives. In the end, however, the course of events showed that the discussion was partly superfluous, since an unexpected amount of material for future examination was collected when the patches were removed and the burn holes were cleaned.

10- One chapter of the story concerns the preparation of the equipment used for the various phases of the work. The Shroud was conveyed on the 'Microtecnica couch' on which it usually lies. This was mounted on a mobile tilting table to ensure a shock-free ride on the very short journey from the chapel to the 'new sacristy'. There the couch was still used on the mobile table, alternately with the 'Bodino couch' and a double table left over from the previous work and adapted for the initial filming stage. The problem of scanning and the movements of the cameras above the surface of the Shroud was resolved by applying a mobile gantry (the "ADL bridge") to the tilting table (devised by ADL in 2000). The sewing operations called for a hard, smooth surface under the sindonic fabric and its new lining to turn back the curved needles of the seamstresses. The 'Bodino couch' was therefore fitted with a glass surface, and upon that the new lining would be laid with the Shroud on top of it. Irene Tomędi placed a videomicroscope (8OX to 450X enlargements) with optic elements attached at the end of an optic fibre cable, equipped with a monitor, a printer and the possibility of digital recording; this ensured perfect vision of all the details of the fabric, allowed to distinguish between pollutants and blood shards and guaranteed safe cleaning by the operators. To these instruments were added a gentle vacuum and an ultrasonic vaporizer; a series of glass slides; and lead weights used to apply slight pressure to smoothen the wrinkles. Much use was made of acid-free Japanese rice-paper to protect the cloth of the Shroud, and to transfer it from one couch to the other a large sheet of strong and easily removable Melinex paper was used.

11 -The conservation program proceeded in three stages: a) removal of the old backing-cloth (the famous 'Holland cloth') and patches, and "stretching" the wrinkles on the backside of the sindonic fabric (21-25 June); b) photography, spectrophotometry and scanning of the front and back (26

June-15 July); c) attachment of the new backing-cloth, first of all in the area of the burn holes and then along the sides; the final photographs of the new image of the Shroud; measurement of the Shroud in its new condition (16-23 July). Stage b), the longest, also included preparation of the new backing-cloth and the initial basting with stitches only on the upper side to ensure that the scanning of the front of the Shroud would provide a definitive vision of the holes already filled by the lining.

As the program proceeded, the seamstresses usually gained time while the technical operators were behind. The two seamstresses were Mechthild Flury-Lemberg and Irene Tomedi. The former had been invited to collaborate during the preparations for carbon dating the Shroud in the mid-80's (she subsequently left the group). Since 1992, however, she never missed any of our meetings. She is today the leading authority on the fabric of the Shroud. Irene Tomedi trained under her at the restoration school of the Abegg Foundation at Riggisberg near Berne, and has worked as a restorer throughout Italy for the last twenty years. There was always a very close understanding between the two.

"We do not underestimate the difficulties of the unstitching", Dr. Flury-Lemberg repeated. From the beginning, an unknown factor was precisely the splendid, but extremely close stitches with which the Poor Clares had attached the Holland cloth and the patches to the Shroud linen. An unexpected help came when Pierluigi Baima Bollone brought small, pointed and very sharp bistouries which worked miracles, in the expert hands of the two seamstresses, replacing their usual slow, awkward and unsafe sewing scissors.

The measurement operators were experts called in by Piero Savarino (Raman spectroscopy was carried out by Drs. Tagliapietra and Corsi, the reflectance and fluorescence measurements by Drs. Pellegrino and Caldironi) and Paolo Soardo's scanning team (Giuseppe Rossi, Paola Iacomussi and Natalia Bo). The fluorescence photographs were taken by Diego Ambroggio and Carlo Marchese, two inspectors from Dr. Maurizio Celia's section of the Turin scientific police force.

12- The most impressive discovery was made when the patches were unstitched, for they were pockets of carbonaceous residues and dusty detritus. It was the confirmation of the necessity of the conservation work that was in progress. But now there was the problem of the collection of all this material, since much of it came from the early history of the Shroud and in any case had been in contact with it for centuries. Piero Savarino, scientific advisor to the Papal Custodian, provided an army of little glass containers which were systematically labeled according to what was taken from the various spots of the cloth, all being marked on a map of a full-scale photograph of the Shroud, the same map already used during the work of 2000. Several maps of the Shroud were employed during these days for various purposes, because the collection of data turned out to be in a variety of forms and it was necessary to provide a guaranteed identification for each datum.

All the day-to-day details of the operations were recorded in the written report drafted by the Committee's secretary, Sister M. Clara Antonini, and her assistants. Some circumstances, however, called for authentication by the Archiepiscopal Chancellor, who acts as an ecclesiastical court notary for all matters concerning the Shroud. This occurred when small threads were noticed protruding from the back of the cloth due to its unevenness and the seamstresses advised their removal. Nothing associated with the Shroud is insignificant; anything could prove to be precious for research. It was therefore necessary to guarantee the authenticity of every tiny remnant or fragment. The same thing was necessary—and was done—for the tiny specimens mentioned above (section 9). The Archiepiscopal Chancellor also checked the work of archiving and collected all the little containers into a large one and applied the archbishop's seal. He himself removed the material, which remains at the disposition of the Holy See, the Papal Custodian and—when the Pope judges it advisable—of those scientists to whom it will be entrusted for future research.

13- Removal of the patches brought to light the sad reality of the effects of the fire of 1532. Some cloth was gained[6], because the Poor Clare nuns had folded inward the damaged edges, but a solution had to be found for the charred margins of the burn holes. Many fragments had already broken away to form the very fine carbon powder under the patches. Evidently the process of carbonization had 'traveled' (as Adler had supposed) and was probably still in progress. What was the best thing to do? Cutting away the charred parts to get back to the undamaged cloth would have produced an unnatural and devastating effect. It was decided to use tweezers to remove material which tended to give way when pulled and to reach the brownish borders—reminders of an ancient disaster. The result was a cloth no longer altered by the intrusion of patches, but still marked in those thin brown borders, the scars left by a dramatic event.

14- The second stage of the operations started with the backside of the Shroud facing upward and ended with the return to view of the image side. The backside confirmed what had already been established by the partial scanning in 2000. On the backside, all the blood was visible, as it had passed through the threads so completely that one could recognize its correspondence with its location on the image on the front. There was instead no recognizable trace of the image visible on the backside. The only debatable point concerned the face because on the backside there seemed to be two locks of hair identifiable. Great attention was thus paid to the gathering of details that could be acquired with all the measuring devices.

While awaiting the analyses which will be made from this data, it was agreed that what seemed to be an impression of the image at only that particular point of the whole surface of the Shroud, could be attributed to the fact that the two locks of hair bear traces of blood that passed from the surface of the face and that at this point, especially on the right side, there is a darker strip on the cloth due to dirtying of some kind.

15- Problems encountered in coordinating the operations, especially to allow time for the delivery of the instruments, meant that on some days less work was done. The time, however, was always filled with other work, such as completing the documentation or stretching the back of the cloth. The biggest problems loomed in preparing the scanning operations. How would it be possible to overspread the enormous surface of the Shroud and handle all the data? Use of the instruments could not extend beyond July because the holiday season was approaching and so scanning had to be only in the A4 format. Consequently, it was necessary to take 102 frames for each of the two surfaces. The time between working hours was exploited to obtain the "back up" of the stored data. In a more appropriate place, the operators themselves will describe the many breathtaking surprises they encountered throughout their work. In this present publication it is not yet possible to offer an appropriate number of scanning reproductions because the time needed for the elaboration of the material and identification of each image goes beyond the time of preparation of this initial presentation, whose purpose is to communicate quickly all that has been done.

16- The new backing-cloth on which the Shroud now rests is a length of raw linen presented by Mechthild Flury-Lemberg. Her father bought it in Holland (another "Holland cloth"!) some fifty years ago for household uses that never materialised. She washed it several times to de-size and soften it, but did not bleach or dye it. It has thus remained a chemically untreated fabric with a deep ivory hue that provides a soft relief for the holes left by the 1532 fire. Its textile structure is normal, therefore much less elaborate than that of the Shroud linen. The two can thus be readily distinguished.

17- The photos taken by Gian Carlo Durante's team (Giuseppe Cavalli, Daniele Demonte, Tiziana Durante)—with the advice of Nello Balossino— had not the advantage of the same preparation worked out in 2000. They nonetheless illustrate the complete reliability of this Studio, which has acquired absolute primary experience in the field of sindonic photography. The backside of the Shroud was photographed with the Shroud lying on the 'third table' supported by small trestles and set at an angle of about 105° with the camera mounted on a staging, whereas the image side, photographed at the conclusion of all the operations, was supported by the tilting table set in a perfectly orthogonal position with the camera on a floor-based tripod. As in the photos of 1997 and 2000, Gian Carlo Durante generously waived his copyright, leaving the Archdiocese of Turin sole proprietor of the photographs.

Especially precious was the identification of some details of the Shroud obtained with Irene Tomedi's microscope. Its objective was mounted on the mobile gantry to allow it to be moved from point to point and then held still while the photos were taken. Attention was primarily directed to the places where the amount of blood was greatest and the advantage of the conservation of extremely suggestive images was immediately apparent. The digital cassette recordings deeply moved those who had the chance to see them in those days. Their evocative effect was particularly accentuated by that of the film produced from the tape. Photos of details that aroused interest were printed immediately by direct connection with the printer.

This microscope was also used to record the details of other fabrics, brought from the Shroud Museum, used in attempts to reproduce the sindonic image, to compare them with the cloth bearing the real image.

18- The gantry attached to the tilting table was dismounted at the end of the second section. Designed by Giangi Ardoino, it had been assembled in record time by the ADL company[7] and proved to be one of the most valuable tools. It ran on rails fixed to the side of the tilting table and at the same time provided transverse coverage of the whole of the Shroud, supporting the instruments which from time to time were used: the scanner, the lens or detector of the videomicroscope, the fluorescence camera and the spectrophotometric sensors. Two tapes fitted with a digital distance numerator automatically measured the shift values and the position of each operation along the short and long sides of the cloth. The mobile gantry did not always solve all the problems (the operators were greatly perturbed when they had to verify if their scanner was also able to take pictures when it was upside-down), but it is sure that many observations would have been unthinkable without the gantry.

19- The final stage of the restoration was entirely in the hands of the seamstresses and left most of the members of the Committee disoccupied. Mechthild Flury-Lemberg ensured the perfect attachment of the sindonic linen to its new backing-cloth while Irene Tomedi concentrated on fixing the burn holes. Their work proceeded apace and their restoration was so invisible that those who looked at what they were doing were unable to distinguish the holes already repaired from the others. The needles were very fine and a bit curved, the silk thread strong, yet almost "disappearing" (like an angel's hair!). Examination of the photos will show how visible the stitching is around the holes.

A heavier thread was used to attach the margins of the Shroud to the backing-cloth. A slight difficulty arose in areas where some parts of the

Shroud cloth had been removed (in the distant past), especially at the ends of the upper strip (in the exposition position[8]). The old Holland lining ran the whole length of the original Shroud and now it was necessary to reconstruct the missing parts. The task was not easy, as the Shroud cloth is not perfectly rectangular, but splays at the four corners. The experience of the seamstresses happily enabled them to cope with the problem. Cardinal Poletto, accompanying Mons. Romeo, Papal Ambassador to Italy passing through Turin, was the first to congratulate the seamstresses on the fruits of their labors.

20- Those who now viewed the Shroud rejoiced in its relaxed beauty. The signs of its vicissitudes remained to tell of the misfortunes this Holy Linen suffered, along the centuries, in its sojourn among men. But now this dramatic past seemed to have taken on an aura of serenity in acceptance of the insults which no longer tried to hide but stood at the side of the great witness of the suffering recorded on the image. It was still the same Shroud, yet pleasingly new because easing of its wrinkles had smoothed away the dour aggression that once so greatly marred the cloth.

Did this newness by any chance extend to the dimensions of the Shroud? The first signs of a slight change had already been discerned by the scanners, since they needed to recalculate the overlap edges for each scan. The verification was made when the work of restoration was complete in order to establish the definitive dimensions of the Shroud in the new situation. The final measurements taken by Bruno Barberis and Gian Maria Zaccone, revealed a difference of several centimeters in the measuring they had calculated in 2000. It has already been observed that the dimensions of the Shroud can vary according to the tension the cloth is subject to. The following data will give an idea of the differences. Referring once again to the exposition position (frontal image to the left, dorsal to the right), the bottom side measured 437.7 cm in 2000 and 441.5 cm in 2002; the top side (less significant, because the ends now consist of the lining only, as two parts of the original cloth were removed in the past) measured 434.5 cm in 2000 and 442.5 cm in 2002; the height at the ends (the significance of which is only relative for the reason just given) was 112.5 cm on the left and 113 cm on the right in 2000, compared respectively with 113 cm and 113.7 cm in 2002.

21-This publication offers the first documentation of the story we have just told. The global photography gives evidence of the new aspect of the Shroud. In the succession of the details, one can follow analytically the development of the work. Some photos show where the work was done and some of the persons who participated. A very small number of scanner images are also included as a foretaste of the scientific publication that will crown all the work.

Those who took part in this round of operations are grateful for the gift they have received from the Lord, the trust reposed in them by the Holy See and the Papal Custodian, and the help received from a countless cohort of collaborators and friends.

Giuseppe Ghiberti

NOTES

* With warm thanks to those who made the English translation, John Iliffe, Dorothy Crispino, and Bruno Barberis.

1 Cardinal Ballestrero's plans after the carbon dating results were directed along the same lines as he himself stated on several occasions, even after his retirement as archbishop of Turin.

2 In this chapel, during the absence of the Shroud, some revisions were made in the monitoring system by Carlo Stroppiana, responsible for the technical section of the Committee.

3 Wanting to be present at the transfer of the Shroud to the choir, he came to Turin from the States but was taken urgently to the Cottolengo hospital where he died in the priest department on 28 February 1993, four days after the transfer took place.

4 The text drawn up on 10 November 2000 proposed the "removal of the Shroud's Holland cloth and patches . . . fixing the edges of the burn holes; application of a new lining". It was also stated that "this proposal stems from the conviction that the present state of the Shroud as such (its own cloth and the Holland cloth) is a threat to its chances of survival and that the solution suggested will result in substantial improvements. The signatories are conscious of the cultural implications of their proposal and advance it solely because they are convinced that it is of advantage for the preservation of the Shroud itself".

5 When the Shroud was transferred after the 1997 fire, the police warned that no place is perfectly defensible. The most effective defense is silence. Those who do not know are not tempted to cause harm.

6 About a centimeter on average, though the amount varied from one place to another.

7 Antonio Gay, the man who began the construction of the gantry, died a few days after the end of our work.

8 The Shroud is usually described as it is seen during an Exposition. The traditional 'Exposition position' is with the frontal image to the left and the dorsal image to the right At the top, a narrow strip is stitched along the Shroud. Some portions of this strip are missing. It is not known when they were removed, nor why.

[Undated, but presumably the same date as the other two documents, i.e., September 21, 2002.]

[For additional information regarding the Restoration, see William Meacham's page: http://freepages.religions.rootsweb.ancestry.com/~wmeacham/shroud.htm.]

APPENDIX M

CORRESPONDENCE BETWEEN RAY ROGERS AND MARINO AND BENFORD IN SEPTEMBER – OCTOBER, 2001

[Personal Communications, reprinted with permission of Joan Rogers.]

Email from Rogers to Marino and Benford on 13 September 2001:

I found a few more fragments of Raes threads. Since they were all picked apart before I got them, I could never tell which were warp and which were weft. I could just make out the twist pattern from these, and all I could see were Z. You said that the cotton threads were all S, didn't you. I could not identify the twist on one with a hand lens. I will mount it tomorrow for a good look. It looks whiter than the others.

I thought that if we could spot a Raes thread that was S, your hypothesis would be proved beyond anyone's shadow of a doubt. Not finding any S thread doesn't prove a thing. Sorry. Incidentally, I could not tell from the Albany figure whether any of the weft threads would be expected to be cotton. What would you expect? Do you have evidence for cotton weft threads in the Raes sample?

I just got an entire CD from Barrie with some of his high-resolution photographs. I'll take a look at them right now.

Email from Marino and Benford to Rogers on 14 September 2001, in response to email of 13 September:

In a message dated 09/13/2001 11:52:31 PM Eastern Daylight Time, mrogers@—- writes:

« You said that the cotton threads were all S, didn't you.»

No. What we found in the literature, according to Raes, was that the thread used to sew the two pieces of material together (the fabric to the seam) was twisted in an S direction. To my knowledge even the sixteenth century patch is twisted in a Z direction.

«1 could not identify the twist on one with a hand lens. I will mount it tomorrow for a good look. It looks whiter than the others.»

This "whiter than the others" observation may be key to the hypothesis of a sixteenth century patch as one would correctly assume that sixteenth century threads would be brighter/whiter than the 1st century counterparts (they would also contain more starch and possibly medieval dyes that were used to match it to the centuries old Shroud). It is likely, according to the location of the Raes samples, that ALL or nearly all of what he was looking at was patch; thus, his fibers might/should be whiter than your original Shroud fibers and should, theoretically, contain different additives, dyes, starches, etc., than your original Shroud fibers. It would be interesting for us to C-14 test the fibers you have from Raes (if there are enough).

« I thought that if we could spot a Raes thread that was S, your hypothesis would be proved beyond anyone's shadow of a doubt. Not finding any S thread doesn't prove a thing. Sorry.»

Once again, the only S-twisted threads, according to Raes, were those connecting the main fabric to the "seam" or tuck as I prefer to identify it. Thus, I *[Sue]* would expect both patch and original Shroud to be in a Z direction.

«Incidentally, I could not tell from the Albany figure whether any of the weft threads would be expected to be cotton. What would you expect? Do you have evidence for cotton weft threads in the Raes sample?»

According to the invisible mending experts I *[Sue]* have consulted, the patch theory would require that both warp and weft threads, in the patch itself, were "new;" thus, theoretically, any of the threads could have contained the blended fabric. However, it's hard to say just how much blended vs. pure thread was used in creating the patch. The literature doesn't specify exactly which thread type, warp or weft, either Raes or Teddy Hall of Oxford identified as cotton.

What I *[Sue]* learned about the invisible mending process that may be important is that about 1/2 to 3/4 inch of completely new material is spliced into the original fabric. The catch is that still another portion of the original, adjacent fabric is somewhat shredded such that streamers of new threads are infiltrated into the original material (not sure if these streamers are warp or weft or even if it's consistent among weavers). It's a little hard to explain this complex mending process without photos. Thus, even though the AMS labs may have unraveled and randomly assigned portions of the subsamples to smaller groups for testing (if they did), it's important to note that, most likely, none of their subsamples would have contained all first century threads.

Hope this helps. I'm sorry that I can't give you more actual details about this area as the documentation available is quite scanty as I'm sure you're aware. Joe and I will reread the Turin Commission Report this weekend and I'll get back to you on any additional clues I might find. Please keep me posted as well.

Also, I just Priority Mailed your packet of materials on our experimental linen sample. Let me know when they arrive as I'm a little concerned with the airmail of late.

Email from Rogers to Marino and Benford on 14 September 2001, in response to email of 14 September:

Thanks for the information. I was just starting a more detailed look at the fragments I have. I have one that looks different. I need to pull a fibril and put it under the microscope, but it gives the appearance of a medieval bleaching process. I will try to conserve enough for a date.

I will try to get a little more information on the starch also.

Email from Rogers to Marino and Benford and also STURP member Dr. Larry Schwalbe on 15 September 2001:

I started looking intently at the fibrils I have left: from the Raes threads. They all looked pretty much as I remembered—but not quite. The surfaces of most are more "frosty" than the fibrils from the center of the cloth. Some do not seem to be frosty, and one, number 14, is entirely different looking than the rest. It is very tightly twisted with a Z twist, it appears to be "stained/dyed" (but don't quote me on that until some more work), and I can't yet see any lignin at growth joints. It does not show the same birefringence as the others, and it doesn't go through extinction under crossed pols the same. It is going to take some more work. Most of the Raes threads don't have much lignin, but some have significantly more than others (I would expect that from observations on the banding).

I can find amorphous material(s) on some Raes threads. I will probably sacrifice a single fibril looking for starch, but I hate to.

No bets yet, but this is fascinating. I have taken about 40 photographs, and I'll get some processed tomorrow. We'll see what you think.

Email from Marino and Benford to Rogers and Schwalbe on 15 September 2001, in response to email of 15 September:

In a message dated 09/15/2001 12:58:27 AM Eastern Daylight Time, rnrogers@—- writes:

« I started looking intently at the fibrils I have left from the Raes threads. They all looked pretty much as I remembered—but not quite. The surfaces of most are more "frosty" than the fibrils from the center of the cloth. Some do not seem to be frosty, and one, number 14, is entirely different looking than the rest. It is very tightly twisted with a Z twist, it appears to be "stained/dyed" (but don't quote me on that until some more work), and I can't yet see any lignin at growth joints. It does not show the same birefringence as the others, and it doesn't go through extinction under crossed pols the same. It is going to take some more work. Most of the Raes threads don't have much lignin, but some have significantly more than others (I would expect that from observations on the banding).»

Can you identify any of the Raes threads specifically as cotton? Would it be worthwhile to have a textile expert independently evaluate the thread types? The "tightly twisted" aspect reminds me of the observations made by the Albany International Research group who noted that some of the threads on the "patched" side of the Zurich sample were considerably tighter/thinner than the "original" side. They concluded this was due to each of the two sides having been woven independently.

The observation of a "frosty" appearance brings to mind the application of the starches used by the medieval weavers as an accessory for their invisible mending. It is also quite characteristic of what I *[Sue]* have seen in all the modern-day linen samples we've tested (this observation was also noted by Al Adler in some of our discussions).

Clearly, the possibility of "staining or dyeing" on any of the Raes fibers is a key variable in assessing the possibility of a sixteenth century patch. Unless a similar dye has been discovered on "non-patched" interior Shroud fibers then all indications would be that all or part of the Raes' sample was a patch. We obtained linen samples from the Italian weaver, Pietro Vercelli (reported in <u>Turin Proceedings</u>, 2000), whereby one was an "unbleached" Shroud linen replica in a 3:1 herringbone pattern and one was "dyed to match" the exact color of the Shroud. This, of course, would have been the preferred sample to use for any restorative work at any time in the Shroud's history (medieval or today).

« I can find amorphous material(s) on some Raes threads. I will probably sacrifice a single fibril looking for starch, but I hate to.»

I *[Sue]* understand your hesitancy but do we have any other choice? As noted above, the presence of starch is one of the indicators of a medieval restoration in the area.

«No bets yet, but this is fascinating. I have taken about 40 photographs, and I'll get some processed tomorrow. We'll see what you think.»

I *[Sue]* am really looking forward to examining these microphotographs. Should you want me to blindly run them by the textile experts we spoke to previously, please let me know. They are all still unaware that the cloth they were asked to examine was the Shroud so their reviews are quite objective.

Looking forward to more updates! Keep up the good work Ray!

Immediate follow-up email on 15 September 2001, from Marino and Benford to Rogers and Schwalbe:

One more suggestion on the Raes threads: we recently noted on our UV fluorescence photography tests our modern-day linen, that the linen itself fluoresced a tremendous amount due to the brighteners. Would it be possible/worthwhile to subject some of the Raes threads, perceived to be dyed, to this test to see if there is a difference in the fluorescence quality? Would we anticipate that the medieval thread would fluoresce differently than the original Shroud fibers? Just a thought since now this testing is possible with Vern Miller, Sam Pellicori and Rand Molnar all on board and doing these tests on our samples anyway. Let me know and I *[Sue]* will forward a query to these guys for a response.

Email from Rogers to Marino and Benford and Schwalbe on 15 September 2001, in response to the two previous emails from Benford and Marino:

I took comparison electronic photographs of the most different-appearing Raes threads. I tried to get them to the same color balance in diffuse, northern sunlight by putting the samples on a 50 per cent gray card; however, I had to keep #14 under a cover slip to protect it.

No.14 is distinctly yellowish to the eye, but that is hard to render in a photograph. The yellow extends into the curled-up parts, but it gets obscured by shadows in any single view. None of the other Raes threads are curled like #14.

I don't have enough undamaged samples to make a statistically-significant study of measurements; however, #14, the yellowish one, tends to be about 0.34-mm diameter, and #4 (the least-damaged "normal" thread) is about 0.16-mm diameter.

I have some old, commercial linen samples that were dyed and naturally aged. I can hardly wait to look at #14's fibrils in comparison with them. Patience.

I have not yet had nerve enough to sample #14 for mounting and closer inspection. I want to make sure we have drained all of the information possible from observations on the intact thread first.

I will have many higher-resolution photographs coming along in about a week.

Please send me your suggestions on observations that can be made on the Raes threads before I start pulling individual fibrils loose for mounting.

Have you sent Luigi Gonella information on your observations? He may have heard your presentation at Orvieto, but he might appreciate being kept informed. May I send him some photo-micrographs?

Second email from Rogers to Marino and Benford on 15 September 2001, in response to the two previous emails from Marino and Benford:

I have not seen any indication of cotton at all. After Raes' report, Joan had been puzzled by not finding cotton in the threads when she looked at them before 1986.

I just tried again to measure comparative twists. I would have to use textile equipment to unwind the thread, and that would ruin some information; therefore, I measured the angle between average fibrils in undamaged thread and the direction along the length of the thread. The strange #14 (obviously tighter twist) shows an angle of 34-40 degrees. But remember, it has a diameter of about 0.34 mm: it is thicker than the other fragments I have. The least damaged "normal" thread shows angles of 26-28 degrees, much less twist, but it is thinner at about 0.16 mm. But I still do not see any evidence for cotton in #14 (or any of the others). I'll have to get fibrils separated from the threads to be sure.

I like your suggestion of looking at fluorescence. In view of my experience with letting samples go before, I have a horror of letting any more threads get out of sight. I also do not feel so confident of the mail system right now. I will try to find a fluorescence microscope I can use here. We will get the information one way or another before the samples are disturbed any more. A textile expert who manipulated the fragments too much could lose considerable information for us. Let's wait on that one.

You said, "As noted above, the presence of starch is one of the indicators of a medieval restoration in the area." It is also an integral part of the production of linen by the technology described by Pliny. The presence of starch will not tell us much. We may make guesses from the amounts, and, given enough work, we could probably determine the source of the starch (potato, wheat, rice, etc.); however, the simple presence of generic starch doesn't say much. Different starch types show different grain morphologies, but normal grains are not visible on/in the threads.

Sorry to be plodding so, but let's get as much information from these last, poor, damaged samples as we can. If we can get enough, perhaps the Vatican will allow more observations and sampling . . . .

Email from Marino and Benford to Rogers and Schwalbe on 15 September 2001, in response to Rogers' two previous emails:

Sounds like you've been very busy!! To respond to your two most recent emails, let's start with your question about Luigi Gonella. Are you thinking that he is still the scientific advisor to the archbishop? If so, this is no longer the case. The current scientific advisor is Egregio Professor Piero Savarino. We did send him, along with the Pope and the new Archbishop of Turin, copies of our C-14 paper but never heard back from them (are you surprised?). Anyway, perhaps a letter from you might get more attention so feel free to send them whatever you think might be of interest. Savarino's address is: Dipartimento Di Chimica Generale Ed Organica Applicata Universita'Degli Studi Di Torino Corso Massimo D'Azeglio 48 10125 Torino ITALY.

When viewing the Raes #14 vs. #4 photomicrographs, I *[Sue]* had a recollection of something Albany International had pointed out in the review of the Zurich C-14 sample. If you look closely, you will see on the top right half of the Zurich sample what appears to be an uncharacteristically thick thread protruding out. They noted that this was "unusual" considering all the threads on the left half are relatively fine and the same size (see the thin thread protruding out on the left side of the Zurich sample). This added to their suspicions of an independently woven patch along with what they noted as the "thick/thin pattern" that is not seen in the left half of sample (others have documented the Shroud threads are generally quite thin throughout). Your #14 thread reminds me of that thick, right-sided Zurich thread.

Yes, I *[Sue]* agree with the starch presence not being a telltale sign of invisible mending. However, if we could determine the origin of the starch on say #14 as being different from a more typical "Shroud-like" #4 thread for instance, then that would be interesting. Should you be able to make such a determination, I will do more research on trends in medieval invisible mending and try to provide evidence for the types of starches they used.

I *[Sue]* will be interested to see if your further fiber analyses come up with any cotton—what tests or resources are you using to make the fiber identifications? If cotton does eventually show up in #14, could the deeper yellowing you noted possibly have been due to lower heat resistance of cotton fibers vs. linen that were disproportionately discolored during the 1532 fire?

I *[Sue]* agree with your ideas about doing the fluorescence tests locally. Your samples are far too precious to this effort right now to trust the fragile nationwide delivery services. Once you get results in this area, we may want to pass them by Vern, Rand, and Sam for their input.

Most fascinating to me *[Sue]* are the distinct diameter (2x!) and twist differences (26-28 vs. 34-40 degrees) between the #14 and the more typical, thinner threads. Of particular note to the C-14 testing is that it is the mass of the threads tested that matters in the overall calculations such that if, for instance, the sixteenth century threads were twice the mass (.34 mm) compared to the original 1st century threads (.16 mm) then this 2x difference will account for a huge shift to the later date even if visually it looks like there may be far fewer sixteenth century threads.

I *[Sue]* haven't had time to reread the Raes report but promise to make time this weekend. I wanted to get these observations to you prior to any irreversible pulling apart of the fibers. Keep me posted and I'll do the same.

Immediate follow-up email from Marino and Benford to Rogers on 15 September 2001:

I *[Sue]* am going to quote from the Raes report in the Turin Commission. I think you'll find his observations noteworthy:

"The size of the threads in piece II seems to be different from that of those in piece I, particularly the weft threads. However, since the size of the threads could only be established by examining a very short length, and there is no indication that the thread is uneven, it is not possible to say whether samples I and II are positively from fabrics of different types of weave.
Various preparations were made up using the fibres taken from the warp and weft threads of fabrics I and II, as also for the sewing thread [the S-twisted thread that united the two disparate pieces]. These preparations were examined under polarized light in order to obtain a better contrast. The raw material used is definitely linen for both pieces of fabric and also for the sewing thread . . . . [H]owever, it should be mentioned that in the preparations made with parts of both the warp and weft threads of the fabric, traces of cotton could be found . . . . For the cotton fibres found in the linen thread the number of re-reversals is approx. 8 per cm, corresponding to the type herbaceum". This type cotton existed in the Middle East. (NOTE: can we also find this imported to/grown in medieval Europe??)
It is not possible to confirm whether fabric I and II are different, although the size of the weft threads is much thicker in piece II. Both linen weft and warp threads pulled from piece I of the cloth show traces of cotton, which seems to indicate that the spinner used cotton as well as linen."
Although it's difficult to discern exactly what constituted Dr. Raes "piece I and II" one thing is for certain—two distinct fabrics were sewn together by an aberrant S-twisted thread. He refers to piece II as being material from "the strip added," which is problematic because we now know

that this "side strip" was not a later addition to the original cloth but, rather, part of a congruent, singular fabric. Considering his sample is adjacent to the large 5 1/2 x 3 1/2 missing panel, it's hard to imagine there NOT being a restorative patch!

Hope this helps.

Email from Marino and Benford to Schwalbe and Rogers on 16 September 2001, in response to email from Schwalbe:

In a message dated 09/16/2001 8:10:30 PM Eastern Daylight time, schwalbe@---- writes:

«The assumption is that each sample consists of two regions. One shown in yellow in Figure 3 is purely of 30 AD manufacture; the other (in pink) is a mixture of 60 per cent material produced in 1500 AD and 40 per cent material produced in 30 AD. Is this understanding correct?»

Not quite. Actually, our hypothesis is that the pink area is <u>entirely</u> sixteenth century patch while the yellow is, predominantly, 1st century original material (since the paper we have learned that this area may include streamers of medieval threads invisibly woven into the area). Given that, let me (Sue) explain the hypothetical parameters applied by Beta Analytic and used in their calculations. As Ray knows, I was not able to quantify the exact amount of 16 century material based on thread size/diameter; thus, I used a hypothetical amount based upon visual inspection of the C-14 subsamples. The sixteenth century "patch," I assumed, was approximately 60 per cent of the total mass of the complete subsample while the original 1st century material then totaled the remaining 40 per cent mass. Based upon these assumptions, Beta Analytic calculated dates using 450 BP (1500 AD) threads (60 per cent) and 1875 BP (75 AD) threads (40 per cent) to achieve the 1210 AD dating (NOTE: because this was only a hypothetical calculation, there are no error bars). Beta Analytic has a preprogrammed proprietary software that performs these calculations and that is why 75 AD was used versus 30 AD, which would have aged the hypothetical sample a little more.

Granted, this is arbitrary and certainly not exact for anyone of the C-14 subsamples; however, it did come remarkably close to the Oxford subsample dates of 1200 AD +/- 30. Ray's colleague may be able to help us quantify the exact ratio of medieval to original at which time we can contact Beta again for a recalculation if need be.

Does this help at all?

Email from Rogers to Marino and Benford on 17 September 2001:

In a message dated 09/17/2001 1:00:12 AM Eastern Daylight time, rnrogers@— writes:

« Joan looked very hard at #1, and she found what appear to be cotton fibrils in the larger end. Is it possible that ALL of the patch was more modern? So far we haven't been able to demonstrate to our satisfaction that any of the threads we have seen are "authentic" Shroud. We'll keep at it, but you may have to modify your 60/40 estimate. John's quantitative analysis may help. We'll see. »

I *[Sue]* have made the statement that, considering the position of the Raes sample, it very well could have been entirely medieval patch. However, using this same position parameter as a variable, I would likewise be surprised if all of the C-14 sample had been all medieval patch. If you take a birds-eye look at that part of the Shroud you'll see what I'm talking about. Of course, at this point, who knows? Should the data demand it we will certainly redo our 60/40 ratio.

Thanks for the #1 photo. No, you hadn't sent that one. Keep up the good work.

Email from Marino and Benford to Schwalbe and Rogers on 17 September 2001, in response to email from Schwalbe:

In a message dated 09/17/2001 8:10:25 PM Eastern Daylight Time, schwalbe@— writes:

« However, if the samples were cut as I suggest above, we should expect to see one or more data from each of the Laboratories to "peg" at 450 BP. I don't see this. I'm sure you guys have thought of this already. Mind helping me out? »

Yes, Larry, we have pondered this whole question of "what if the labs cut the piece in half such that the 1st century material was on one side and the sixteenth century on the other?" Certainly, according to the hypothesis that each side contained pure threads from each of these time periods, your suggestion of, at least, one 1500 AD date and, my *[Sue]* thought of, at least, one older date would be expected. Several possibilities arise:

1) our hypothesis is wrong and some other mechanism is responsible for

the skewing of the dates such that it caused the date spread to fall outside normal statistical parameters in a coincidental angular skewing along the notable demarcation line;

2) both the "1st century side" and "sixteenth century side" were, in fact, a mixture of both older and medieval threads; thus, no matter how the sample was cut, the threads were mixed;

3) once the labs cut and cleaned the *samples*, the 1st and sixteenth century threads became intermixed in their subsamples.

Although I *[Sue]* have speculated (and Ray has recently also suggested), that the Raes sample may be all "patch;" I would be highly surprised if this were the case with the C-14 sample due to the notable weave differences from side to side with one side appearing almost identical to other Shroud samples plus the difference in locations (Raes is directly in line with the patch area demarcation). However, I have little hard data to back up this speculation with a couple notable exceptions. Oxford reported that one of its subsamples came in at 1182 AD. If, indeed, we are looking at a purely sixteenth century patch then this is hard to accept given the error ranges quoted by Oxford. Now, that doesn't rule out an earlier patch of that area prior to the sixteenth century patch to help balance the later threads but does make a purely sixteenth century date unlikely.

On the other side of the equation, obtaining a 1500 AD date, keep in mind that Arizona only reported 4 of its 8 subsample dates. One of their dates was 540 +/- 57 which comes out to a possible year of 1467 AD. Pretty close to pure sixteenth century I would say!

Another report according to Ken Stevenson was, "According to their own published reports, they [Dr. Tite's C-14 researchers] discarded readings that didn't fit what they wanted. From their own figures, they were as much as 400 years off on the low end and on the high end 1500 years off which is pretty significant" (*Catholic Counter Reformation in the 20th Century*, Dec. 1990).

Does this help at all or confuse things even more? :) Let me know your thoughts.

Email from Marino and Benford to Rogers on 18 September 2001, in response to his email of 17 September 2001:

Super work! Your findings are indeed quite compelling and exactly the type of empirical data that our theory requires. The microphotograph is excellent (keep them coming!)

A question: did you observe the same magnitude/intensity/type of Becke lines on the Shroud samples as you did on the Raes threads? This might be an interesting comparison or contrast (when your eyesight returns of course!).

Also, it seems your finding of the lignin in the Raes sample is a dead giveaway that the threads are more modem than the bulk of the Shroud fibers. Is there any way to determine a "half-life" of lignin in an aerobic environment? This would be an interesting calculation to help determine age of the patch.

Let us know when we can break out the champagne!!

Email from Rogers to Marino and Benford on 19 September 2001:

With regard to your image hypothesis, would you please look at the x-ray fluorescence paper again and, perhaps, talk with Larry? I believe that locations 2-7 were in a non-image area. I did not take notes on the locations, but Larry would have the original data. There are also detailed photographs and x-ray-transmission films of the area. I am not yet convinced that there is any significant difference in Ca. Location 19 shows different reflectance density (a band of warp thread of different chemical characteristics), x-ray density, iron, and Sr. Why don't you ask Larry?

I am attaching photomicrographs of Kate Edgerton's "primitive" linen and fibrils from Raes #5. You can see that there is much more lignin at the growth bands in Kate's sample than there is in 'Raes'. 'Raes' sample does not look like modem, Cl-bleached material, but it certainly does not look like "primitive." Two of the four fibrils in the view of Raes #5 are cotton. They are on the left. I'll know more when we make a more detailed quantitative study on Shroud fibrils, but I remember remarking on how easy it was to observe lignin on them even though I could not get a spot test.

I'll talk with you soon with more photographs.

Email from Rogers to Marino and Benford on 20 September 2001:

I have spent five hours at two tapes today, and it looks like the rest will take more than a week with luck.

My tape from the Holland cloth didn't get much use (I doubt anybody prayed to it either), so it has lots to offer. It is loaded with cotton, but some shows a much shorter twist than Raes reported. Whether that came from the Shroud or not is your guess. The Holland-cloth linen is very clean with little lignin.

At first count, the Raes fibrils look more like the Holland cloth than the Shroud.

I have not yet found any cotton on 1HB, a tape I pulled from the right foot of the image. It has blood flecks on it, and I have found several image fibrils. There seems to be appreciably more lignin at the growth joints. I have photographs for you.

If the lignin amounts hold up in other Shroud areas, lignin will provide a convincing difference between the Raes samples and the Shroud. Old technology should show more lignin than medieval samples, and it should vary from sample to sample.

I got an e-mail from Vern [Miller], and I answered him. If he has a UV photograph of the area from which the 14C sample was cut, it will be interesting to see whether it shows the same background fluorescence as the Shroud. If my hypothesis about the Saponaria means anything, there should be next to no fluorescence in the patch area.

We'll see.

Second email from Rogers to Marino and Benford on 20 September 2001:

Lignin is one of the most complex molecules that has ever been studied. It is the ultimate high polymer (macromolecule). All of the lignin in a tree is one molecule. When the tree is cut down, it becomes several fragment molecules. The only way you can study it is to chop it up into smaller fragments chemically.

One common fragment shows phenyl-isopropanoid units. The phenyl part is often a 4-hydroxy-3-methoxy- unit. When this is broken off of the huge molecule by heat or other attack, it produces 4-hydroxy-3-methoxy benzaldehyde, vanillin. The rest of the molecule is still there.

We use the evolution of vanillin to identify lignin on materials. Since heat and chemical attack (including enzymes from microorganisms) can remove the vanillin easily, there is less and less of it to detect as the lignin ages or is heated. That is a very, very small fraction of the original complex molecule. What is left is very easy to observe in its original location, like at growth rings of linen, but it gives less and less of a test.

And, no, Saponaria was used in parts of the world for a very long time, and I think it still is in the Near East. The presence of Saponaria and starch doesn't tell us much about the age of the cloth, but I would be mightily surprised to find it on the Holland cloth.

Email from Rogers to Marino and Benford on 22 September 2001:

No feedback yet and no UV fluorescence photographs of the Raes area from Vern yet.

I will start scanning a few photographs as time allows and filing them in my computer. I don't think an infinite number of photomicrographs showing lignin are much better than a few (statistically maybe), but no matter what you do somebody isn't convinced (always). I have yet to make a detailed study of all of the Raes threads. I got sidetracked when I saw the splice. There may be something else there. I may have found a little evidence for older Shroud fibrils interwoven with Raes stuff, but I can't be sure.

I plan on sacrificing a few Raes fibrils just to confirm the presence of starch.

Mainly, I think the most important observation hanging fire is whether or not we can prove that the 14C sampling area is devoid of fluorescence (or shows a plaid pattern in some places).

Any other suggestions?

John Petrovic, a materials scientist, keeps telling me that the only way to look at fibrils is to section them. Sure. I thought of that years ago, but I don't have any way to do it. He wanted me to cut an image slide in sections with a diamond saw—like I could ever replace the slide. I can just imagine what the adhesive on the tape would do. I still can't find documentation of Al's [Adler] observation on the sectioned fibrils. Do you have anything on that?

He told me, but that doesn't carry any weight.

John also has a paper on new observations of lettering around the face of the image. The paper indicates excellent image analysis methodology, but we saw nothing by any of our techniques. He thinks it could be on the back surface. I don't think so. First, nobody would have been allowed to paint something on the Shroud—ever. Second, if they did, the paint should have left traces, and we saw no evidence on the back surface or from spectra, or x-ray fluorescence. An ink would most likely have had iron and tannic acid in it. Squid ink never goes away. Plant-gum inks/paints don't go away either. Third, the observation has not been confirmed, and there are lots of subjective elements in an image analysis. Fourth, the person used Enrie's [1931] photographs, not the best for analysis. You don't know somebody who would like to confirm another "I think I saw" exercise, do you? I'm tired of chasing phantoms.

Email from Rogers to Marino and Benford (and four others) on 1 October 2001:

Worthy Researchers:

I am just now finishing the chemical study on the archived samples from the Shroud. My results do not agree with the statements of the textile experts...

I have documented all of my observations with photographs, photomicrographs, and any necessary references. The photographs should be available today, but they will require a huge file for transmission via e-mail. I would of course, send you anything I have that you would like to have; however, I will winnow the mass as soon as possible to make a manageable file.

A summary of the salient observations follows.

1) Only one small spot of starch was identified on Raes threads with iodine.
2) All Raes threads show a "frosty" surface. They are coated with an amorphous, yellow-brown material. The color varies in intensity among samples. Some colored material is seen in the linen medullas; therefore, it was added to the surfaces of threads as a liquid. The frosty colored layer is unique to Raes threads.
3) There is absolutely no encrustation on Shroud fibrils, except in blood areas.

4) The frosty coating softens and swells in water. Its color but not the crust is eliminated by 6N HCI, and the encrustation is eliminated by concentrated hydrochloric acid (con HCI). The encrustation is not a mordant. Hydrous aluminum oxide, the mordant for red alizarin dye, is soluble in 6N HCI.

5) There is no fluorescence in the Raes threads, a 20 BC Dead Sea linen sample, or

Shroud fibrils. Modem white linen shows a bright, blue-white fluorescence as a result of the use of fabric brighteners.

6) The cotton fibrils on the surface of the Holland cloth (only superficial samples were obtained) and inside the Raes threads are all what Raes identified as Gossipium [sic] herbaceum, the ancient Near Eastern variety (1.25-mm spacing between reversals).

7) There is only a slight traces of herbaceum cotton on Shroud samples. There are traces of modern cotton on many tapes. Note that we used cotton gloves to protect the Shroud during the 1978 studies. There is one lavender modem-cotton fibril on the 1 EB tape.

8) There is a great variation among the fibrils on Shroud tape samples from different areas of the cloth in the amounts of lignin seen at the linen growth joints. Some joints are heavily encrusted with lignin.

9) Raes threads, fibrils from the Holland cloth, and modem linen have much less lignin at growth joints, and the amounts are quite consistent throughout a sample.

10) Linen made recently by the ancient technology shows heavy encrustations of lignin at growth joints.

11) Image areas show large numbers of yellow fibrils as reported by Skirius at the McCrone Institute. These fibrils do not show paint media or pigments. Their chemistry has been determined by STURP.

12) All of the Raes samples show colored amorphous encrustations. None of the Holland fibrils or Shroud fibrils do.

13) Some blue lakes can be seen on Raes #14, and they probably appear on other samples. The color and appearance indicate traces of alizarin on crystals of calcite in the cloth.

14) Bright red lakes can be seen on Raes #14. They are probably alizarin on a hydrous aluminum oxide mordant.

15) Raes #14 shows the largest amount of yellow-brown encrustation of any of the samples observed. The encrustation is not removed by organic solvents.

16) Scorching damage can easily be observed in the medullas of tape sample 11B, the scorch control sample. There is no similar scorching in the medullas in Shroud fibrils.

17) Iodine on unwashed #14 gives very few blue flecks. There is very little starch on the Raes samples.

18) The colored encrustation does not seem to stick to linen. Some linen fibrils appear to be nearly clean, but the cotton fibrils can be heavily encrusted in the same thread sample. This suggests that the cotton was added to the Raes threads to make dyeing possible. The cotton in the threads would have made color matching easier. Linen is difficult to dye or stain. The

commercially-produced Holland cloth may have contained small amounts of cotton for the same reason.

19) When I teased Raes #14 open at one end, the center of the thread appeared to be clear, nearly completely colorless. The outside of that thread showed the heaviest encrustation and deepest color of any of the samples, except one end of Raes #1 (the spliced thread). This observation suggests that the color and its vehicle were added by wiping them as a viscous liquid on the outside of threads that were to be used in the presumed reweaving. The threads were not vat dyed. The object must have been to match colors.

20) After treating the frosty fibrils in concentrated HCI, the color and frosty crust are completely removed. Fibrils of #14 are clear and clean. Some polysaccharides are easily and quickly hydrolyzed in con. HCI. This suggests a plant gum that is largely composed of pentose-sugar units.

21) Raes #14, after cleaning with HCI, gives a light-blue color with iodine. Apparently there had been starch on the cloth before the stain was put on. Starch is harder to hydrolyze than are gums.

22) Iodine on unwashed, frosted Raes threads gives a bright-yellow coating that is highly visible. Plant gums show this characteristic. Solutes in a liquid phase that is in contact with another, immiscible phase distribute themselves between the phases according to fixed "distribution coefficients." For example, iodine distributes between an aqueous layer and chloroform to show the intense violet color of molecular iodine in the chloroform. It shows a yellow to brown color in alcohols and other solvents that contain hydroxyl groups. Sugars all contain hydroxyl groups. The "frosty" coating is almost certainly a plant gum. The most probable gum is gum Arabic, an acacia gum that is mostly pentose units, because it is relatively easily soluble in water. Gum Arabic has long been popular for textile applications. Agar-agar, gum tragacanth, and flax-seed gum are less popular than gum Arabic for textile work. Gum Arabic, agar-agar, and gum tragacanth all turn bright yellow in iodine water. The definitive identification of specific gums is a major task.

23) After drying the gum that was yellow in iodine solution, it is colorless. The iodine has vaporized completely. It did not react with the substrate. This is important, because it shows that the yellow did not involve iodine-catalyzed dehydration or an iodinization reaction. It was pure solution. The immiscible solvent phase is almost certainly a plant gum on the surface of the linen (cellulose) fibrils.

24) The yellow colors of gums in iodine are amorphous. This helps confirm the fact that there was no chemical reaction.

25) No dye/stain remains after treatment with iodine in water and washing with pure water. One dye used must have been alizarin (Madder root). Madder has been used with an alum (hydrous aluminum oxide) mordant to produce a beautiful red color for thousands of years.

Other mordants produce different colors, including blues with calcium compounds. A mixture of mordants with alizarin could produce any shade of yellow or brown that was desired.

26) After encrusted fibrils on a microscope slide have been wetted with water and allowed to dry, it is easy to observe the gum that dissolved and

migrated away from the fibrils. The easy solubility indicates gum Arabic.

27) I could observe a significant amount of herbaceum cotton on the Holland tapes, but there was absolutely no encrustation. There is no encrustation on image fibrils. The encrustation is unique to the Raes samples.

28) The Raes samples are not representative of the main cloth of the Shroud of Turin.

The question is, where do we go from here?

Regards,

Ray

APPENDIX N

APPENDICES OF LETTER OF 5 AUGUST 2003, FROM WILLIAM MEACHAM AND RAYMOND ROGERS TO CARDINAL SEVERINO POLETTO OF TURIN
[Reprinted with permission of William Meacham.]

Appendix I -Material Requested

—30 mg of carbon dust and fiber fragments removed from TS area, for sample characterization, pretreatment and radiocarbon measurement

—30 mg of carbon dust and fiber fragments removed from T11 area, for sample characterization, pretreatment and radiocarbon measurement

—weft fiber no.10 removed from the reverse side of the Shroud, for study of contamination possibilities

—a fiber of 1 cm length from the "reserve" piece taken in 1988, for study of contamination possibilities

Appendix II -Comments on the Previous C 14 Sample

Since the C14 dating of the Shroud was announced in 1988, there have been doubts expressed as to the nature and reliability of the sample taken. Garza-Valdez, supported by the microbiologist Mattingly, claimed that there was a substantial "bioplastic coating" on Shroud fibers that constituted contamination and skewed the C 14 date. Marino and Benford, supported by weaving specialists, claimed that the area of the C14 sample had been partially re-woven.

Prof. Adler had begun to study these claims. In a paper published in 1998, he noted that "a great deal of variability was evidenced in the radiocarbon samples. Some of the patchy encrustations were so thick as to mask the underlying carbon of fibers . . . "

Over the last two years, Rogers examined the claims of Garza-Valdez/Mattingly and Marino/Benford, at first with considerable skepticism, but he found that fibers of the "Raes sample" adjacent to the C 14 sample did indeed have a coating of some kind, and did indeed have quite different chemical characteristics to fibers from other parts of the cloth.

After a considerable number of tests on samples taken by STURP, Rogers found that no sample from the main part of the Shroud showed any feature even remotely similar to the coating in the anomalous Raes/C-14 area. These findings have been published in detail with illustrations in the following article:

http://www.shroud.comlpdfs/rogers2.pdf.

In summary Rogers found that the area of the Raes and radiocarbon samples was anomalous, and had the following chemical and physical characteristics:

1) It did not fluoresce, and therefore its chemical composition was different from the main cloth. This is seen clearly and beyond doubt in the fluorescence photographs taken by STURP in 1978. There is absolutely no question about this fact.

2) The yam in that area was coated with a gum that contained both dyes and mordants (common technology through millennia for dyeing linen). It had been colored for some purpose. Most of the added color appears on the outer surface of the yam in that area. Photomicrographs document this fact. None of the main part of the cloth had any of this gum-dye-mordant coating.

3) The linen had been bleached by a different technique than the main part of the cloth: it shows very little lignin at growth nodes.

4) The lignin in the anomalous area gives the microchemical test for vanillin, a component of lignin that decreases with time. The lignin in the main part of the Shroud does not give the test (nor does lignin from Dead Sea Scroll wrappings). It is reasonable to conclude that the anomalous area has a different age than the Shroud, and that it is younger than the main cloth.

5) As Raes observed, there is cotton in the yarn of the sample taken for him. It is easy to find inside the segments of yarn. The only cotton that is found on the main part of the cloth is a superficial impurity.

6) SEM analyses by Adler proved that fibers from the anomalous area have twice (2X) the concentration of aluminum as other areas. Aluminum is used as a mordant for the ancient Madder root dye that exists in the anomalous area. Microscopic views, documented with photomicrographs, prove the presence of Madder dye on hydrous aluminum oxide mordant.

7) Madder root dye is largely alizarin and purpurin. These can easily be detected in the anomalous area. No other area of the Shroud is coated with Madder root dye. Alizarin has been used for over a century as an acid-base indicator in chemistry: its properties are known in detail, and its presence in the area has been documented with photomicrographs.

8) The hydrous-aluminum-oxide mordant is instantly soluble in hydrochloric acid. The color of fibers from the anomalous area changes instantly when treated with the acid, and the colors obtained depend on the pH of the solution (as expected from the dyes).

9) The gum coating on the outside of the yarn is soluble in water. It can be observed under a microscope, and the soluble gum is redeposited when the water is allowed to evaporate. The gum is not a biogenic polymer (as Garza Valdes and Mattingly believed), and it does not give any test for proteins. The gum quickly hydrolyzes in acid, and it hydrolyzes somewhat more slowly in sodium hydroxide solution. It gives the color test with iodine that is common to plant gums like gum Arabic (bright yellow). There is nothing like that on the rest of the cloth. Such gums were items of commerce for millennia, it was not a natural impurity on linen, and it was used to stain/dye the yarn. Photomicrographs are available to document these observations.

10) Careful microscopic viewing of yarn segments from the Raes sample showed a unique, end-to-end splice (photomicrograph available). The main part of the cloth was woven using overlaps of yarn when one batch of yarn ran out and another was added to continue weaving.

All of the above observations lead inevitably and outstandingly to a single conclusion: the Raes/C14 area is quite different from the rest of the cloth. The radiocarbon sample was NOT representative of the main part of the cloth. The radiocarbon date was invalid; it was run on a spurious sample.

APPENDIX O

MAJOR SHROUD RESEARCHERS SINCE 1898

I had originally intended to compile a list of all the major sindonologists since 1898, when the first photographs of the Shroud were taken and modern scientific study began to include as one of the appendices to include in the book. Although I originally did not have a deadline to finish the book, one arose, which meant that finishing this appendix, so large in scope, in time for the deadline would have been pretty much impossible. The fact that I wouldn't be able to finish in time for the deadline turned out to be a blessing in disguise. The Shroud Science Group to which I belong has a Wiki, which means that all the researchers on the group, about one hundred thirty from all over the world, would be able to help edit the data, making it more accurate than I would have been able to, with the added advantage that it would enable it be constantly updated as opposed to the static print version. I was amazed when I went through my vast collection of material how many researchers there have been and are.

I have divided them into two groups: 1) those skeptical of the Shroud's authenticity (i.e, it's not a first-century burial cloth) and 2) those that are either pro-authenticity (it is a first-century burial cloth) or neutral (i.e, undecided). (In cases where the researcher seemed neutral, I couldn't actually even be 100 per cent sure that they were neutral but in cases like these the researchers seemed to lean more toward pro-authenticity as opposed to being skeptical. I also intentionally refrained in these categories from identifying the Shroud with Jesus. Needless to say, there are so many varying beliefs of researchers regarding the Shroud, it's impossible to come up with perfect categories.) I have restricted the information to listing a person's name (and added if they are/were a Reverend or Sister, a doctor or a Ph.D. in order to show some academic credentials) and their country of origin or domicile for their Shroud work. If their country is uncertain, a question mark is present. If a person is deceased, there is an asterisk next to their name. Those who are on the lists have done at least one of the following:

* Studied the Shroud directly or as part of a scientific group or commission

- Written a book on the Shroud or significant amounts of Shroud material in non-Shroud books
- Written a major article on the Shroud in a journal or periodical (newspaper) article authors are not included if that's the only medium they've used)
- Presented a paper at a Shroud symposium or helped organize the symposium
- Have been involved with a Shroud photo exhibit
- Are/were part of a Shroud center
- Have lectured on the Shroud
- Appeared or have been involved in the making of Shroud documentaries
- Have given radio interviews on the Shroud
- Have produced art works or plays based on the Shroud
- Have a Shroud website or blog or are part of a Shroud group on the Internet

Obviously a large listing like this is not going to be 100 percent accurate, even with multiple editors. Neither is it feasible to go beyond name and country. However, it does give one a good idea of the amazing numbers of people that have actually been involved in sindonology since 1898. (One can't assume that all Reverends will be in the pro-authenticity camp—there are many who are in the skeptical category). It is also clear that there are considerably more researchers who are pro-authenticity or neutral than ones who are skeptical. The usual stance for the pro-authenticity camp is that the Shroud wrapped the historical Jesus. The usual stance for the skeptic is that the cloth was forged in the Middle Ages. However, there are some researchers who believe that the Shroud is authentic but may not be of Jesus and/or may not have originated from the first century. I have listed those researchers in the pro-authenticity/neutral list. The lists will be updated as new information is received.

To see these lists, go to:
http://shroud.wikispaces.com/Shroud+Researchers.

The author's late wife, M. Sue Benford, had her autobiography <u>Strong Woman: Unshrouding the Secrets of the Soul</u> published in 2002. Cradle Press republished her book in 2011. It is a wonderful complement to <u>Wrapped Up in the Shroud: Chronicle of a Passion</u>. Both books are available through *amazon.com*.

To contact the author, please send an email to JMarino240@aol.com.

CPSIA information can be obtained at www.ICGtesting.com
Printed in the USA
LVOW111116190212

269367LV00004B/18/P